LOCKERBIE THE TRUTH

Also by Douglas Boyd

Histories:

April Queen, Eleanor of Aquitaine
Voices from the Dark Years
The French Foreign Legion
The Kremlin Conspiracy: 1,000 Years of Russian Expansionism
Normandy in the time of Darkness: Life and Death in the Channel Ports 1940–45
Blood in the Snow, Blood on the Grass: Treachery, Torture, Murder and Massacre – France, 1944
De Gaulle: The Man Who Defied Six US Presidents
Lionheart: The True Story of England's Crusader King
The Other First World War: The Blood-Soaked Russian Fronts 1914–22
Daughters of the KGB: Moscow's Cold War Spies, Sleepers and Assassins
Agente: Female Spies in World Wars, Cold Wars and Civil Wars
The Solitary Spy: A Political Prisoner in Cold War Berlin
Red October: The Revolution That Changed the World

Novels:

The Eagle and the Snake
The Honour and the Glory
The Truth and the Lies
The Virgin and the Fool
The Fiddler and the Ferret
The Spirit and the Flesh

LOCKERBIE THE TRUTH

DOUGLAS BOYD

The History Press

This book is dedicated to the memory of 270 people of all ages who died in an act of mass murder on 21 December 1988 above and in the town of Lockerbie and in homage to the individuals and families who lost their loved ones on that night but were denied justice and closure by government agencies in the USA and the United Kingdom.

First published 2018

The History Press
The Mill, Brimscombe Port
Stroud, Gloucestershire, GL5 2QG
www.thehistorypress.co.uk

© Douglas Boyd, 2018

The right of Douglas Boyd to be identified as the Author
of this work has been asserted in accordance with the
Copyright, Designs and Patents Act 1988.

British Library Cataloguing in Publication Data.
A catalogue record for this book is available from the British Library.

ISBN 978-0-7509-8577-2

Typesetting and origination by The History Press
Printed and bound in Great Britain by TJ International Ltd

CONTENTS

Part 3

Part 4

LIST OF ABBREVIATIONS
AND ACRONYMS

AAIB	Air Accident Investigation Branch (of British Ministry of Transport)
ACSSP	Air Carrier Standard Security Programme
ATC	air traffic control
ATS	air traffic system
AWACS	airborne warning and control system
BfV	Bundesamt für Verfassungsschutz
BKA	Bundeskriminalamt (West German anti-terrorist police)
BND	Bundesnachrichtendienst
CCRC	(Scottish) Criminal Cases Review Commission
CIA	Central Intelligence Agency
CIC	Combat Information Centre
DEA	(US) Drugs Enforcement Agency
DIA	(US) Defense Intelligence Agency
ETA	estimated time of arrival
FAA	(US) Federal Aviation Authority
FIR	flight information region
GID	(Jordanian) General Intelligence Directorate
GSG-9	Grenzschutzgruppe 9
ICAO	International Civil Aviation Organization
ICJ	International Court of Justice

IDF	Israel Defense Forces (Israeli armed forces)
IED	improvised explosive device
IFF	Identification friend or foe
LICC	Lockerbie Incident Control Centre
METFC	(US) Middle East Task Force Command
MI6	(British) also known as SIS – Secret Intelligence Service
MOIS	(Iranian) Ministry of Intelligence and Security
NSC	(US) National Security Council
PFLP	Popular Front for the Liberation of Palestine
PFLP–GC	Popular Front for the Liberation of Palestine – General Command
PLF	Palestine Liberation Front
PLO	Palestine Liberation Organisation
PO	petty officer
PPSF	Palestine Popular Struggle Front
RARDE	Royal Armaments Research and Development Establishment
TADMUS	Tactical Decision Making Under Stress
TN	tracking number
UAE	United Arab Emirates
UAR	United Arab Republic
USN	United States Navy
WMD	weapon(s) of mass destruction

INTRODUCTION

This is a real-life whodunnit, without the final scene where the master detective calls all the suspects together and reveals who committed the crime – which, in this case, is mass murder.

It is a scandal that, thirty years after the worst civil aviation accident in British history, we do not *officially* know for certain who blew up the Pan American Boeing 747-121 Clipper, registration N739PA, named *Maid of the Seas* above a small Scottish town on 21 December 1988, causing 259 deaths in an awful night when bodies and body parts of passengers and crew rained down from the sky onto Lockerbie. Amazingly, only eleven other people were killed on the ground although large parts of the Boeing jumbo jet fell on or just outside the town, causing a fireball 300ft high.

In the following days and months, thousands of police, military personnel and specialised investigators of the Ministry of Transport Air Accidents Investigation Branch (AAIB) scoured southern Scotland, finding debris over an area of 1,500 square miles. Investigators from the US Federal Aviation Authority took part and representatives of the FBI and CIA were present for reasons not divulged. Three years of the joint British/US investigation involved 15,000 statements being taken, producing as many questions as answers.

An improvised explosive device inside a modified Toshiba radio cassette player similar to the one that brought down the Pan American flight which crashed on Lockerbie had recently been seized from the Popular Front for the Liberation of Palestine – General Command (PFLP-GC) terror group by West German anti-terrorist police, but the Palestinian and Syrian terrorists and bomb-makers concerned were then released by a German judge 'for lack of evidence' connecting them with a substantial cache of weaponry and bomb-making equipment in their possession.

So, was this criminal act of mass murder the work of that breakaway Palestine Liberation Organization (PLO) faction, hoping to disrupt ongoing talks between Washington and Yasser Arafat's mainline PLO, which, as a gesture to show that it had renounced terrorism, had given warning that something like this might happen? Was it the work of the Abu Nidal / Fatah group, as seemed to have been indicated in the mysterious warning by a man with an Arabic accent who telephoned the US Embassy in Helsinki a couple of weeks earlier? Was it the revenge of the Iranian Government for the unprovoked shooting down by missiles from the USS *Vincennes* five months earlier of an Iran Air Airbus A300 B2-203 on a scheduled flight while over Iranian territory above the strait of Hormuz, causing 290 innocent civilian deaths? Was it the act of an intelligence officer of Colonel Muammar Gaddafi's Libyan Arab Jamahiriya, whose agents in Africa had been found ten months earlier allegedly carrying *similar* components for a Semtex bomb? Was it the FBI, which was implicated in the deliberate falsification of evidence in its forensic laboratories between the Lockerbie bombing and the trial eleven years later? The *pièce à conviction* was said in court to be a tiny fragment of a circuit board made by a Swiss firm that had supplied similar boards to Libya and the Stasi, but this may not ever have been on the Pan Am 747. The technician who made it admitted to lying in court and stealing a circuit board, which he gave to a Lockerbie investigator to be used as fabricated evidence.

Eleven years after the fatal night, three senior Scottish judges, under pressure to come up with a culprit at the court hearing on neutral territory in the Netherlands, pinned the blame on a Libyan Arab Airlines security officer and freelance businessman named Abdelbaset al-Megrahi, largely on the evidence of a Maltese merchant who identified al-Megrahi as a customer who had, *eleven years before the trial*, bought some clothes that *may* have been in the suitcase with the Lockerbie bomb. Not only did the Maltese merchant change his statement eighteen times, but shortly before the identity parade he had seen a recent photograph of al-Megrahi in a magazine article linking him with the crash. In court, all the Maltese witness said was that al-Megrahi *resembled* the long-ago customer.

The court chose to believe that the bomb which al-Megrahi allegedly used to destroy Pan Am Flight 103 had been smuggled in an unaccompanied suitcase onto Air Malta flight KM 180 in Luqa Airport on the morning of the fatal day, flown to Frankfurt and trans-shipped that afternoon onto Pan Am feeder flight 103A to London and there placed on board *Maid of the Seas*. There was a more rational conclusion that did not implicate al-Megrahi. It made far more sense for professional terrorists with experience of sabotaging aircraft to introduce the suitcase containing the improvised explosive device into the baggage system at London's Heathrow Airport, rather than send it on two previous flights, at any point during which it could have detonated prematurely or been detected when on the ground between flights. But the court that condemned al-Megrahi to life imprisonment was not told that the baggage area in Heathrow's Terminal 3 was reportedly broken into by a person or persons unknown under cover of night a few hours before Flight 103 took off for New York.

Al-Megrahi was found guilty of murdering the 270 Lockerbie victims. Official UN observer at the trial Professor Dr Hans Köchler repeatedly declared – in 2001, 2002, 2003, 2005 and 2007 – that the verdict was a spectacular miscarriage of justice. That opinion was shared by many other legal figures and, perhaps surprisingly, by relatives of the victims present in court, who surely had every reason to want a conviction. In June 2007 the Scottish Criminal Review Commission found that al-Megrahi *might* have suffered a miscarriage of justice. After serving ten years of his sentence, he was liberated on the compassionate grounds that he was suffering from incurable prostate cancer with a short time to live. Yet he lived for two more years. So, was the allegedly compassionate release really a cover-up to avoid the embarrassment of new evidence being produced at his scheduled second appeal?

Nothing in the investigation of the Lockerbie crash and the trial of the man found guilty for it can be taken at face value.

PART 1

1

IN THE BEGINNING

Thirty years after the tragedy which saw nearly 300 people simultaneously murdered in December 1988, the name of Lockerbie is still a synonym for mass murder.

Actually, there are twice as many victims in this story and half of them died five months earlier. The sequence of events really begins shortly after the 1979 Islamic Revolution that deposed Iran's last shah, Mohammad Reza Pahlavi, and replaced his British- and American-backed regime by a theocratic government headed by Ayatollah Ruhollah Khomeini. In the revolutionary disorder, many senior Iranian officers were executed as being loyal to the shah, with command of some military units being taken over by imams. This led Iraq's Baathist dictator Saddam Hussein to revive the millennial Persian–Arab conflict by invading Iran on 22 September 1980, using as his *casus belli* a dispute about the common border of the two countries in the Shatt el-Arab waterway. The real reason for the invasion was to capture Iranian oilfields. Far from being a primitive squabble between 'people in faraway countries', as Neville Chamberlain might have said, this war was the first one in which modified Soviet ballistic missiles were used by both sides, and chemical weapons claimed thousands of victims. It continued for nearly eight years at a cost of some 1.5 million lives, half of them civilians shot by small-calibre projectiles, blown to pieces by artillery shells and bombs or killed by poison gas.

Having, like Britain, previously supported the corrupt regime of the Shah of Iran in return for controlling the country's oil supplies, the USA was not unnaturally suspected of giving support to anti-Khomeini elements in the hope of regaining control of the Iranian oil. In fact, the CIA had been running a significant number of agents inside Iran and the tension between Washington and Tehran reached ignition shortly after US President Carter announced on 23 October 1979 that he was allowing the exiled shah into the USA for treatment of his late-stage terminal cancer. American diplomats in Iran were aghast, knowing that this was the last straw for all Iranians who suspected US interference in their affairs. They were right to be horrified. On 4 November allegedly spontaneous rioting by 'students' ended with sixty-six American diplomats and other US nationals taken hostage by the rioters and confined in the US Embassy in Tehran. One woman and two Afro-Americans were released on 19 November after praising the aims of the revolution in front of cameras and microphones; the following day four more women and another six Afro-Americans were also released. After one more prisoner was freed, suffering from belatedly diagnosed multiple sclerosis, the remaining fifty-two hostages were held for a total of 444 days.

Diplomatic negotiations and sanctions failed to secure the release of the hostages. On 20 March 1980 at a top-level meeting in the White House, a blockade of all Iranian ports was debated, for both imports and exports. More aggressively, Admiral James Lyons drew up a plan for carrier-based US marines to take by force and occupy the undefended Kharg island in the north of the Persian Gulf, where 95 per cent of all Iranian oil exports was piped into waiting tankers. He promised that would bring Tehran to its knees inside two weeks. Fortunately for the hostages, who would have been subject to retaliation, cooler heads prevailed. Instead, President Carter did approve a rescue operation dubbed Eagle Claw using Rangers and newly formed Delta Force units based on the massive American aircraft carriers USS *Nimitz* and USS *Coral Sea*, which were on station in international waters near Iran. The essence of the plan was to take advantage of the Iranians' preoccupation with their war against Iraq to land the special forces from military helicopters near Tehran, where they would be picked up and transported by CIA sleepers into the capital to kill the guards at the embassy and drive the hostages to a sports stadium nearby. There, the helicopters would land to spirit rescuers and rescued away to safety.

On 24 April 1980 the rescue attempt failed catastrophically after two helicopters were put out of action by dust storms encountered during the mission – which, due to the extreme secrecy surrounding Eagle Claw, lacked any current meteorological information. A third helicopter crashed into a fixed-wing aircraft, killing eight soldiers. This was a high cost in lives for a failed rescue operation. Removed from the embassy and dispersed all over Iran to prevent any further American rescue attempt, the unlucky fifty-two were eventually released on 20 January 1981 after mediation by Algeria and the payment of a king's ransom: 50 tonnes of gold worth $7.98 billion.

In early 1983 US President Reagan's National Security Council (NSC) expressed the view that the Iraq–Iran conflict might spread to other Middle Eastern countries and his National Security Planning Group considered that the conflict must lead to higher oil prices and/ or disrupt oil supplies from the region. The war was also taking its toll at sea, with Iraqi missile attacks and bombing of Iranian shipping and offshore oil platforms leading Tehran to retaliate against ships in the Persian Gulf that belonged to Arab states giving Saddam Hussein huge loans to bolster his war effort. In one three month period, February to April 1984, Iraqi aircraft sank or heavily damaged sixteen ships,[1] mostly tankers that exploded in huge fireballs with some loss of life. Wrongly blamed by Arab states supporting Iraq for starting what was called 'the tanker war', Iran eventually replied in kind. This resulted in the US Navy (USN) launching Operation Earnest Will in July 1987, during which American warships escorted reflagged Kuwaiti oil tankers safely through the Persian Gulf. There were frequent firefights between US warships and a flotilla of armed speedboats built by the Swedish company Boghammar AB and capable of reaching speeds of 45 knots. Armed with 12.7mm heavy machine guns, rocket launchers and mortars, they were manned and operated by the Iranian Guardians of the Revolution paramilitary navy, which regarded the Iranian Navy as politically unreliable because its personnel was averse to martyrdom!

The war in the Persian Gulf was a dirty affair, even by the standards of undeclared warfare. It reached its nadir at the Conference of the Organisation of Islamic Cooperation at Kuwait in January 1987 when delegates debated the treachery of the USA, which insisted on a worldwide blockade of Iran and yet was supplying arms shipments to Tehran in the Iran–Contra deals negotiated by Colonel Oliver North. None of the speakers gave much credibility to the Reagan administration's excuse that this was a rogue operation, not approved by the White House.[2]

Readers whose memories go back no further than the two Iraq wars involving Western coalition forces – Operation Desert Storm in 1991, triggered by Iraq's invasion of Kuwait the previous year, and the war of 2003 ironically dubbed 'Iraqi Freedom' and spuriously justified by claims from US President George W. Bush and British Prime Minister Tony Blair that Saddam Hussein was about to use weapons of mass destruction (WMDs) – none of which were ever found by UN inspection teams – may be surprised to learn that, in the preceeding eight-year war between Iraq and Iran, geopolitical considerations had aligned America and its allies on the side of Saddam Hussein. This was despite Iraq's close ties with the USSR throughout the Cold War and the fact that it had been placed on Washington's List of State Sponsors of Terrorism on 29 December 1979 for its support of the Abu Nidal and other terror groups. Yet, throughout the Iran–Iraq War the USA remained officially neutral, although supplying political support and some aircraft to Saddam Hussein. When, in March 1982, Iran launched a successful counteroffensive, the USA upped its level of support for Iraq to prevent an Iranian victory and helpfully removed Iraq from the List of State Sponsors of Terrorism, so that American arms manufacturers could legally supply arms to Iraq; sales to Iraq reached a record high in 1982.

During the Cold War neither NATO governments nor those of the Soviet Union's Warsaw Pact countries wished to become directly involved, so they supported proxy wars instead. Yet, in June 1987, when US Defense Secretary Caspar Weinberger and Assistant Secretary of Defense Richard Armitage visited Hawaii, Admiral James 'Ace' Lyons, Commander-in-Chief, US Pacific Fleet defied the normal channels of communication by lobbying them to 'take the war to the enemy' by exploiting an operational advantage that would come in August when the aircraft carrier USS *Constellation* and her battle group, deployed to the Gulf of Oman in support of Earnest Will, was due to be relieved by USS *Ranger* and her battle group. With two carrier battle groups briefly on station during the handover, plus the recommissioned Second World War battleship USS *Missouri* and five other warships tasked to Earnest Will, Lyons argued there was a short window of opportunity to destroy the economy of the Islamic Republic of Iran by taking out harbours, oil installations and strategic targets inland in one massive blow before the Iranians had time to react.

Whatever Weinberger and Armitage thought of the idea, President Reagan's National Security Adviser Lieutenant General Colin Powell blocked the idea. Yet in October 1987 US warships attacked Iranian offshore oil platforms in retaliation for an Iranian attack on a US-flagged Kuwaiti oil tanker. On 14 April 1988, the American frigate USS *Samuel B. Roberts* was badly damaged by an Iranian mine, with ten sailors wounded. The American response four days later, dubbed Operation Praying Mantis, was an attack on Iranian vessels in Iranian waters, which sank or damaged half of Iran's small navy in a few hours, including the two British-built frigates *Sahand* and *Sabalan*.

The choke point for international shipping carrying supplies to Iraq at the head of the Persian Gulf and conveying in the other direction one-fifth of the world's oil exports each day was at the Strait of Hormuz – the narrow passage leading from the Gulf of Oman to the Persian Gulf. Because the strait is only 21 nautical miles across at its narrowest point, internationally designated seaways through it traverse what would otherwise be territorial waters of both Iran to the north and Oman to the south. US Navy warships on escort duty also used these seaways under an Iranian law of 1934, as amended by a law of 1959.[3] On Sunday, 3 July 1988, one of these was the heavyweight Ticonderoga-class guided missile cruiser USS *Vincennes*, commanded by Captain William C. Rogers III.

Vincennes was the most sophisticated ship in the US Navy, costing more than $1 billion. Crewed by about 400 officers and ratings, she had two 5-inch guns and a range of other anti-ship and anti-aircraft weaponry. Most importantly, it had Aegis, a state-of-the-art seaborne alternative to an Airborne Warning and Control System (AWACS) aircraft covering the Strait of Hormuz, supposedly giving a similar degree of accurate, detailed real-time analysis of airborne and surface activity and communications in the region.

What sort of man was the captain of *Vincennes*? In view of what was about to happen, it seems incredible that Rogers was a son of a Second World War US Navy psychologist and himself a university-qualified psychologist. Having enlisted in the navy at the mature age of 27, this was his twenty-third year of service after two years of teaching high school science in civilian life. His attitude to authority was not what one might expect from a former schoolteacher. That was made clear when he sent only a lowly lieutenant from his crew to the important briefing on the rules of engagement in the Gulf on being posted there in May 1988. When officers of the departing USS *Wainwright* offered to brief their replacements on the current situation, they were cold-shouldered with, 'Aegis will sort all that out'. In war games at Tactical Training Group, Pacific, Rogers had both ignored instructors' advice and repeatedly violated the rules of engagement laid down.[4] Once on station in the Gulf, where his mission was to supervise and, if necessary, back up smaller naval craft escorting tanker convoys, Rogers chafed at the bit, frequently pleading with his superior, Rear Admiral Anthony Less, for a more aggressive role for *Vincennes* – one message specifically asking permission 'to go into harm's way, for which [*Vincennes*] was intended'.[5]

Rogers, who had been given command of the missile cruiser *Vincennes* in April 1987, was from the same mould as Admiral Lyons.

Since joining Operation Earnest Will, Rogers had earned a reputation among other USN captains in the region for extreme aggressiveness and his ship was given the nickname 'Robocruiser' after the cartoon character Robocop, always spoiling for a fight. It seems that he thought the moment had come on 3 July 1988 to seize the mantle of Lyons. That morning, *Vincennes* was 40 nautical miles north of its station allotted by Middle East Task Force Command after Roberts had received reports from the USS *Montgomery* in the Strait of Hormuz of some gunfire from Iranian speedboats in the area. Driven by the 80,000 horsepower of its four gas-turbine engines, *Vincennes* travelled towards the location at 30 knots until Rear Admiral Less at Fleet Headquarters in Bahrain ordered Rogers to stay clear of the area and instead despatch a Seahawk SH-60B LAMPS helicopter to assess the scene *at a distance*. The pilot reported back that a small number of the fast Iranian Boghammars were routinely harassing a German-flagged Pakistani freighter, the *Dhaulagiri*, but not attacking it.

Rogers headed north again, still making 30 knots. Passing the *Dhaulagiri*, he ignored a signal from it reading *A-OK*. At 0840 the Omani coastguard radioed the Iranian small craft to clear the scene. The coastguard also warned *Vincennes* that its excessive speed and aggressive posture were not acceptable in Omani waters. Almost simultaneously, Fleet HQ in Bahrain ordered Rogers to return to his allotted station, leaving the Seahawk helicopter to observe. Rogers grudgingly complied until the co-pilot of the helicopter radioed that he was taking airburst fire from the gunboats. In fact, one Iranian Revolutionary Guard boat near the freighter quite reasonably fired ten warning shots well ahead of the Seahawk when it intruded into Iranian airspace. It also defied the rules of engagement, ignoring the agreed 4-mile separation by approaching to within half that distance of the Iranian boats.

Taking this as sufficient reason to send his crew to battle stations, Rogers ordered full speed and headed north again to engage the Boghammar speedboats that were 'attacking' his helicopter. The $400 million Aegis combat information system on board *Vincennes*, with its three-dimensional phased-array AN/SPY radar, was not designed for skirmishes with small boats, but for all-out war with the Soviet Navy, being capable of tracking simultaneously up to 100 incoming enemy missiles or attacking aircraft and launching missiles to destroy them. As the small patrol boats bobbed up and down in the swell, well inside Iranian waters, they kept disappearing from the American radar. In line of sight, the poor visibility due to a sand haze permitted only momentary glimpses of their wakes from the deck of *Vincennes*, although the very high-powered binoculars of the lookouts *seemed* to show two small craft headed towards *Vincennes*.

The Revolutionary Guards commander in Bandar Abbas was a young 'student' named Ali Fadavi. As *Vincennes* and *Montgomery* entered the Iranian exclusion zone, he ordered one Boghammar to suss out *Vincennes*' intentions. The speedboat made a fast pass with crewmen on both sides staring at each other close-up. Rogers informed Bahrain that he was being attacked and announced his intention of opening fire on the Iranian boats. Apparently unaware that *Vincennes* was then 50 miles north of its correct position, Admiral Less approved Rogers' request to defend his vessel against the Iranian 'attack'.

At 0941 his navigation officer informed Rogers that *Vincennes* had just left the international seaway and crossed into Iranian territorial waters. At 0943 the two American warships opened fire on the gunboats with their 5-inch guns at approximately 8,000 yards' range. A radar-directed barrage of some 100 shells commenced, which eventually damaged one Iranian boat and set two others on fire, sinking them.[6] Twenty-five miles to the east, Commander David Carlson, captain of USS *Sides*, had heard Rogers' communications with Bahrein and was horrified. He knew that it was extremely unlikely that the lightweight fibreglass Iranian craft would attack the heavily armoured and armed *Vincennes*, because that would end in their annihilation. By attacking them, Rogers was committing an act of war, when his mission in Operation Earnest Will was to *prevent* escalation.

The Iranian national carrier Iran Air had a twice-weekly scheduled flight due to depart that morning from Tehran, destination Dubai, with a brief stop at Bandar Abbas Airport in southern Iran, after which, designated IR655, it was to use an internationally recognised civilian aviation route code named Amber 59 across the strait on its 140-mile flight. The captain of the Airbus operating this flight, an A-300 B2-203 registration EP-IBU, was Mohsen Rezaian, an experienced pilot with 7,000 hours of flight time, of which 2,000 hours were on Airbus A-300 aircraft. The Bandar Abbas–Dubai sector was part of a regular passenger service that Iran Air had operated for over twenty years using Air Traffic System Amber 59 or ATS route A59. This regular flight was dubbed 'the Haj flight' by watching American monitors because it was heavily used by Iranian pilgrims to Mecca, as it was on 3 July 1988, a few days before the important ritual of Eid al-Fitr that ends the fasting month of Ramadan.

Captain Rezaian was familiar with the route, having flown it many times in the past two years. His second officer was also experienced, as was the flight engineer. All three flight deck crew held valid commercial pilots' licences. A subsequent investigation by the International Civil Aviation Organisation (ICAO) found no evidence that any one of them was physically or psychologically unfit. The report of that investigation states that the timetable of commercial flights using this route dated 28 June 1988, including the one flight due to take place in the morning of 3 July 1988, was available on board all US naval vessels in the region. On that day, there were three US warships present in the area. All had received the civilian flight schedule for the region dated 28 June showing that the only flight due to leave Bandar Abbas Airport on the Iranian side of the straits that morning, after its scheduled stopover there, was IR655. In the ICAO report, times are given in Coordinated Universal Time (UTC), i.e. Greenwich Mean Time. The local time was four and a half hours in advance of this. The following is in corrected local time.

Captain Rezaian's Airbus A-300 took off from Bandar Abbas twenty-seven minutes late, due to a passenger having visa problems, at 1117 Tehran time, or 0947 as shown on board the US ships.[7] US personnel monitoring Iranian civil aviation frequencies heard Bandar Abbas tower clear the Airbus to use the airport's runway 21.

On board, according to the passenger list later supplied by the Iranian Government to the International Court of Justice were 238 Iranians – many of them on pilgrimage to Mecca – plus thirteen citizens of the United Arab Emirates, ten Indians, six Pakistanis, six Yugoslavs and one Italian. The flight deck and cabin crew numbering sixteen brought this to a total of 290 people on board, including sixty-six children.

At 1119.18 Captain Rezaian notified Bandar Abbas tower that he was on track and climbing from 3,500ft to 14,000ft, destination Dubai International Airport. He estimated reaching the MOBET reporting point at 1122 and reporting point DARAX at 1128, to land in Dubai at 1145. IR655 transmitted the same information to Tehran air traffic control (ATC) when the aircraft was at 7,000ft and still climbing. In accordance with international aviation practice, all these transmissions were in clear English, as was Tehran's transmission of this flight information to United Arab Emirates (UAE) ATC on the other side of the straits and the acknowledgment by UAE ATC. Two USN frigates in the area – USS *John H. Sides* and USS *Elmer Montgomery* – identified IR655 on their radar screens as a civilian aircraft 4 miles off the centre line of the 20-mile-wide international air corridor.

The USA had issued a Notice to Airmen, conventionally called a NOTAM, warning that aircraft in the region, even if taking off from a regional airport, must not come within 5 nautical miles of an American warship at an altitude of less than 2,000ft. Doing so would be deemed an attack profile and risk the warship launching 'defensive measures', i.e. shooting down the perceived threat. At 1121.30 Tehran asked IR655 to notify when it reached 14,000ft at reporting point DARAX, where the Tehran Flight Information Region (FIR) ended and the UAE FIR began. Asked by Tehran to confirm that IR655's transponder was squawking the allotted Mode 3 identification code 6760, Rezaian replied, 'Affirmative'.

By that stage, the large display screens in the darkened combat information centre (CIC) of the USS *Vincennes* had been showing the plot of IR655, designated as TN (for tracking number) 4131 for several minutes.[8] At 1124 IR655 transmitted its last message to

Bandar Abbas, giving its position at reporting point MOBET. This was acknowledged and Rezaian replied in the normal courtesy of civil aviation communications, 'Thank you. Good day.'

According to the American Government, the crew in the Aegis combat information centre aboard *Vincennes* incorrectly identified the Iranian Airbus as an attacking F-14A Tomcat fighter despite the fact that its transponder was squawking call-sign 6760 in Mode III, which clearly identified it as a civilian aircraft. The Tomcat was a supersonic variable-geometry interceptor made by US constructor Grumman in service only with the US Navy and the Islamic Republic of Iran Air Force which had inherited seventy-nine of them, plus spare engines, other parts and compatible armament, including AIM-54 Phoenix air-to-air missiles that were supplied at a cost of $2 billion to the shah before the Islamic Revolution in 1979. The shah, being a trained military pilot, wanted the F-14 to intercept Soviet Mig-25 Foxbat reconnaissance aircraft that regularly overflew Iranian territory.

At least, that was the official reason for the purchase, but many elements in this story are not what they seem at first sight. The Soviet overflights were Moscow's reaction to increasing pro-US intelligence-gathering by Iranian and American units based close to the Iran–USSR border, a major task of which was Operation Dark Genie: the exploring of routes by which US bombers could penetrate the Soviet Union via Iran with least radar vulnerability and the execution of high-altitude photo reconnaissance of new military bases in that period of the Cold War before satellite surveillance was possible. It is relevant to what happened on 28 June 1988 that the F-14s supplied to Iran were constructed and supplied to Iran by an American company. So the US Navy well knew that they were configured for air-to-air combat, not for attacking surface craft.

2

MEDALS FOR MURDER

In the tense atmosphere of *Vincennes'* windowless, dimly lit CIC, with all the display screens more resembling an arcade of video games than the real world outside, the men monitoring the large-screen displays had been briefed that the Iranian F-14s carried non-guided bombs, Maverick missiles and unguided rockets. The *Vincennes* crew later claimed to have made ten attempts to contact the aircraft taking off from Bandar Abbas and warn it off, using both military and civilian radio frequencies without receiving any reply. Later allegations by CIC personnel aboard *Vincennes* were quite different and smacked of collusion. Several of them reported a squawk in Mode II – the military IFF mode – indicating an Iranian F-14, although none of the *Vincennes* data recorders showed any IFF response other than Mode III, Code 6760. It was alleged later that a petty officer in the CIC forgot to reset the range of his IFF set and mistook the squawk from an Iranian military aircraft on the ground at Bandar Abbas as coming from the transponder of TN 4131.

Since the so-called black box flight recorders of the Iranian Airbus still lie at the bottom of the strait, it will never be known whether Capt Rezaian ignored the American challenges or simply did not hear them because he was talking to Bandar Abbas and Tehran at the time. In any case, the official ICAO report stated that these attempts to contact Iran Air 655 were sent on the wrong frequency and addressed to a non-existent Iranian F-14. So, even if they had been heard on the flight deck of the Airbus, Rezaian would have had no reason to think that the aircraft being warned off was his, any more than he could have known an American warship lay ahead, more or less under his regular flight path well within Amber 59.

According to the ICAO report, the height and speed of the Airbus, and the size of the radar echo from this large commercial airliner measuring 177ft long by 171ft wingspan, as against the 62ft length of a two-seater supersonic Grumman F14 Tomcat and wingspan only 38ft in swept-wing attack profile, should have told the operators in the CIC of *Vincennes* beyond any doubt that the echo on their screens of Rezaian's Airbus could NOT be a much smaller and faster F-14 descending at less than 2,000ft on an attack run. Although the large-screen displays rather strangely did not give the altitude of the plane being tracked, other operators in the CIC did have this information. Even if the echo had been from an Iranian F-14, it was in Iranian airspace and still climbing, thousands of feet higher than an attacking fighter in a combat dive. Later American allegations that the Airbus was 4 miles outside Amber 59 were blatant lies, and had *Vincennes* been in its allotted station there could never have been any assumption on board that TN 4131 was headed towards an American missile cruiser involved in a pointless and unprovoked skirmish with the Revolutionary Guard boats.

The *Vincennes* attack radar, which functioned as an electronic path, along which a smart missile could travel unerringly to the target, was locked on to, or 'painting', the Airbus. This caused Commander David Carlson aboard USS *Sides*, the frigate nearest to *Vincennes* at the time of the incident, to observe that the pilot's failure to take any evasive action confirmed its civilian status, since Rezaian and his flight deck crew had no way of knowing that their aircraft was being targeted, whereas the pilot of an Iranian military aircraft would have been warned by his own onboard systems the second he had been 'painted', and immediately peeled away, to avoid a missile launch that would blow him out of the sky. Testimony from those aboard

USS *Sides* corroborates the Airbus flight path and the Mode III IFF squawk. Yet, it seems that *Vincennes* had no communications receivers able to monitor civil aviation frequencies, other than the International Air Distress frequency. After the shoot-down, all USN warships in the Persian Gulf were equipped with tunable VHF receivers, able to listen in to traffic on civilian frequencies.

Carlson later jeopardised the rest of his service career by going into print, saying that the events of that morning marked the 'horrifying climax to Captain Rogers's aggressiveness', which he first observed on 2 June 1988, when Rogers sailed *Vincennes* threateningly close to an Iranian Navy vessel making a lawful search of a bulk carrier and launched a helicopter within 3 miles of an Iranian Navy vessel in defiance of the rules of engagement requiring the 4-mile separation and opened fire on Iranian patrol boats.[1] Carlson also commented that Iranian vessels he had encountered in the area during the month prior to the incident were both non-threatening and professional.[2] Listening in to Rogers' announcement to US Middle East Task Force Command that he was going to shoot down the approaching aircraft, Carlson, who was under tactical control of Rogers on *Vincennes* at the time, is reported to have been thunderstruck, saying to personnel with him on the bridge of USS *Sides*, 'Why, what the hell is he doing?' With a real-time data link between the CIC in *Vincennes* and *Sides*, Carlson knew *exactly* what was being shown on the screens in front of Rogers' CIC crew. Let alone its size, how could TN 4131 be an F-14 in attack profile at less than 2,000ft, when it was already visibly at 7,000ft and still climbing?

Rogers had apparently been informed by his air warfare coordinator Commander Scott Lustig that the tracked aircraft designated TN 4131 was diving. Lustig was a well-liked officer, but had never been in combat before and apparently lost his nerve in the confusion of the skirmish with the surface craft combined with the new perceived threat. Carlson later wrote in the US Naval Institute journal *Proceedings* that he had 'wondered aloud in disbelief' on hearing of *Vincennes*' intentions to effect a shoot-down, and wondered at the time whether the crew of Rogers' ship 'felt a need to prove the viability of Aegis in the Persian Gulf, and ... hankered for the opportunity to show their stuff'.[3] He also wondered what such a heavyweight and costly vessel as *Vincennes* was doing skirmishing with highly manoeuvrable Iranian small patrol boats. It was, as a *Newsweek* journalist later remarked, like shooting rabbits with a radar-guided missile.[4]

A detailed analysis of 'the *Vincennes* incident' by three researchers at Massachusets Institute of Technology[5] cited Petty Officer Andrew Jackson in the Aegis combat information centre aboard *Vincennes* during the shoot-down as correctly attempting to consult commercial air traffic schedules to check the possibility that the plot designated TN 4131 did represent a commercial airliner. In this he was handicapped by (1) the poorly lit CIC losing *all* lighting each time *Vincennes* fired on the Iranian patrol boats; (2) his uncertainty how to read the schedules, since the ship was on Bahrain time and Iran Air's schedules showed Tehran time and (3) the Airbus had taken off twenty-seven minutes later than scheduled.

In addition, *Vincennes* had a 'foul bore' – a shell jammed in one gun that could not be fired at the Iranian patrol boats. To compensate for this, Rogers executed a violent manouvre, turning 50 degrees at 35 knots to bring another gun to bear on the small craft. When *Vincennes* heeled right over at this speed, papers and other objects on the CIC crew's desks that were sent flying onto the floor included the commercial air traffic schedule Jackson had been trying to read.

To that unfortunate combination of circumstances must be added that Rogers in his darkened control cockpit next to the CIC was continuing personally to oversee his pointless skirmish with the Iranian patrol boats – for which sort of engagement *Vincennes* was not designed. Lustig was later described as 'increasingly hysterical'[6] and appears to have assumed that the presence of those craft and their warning fire to drive the intruding American helicopter back into international airspace were a deliberate decoy operation to distract attention from the approach of a hostile aircraft. Somehow, the Aegis system confused TN 4131 with the trace of a US naval jet descending to land on a USN carrier in the Gulf of Oman and Rogers was told that 'his' TN4131 was diving. His multi-tasking confusion and the general sense of urgency on board *Vincennes* generated a variation of the 'fog of war' labelled 'scenario fulfilment' by military psychologists, in which the stress of combat causes men to blot out alternative possibilities and focus on one alone – in this case, the wrong one.

The personnel in the *Vincennes* CIC had been trained to handle multiple simultaneous attacks without panicking. Yet, with the misidentified aircraft 11 miles distant, Rogers reached up and turned the key in his cockpit that empowered the Aegis weapons control system to fire missiles. The young lieutenant at the console was so panicked by what was happening that he fumbled the firing switches several times until an older petty officer leaned across him and hit the switches. Two supersonic SM-2MR surface-to-air missiles erupted from the forward turret of the cruiser, to follow the attack radar path to the target. A few seconds later both of the missiles hit IR655 – one on the Airbus's wing and the other on its tailplane – at a range of 8 nautical miles and an altitude of 13,500ft, blowing one wing with its engine completely off.

On board *Vincennes* a lookout came onto the bridge and announced that the falling debris was far too large to be from an F-14. The crew of USS *Montgomery* saw a wing and engine pod fall into the sea. The chief radar operator on USS *Sides* told Carlson that the destroyed target was probably a 'commair' or commercial aircraft. Without knowing how many people had been on board, Carlson was almost physically sick. By then, all 290 people on board the Airbus were dead. At noon that day, Iranian helicopters and patrol boats were searching the Strait of Hormuz and recovering bodies, body parts, luggage and wreckage. According to an article in *Washington Post* next day – Independence Day in the USA – President Reagan at the presidential country retreat of Camp David in Maryland said that this was a 'terrible human tragedy', but that the *Vincennes* missile launch was 'a proper defensive action'. At the same time, Iran was accusing the USA of a 'barbaric massacre' and vowing to 'avenge the blood of our martyrs'.[7]

In the absence of any gesture of guilt or atonement by the USA, the events of that fateful morning are fully documented in a 'memorial' submitted to the International Court of Justice on 24 July 1990 by the Islamic State of Iran, stating that:

> the use of force by the United States naval units in destroying IR 655 and the killing of its passengers and crew violated the most fundamental principles of international law, including specific provisions of the Chicago convention and the Montreal convention which govern and protect international civil aviation. The shooting down of the aircraft also violated Article 2[4] of the United Nations Charter and rules of customary international law prohibiting the use of force. In unlawfully intruding into the Islamic Republic's internal and territorial waters, in breaching its stated neutrality in the area, in endangering civil aviation generally and in destroying the aircraft, the United States also violated the Islamic Republic's sovereignty and the principle of non-intervention as well as the principles of neutrality enshrined in the Hague Conventions of 1907. All of these actions were in breach of the Treaty of Amity, Economic Relations and Consular Rights between the United States and Iran, customary practice and rules relating to the Law of the Sea, including those reflected in the 1958 Geneva Conventions on the Law of the Sea and the 1982 United Nations Convention on the Law of the Sea, as well as the provisions of Chapter VII of the United Nations Charter. This case also involves a flagrant violation of the principle of non-interference in the affairs of a sovereign State and of elementary principles of humanity and norms of international behaviour.[8]

As to why it had taken two years for it to be submitted, the memorial continues:

> Despite these [and] numerous [other] violations of international law, the United States has refused to accept responsibility [although] immediately after the incident, the Islamic Republic [of Iran] referred the matter to the Council of the International Civil Aviation Organization [the ICAO Council]. Although on previ-

ous occasions the ICAO Council had condemned the actions of members who had shot down civil aircraft, it took no such action in this case.

The ICAO is a specialised agency of the United Nations Organisation based in Montreal, Canada. Why did it not condemn the act that caused the destruction of the Airbus and the deaths of 290 persons?

Although it begins with the Islamic formula 'In the name of God', the Iranian memorial to the International Court of Justice is written in legally precise English, being based largely on the Report of the ICAO Fact-Finding Investigation into the incident issued in November 1988. Substantial parts of that report use material from the report of the inquiry by the US Department of Defense, a declassified version of which was issued on 28 July 1988. However, that version of the latter report had been heavily redacted, with *hundreds* of passages being deleted. In some cases, this was to conceal names of participants, but in other cases whole paragraphs had been removed. As the memorial comments dryly, 'the extent of these deletions, especially where critical aspects of the incident are being discussed, suggests that there were other motives at work'.

USS *Vincennes* also had a black box of sorts, on the magnetic tape of which voice communications and data from all the combat and communication systems were recorded. This was available to the USN investigation board convened by Rear Admiral William M. Fogarty at Bahrain beginning on 6 July 1988. Formal hearings began a week later, and the board's report was delivered to the Department of Defense in Washington. Even in its redacted, published form, there is a striking variance between the data recorded by the SPY-1A system and what its human interpreters were reporting. This showed that verbal combat information was passing up the chain of command *contradicting* the evidence from the electronic systems on board.

President Reagan deputed Vice President George H.W. Bush to defend Rogers' action at the UN on 14 July, but when an assistant secretary of state tried to obtain firm facts from Admiral William Crowe's staff at the Pentagon in order to brief Bush for this, a curtain of silence descended, behind which lies and misleading half-truths, including denials of any cover-up, falsified data from Aegis and mis-reporting of the position of *Montgomery*, continued in the attempt to deny the truth.

Yet, on paragraph 4 of page E08 of the US Defense Department report published on 28 July, the following can be found:

> Iran Air flight 655 took off on runway 21 [heading 210 degrees true], was directed by the Bandar Abbas tower to squawk IFF mode III code 6760, and began a normal climb out to assigned altitude of 14,000 feet for the flight, which lasted a total of 7 minutes before the plane was hit by the missiles from USS VINCENNES. The pilot remained within the Amber 59 air corridor [20 miles wide, 10 miles each side of centerline], made a routine position report to Bandar Abbas departure control at approximately 0654 Z [or UTC, i.e. 1124 local time], and was ascending through 12,000 feet at a speed of approximately 380 kts at the time of making his report.

The Iranian memorial to the International Court of Justice continues:

> It must be concluded from this that at the time the United States knew these facts either from the *Vincennes* itself or from other ships in the area or through its own monitoring and intelligence network. In other words, the United States had full independent knowledge of the actual radio communications that passed between IR 655 and the various ground stations [to which it was reporting]. United States forces in the area knew which runway had been used and that the Bandar Abbas tower had directed Capt Rezaian to set the Airbus' transponder to squawk code 6760 on Mode III [the normal civilian aircraft squawk mode]. It knew that IR 655 was to make a normal climb within corridor A59 to its cruising height of 14,000 feet [normal for such a short flight]. It knew that the last communication from IR 655 took place at 0654 [or 1124 local time]. Despite this knowledge and despite all the other clear indi-cations that IR 655 was a civilian aircraft which posed no threat to

anyone, the *Vincennes* requested and was given permission by the U.S. Middle East Task Force Command to shoot down the plane.

Despite these numerous violations of international law, the United States has refused to accept responsibility [for the shoot-down]. Immediately after the incident, the Islamic Republic [of Iran] referred the matter to the Council of the International Civil Aviation Organization. [Because the ICAO Council took no action in this case] it is partly as a result of this unequal treatment that the Islamic Republic has been compelled to file its Application as an appeal from the ICAO decision under Article 84 of the Chicago Convention. In addition, the Islamic Republic applies independently to the [International] Court [of Justice] under Article 14[1] of the Montreal Convention and Article XXI[2] of the Treaty of Amity.[9]

The guided missile cruiser *Vincennes* being among the most techno-logically advanced vessels in the US Navy, the information gathered by Aegis was displayed on numerous screens in the CIC, one at least of which should have been showing the identification code being squawked by IR655 as well as its height, speed and direction.

Captain George Gee, Director of the US Navy's Surface Combat Systems Division, testified to the US Senate that the crew of the *Vincennes* had routinely trained in exercises simulating simultaneous attacks *by thirty or forty aircraft and/or missiles*. Although the Aegis soft-ware and hardware was very sophisticated, the information displayed in the CIC was clear and simple. So, it is hard to understand how it could be misread to show the far larger and much slower Airbus climbing *upwards* to 14,000ft as a faster and smaller supersonic fighter in a *descending* attack profile. It is relevant that Cdr Carlson, com-manding the frigate USS *Sides* that day, wrote in the September 1989 issue of *Proceedings*, published by the US Naval Institute:

Having watched the performance of the *Vincennes* for a month before the incident, my impression was that an atmosphere of restraint was not her long suit.[10]

He also wrote:

> The helicopter drew fire because it was a nuisance to the IRGC [Iranian Revolutionary Guard] boats. The *Vincennes* saw an opportunity for action, and pressed hard for Commander Middle East Force to give permission to fire. De-escalation went out of the window. Equipment failed. The fog of war rolled in.[11]

After a gross error by military or naval personnel occasioning unwarranted loss of life, their lips are often sealed by the award of medals and citations, 'proving' that everything was correctly done. To keep their mouths shut, the crew of *Vincennes* were all awarded combat action ribbons. According to *The Washington Post* dated 23 April 1990, Rogers was awarded the Legion of Merit for his performance in the Persian Gulf on 3 July 1988. The citation included the words:

> The President of the United States takes pleasure in presenting [the award to Capt Rogers]… for exceptionally outstanding service as commanding officer USS *Vincennes*. During the course of Persian Gulf operations, Capt Rogers' tactical skills and calm direction enabled his crew to successfully engage seven heavily armed, high-speed Iranian surface craft attacking *Vincennes*. As a result, five craft were destroyed and two retreated. Capt Rogers' dynamic leadership, logical judgement and unexcelled devotion to duty were in keeping with the highest traditions of the US Naval Service.[12]

Lieutenant Commander Lustig, the air-warfare coordinator on board *Vincennes*, won the US Navy's Commendation Medal for 'heroic achievement' on 3 July 1988. The citation continued:

> Throughout he maintained an exceptionally smooth flow of information and rapidly assimilated attack data to provide clear, concise flow of information to commanding officer and higher authority. As a result he was able to precisely complete the firing procedure.[13]

On 3 July at the first press conference in Washington, Chairman of the Joint Chiefs of Staff, Admiral William J. Crowe and Secretary of Defense Frank Carlucci maintained that IR655 had been shot down at the height of 9,000ft while descending at what was called 'the high speed of 450 knots' directly towards USS *Vincennes*. Testifying later before before the House of Representatives' Armed Services Committee, Crowe asserted that there there had been no cover-up. Yet, according to Admiral Fogarty's report dated 19 August, which was based on recorded data from *Vincennes*, the Airbus was clearly ascending through 12,000ft at the lower speed of 380 knots.[14]

Rogers remained in command of *Vincennes* until May 1989 and was then posted as commanding officer to the USN Tactical Training Group at Point Loma, where fast-track officers were trained in handling combat situations.

Ali Akbar Velayati, Foreign Minister of the Islamic Republic of Iran, pleaded before the UN Security Council for recognition and condemnation of what had happened on 3 July in and over the Strait of Hormuz. Leading the US delegation, Vice President George H.W. Bush used lies – particularly the assertion that Iran Air 655 had strayed outside Amber 59 – to blame Iran for the shoot-down. The United Nations refused to condemn the actions of USS *Vincennes*. Nobody, it seems, took seriously the stated intention of Iran to 'avenge the blood of our martyrs'.

Eight years after the shoot-down of IR655 the administration of President Bill Clinton reached a settlement at the International Court of Justice which included the statement that …

the United States recognized the aerial incident of 3 July 1988 as a terrible human tragedy and expressed deep regret over the loss of lives caused by the incident.

Yet the USA still did not admit legal liability or formally apologise to Iran. In the 1996 settlement, Washington paid the Iranian Government $131.8 million 'without prejudice', including $61.8 million for the victims' families in compensation for their loss, calculated at $213,103.45 per passenger. In exchange, Tehran agreed to drop its case against the USA in the International Court of Justice.

Government denials and failure to punish those directly responsible notwithstanding, the USN did take steps under the subsequent Clinton administration to ensure that this sort of incident did not occur again. The Tactical Decision Making Under Stress, or TADMUS, programme resulted in a redesign of the visual interface for the Aegis system, finally making it clear whether a tracked aircraft is descending rather than climbing!

3

THE *QISAS*

In the earliest known code of laws, laid down by Hammurabi, sixth king of Babylon *c.* 1750 BCE, the formula for legal revenge is close to the Old Testament formula: 'an eye for an eye, a tooth for a tooth, a hand for a hand, a foot for a foot.'[1] The European principle of legally justified revenge or *lex talionis*, to give it the medieval Latin title, was a restatement of the principle that punishment should fit the crime by inflicting on the perpetrator of the crime the same hurt, damage or loss he had inflicted on his victim. This principle is still an active part of the sharia law, under which Iran is governed, and legally sanctioned revenge is known as *qisas*.

To avoid a killing in revenge for a killing in the manner of a Mediterranean feud, blood money calculated according to the injury or wrong suffered may be accepted by the victim's family. A European friend of the author, who happened to kill a native of one of the Gulf states in a motoring accident, was saved from death at the hands of relatives of the dead man by the ruler of the emirate going out in the middle of the night personally to hand the right amount of blood money to the bereaved family in an act of atonement before revenge could be planned.

It is therefore possible that an immediate apology by the USA for the shoot-down of IR655, accompanied by the donation of an appropriate amount of blood money to the families of the passengers and crew of IR655 – and compensation to Iran Air for the loss of the aircraft – might have ended the unfortunate business of the shoot-down by *Vincennes*. Instead, Vice President George H.W. Bush, who later became US President, said, 'I will never apologise for the United States of America, ever. I don't care what the facts are. I'm not an apologise-for-America kind of guy.'[2] It was not the first time he had made this boast, but it was amazingly ill-advised for a senior American politician to utter this arrogant assertion in public less than one month after the shoot-down.

A documentary shown on the Al Jazeera satellite television channel on 11 March 2014 included an interview with Abolghasem Mesbahi, formerly a senior officer of the Iranian Ministry of Intelligence and Security (MOIS), also known by the acronym Vevak from its full Farsi title *Vezerat-e Ettela'at-e Keshvar*. When interviewed, Mesbahi was living under a witness protection programme in Germany. According to his statement to camera, in the absence of any American apology or acceptance of responsibility or offer of compensation for the *Vincennes* downing of IR655 in 1988, Iran's supreme leader Ayatollah Khomeini ordained *qisas*. Under the sharia law principle of like-for-like punishment, this required the swift destruction of an American aircraft with a similar number of, preferably American, passengers and crew on board. MOIS worked directly under the supreme leader and, according to Mesbahi, accepted without question the principle of *qisas* for the shoot-down.[3] It is not hard to see why, given Washington's refusal to acknowledge what one of its warships had done. However, with no wish to worsen its status as a pariah state in the view of the West, MOIS deemed it impolitic for identifiably Iranian agents openly to kill so many Westerners. Who knew where that could lead?

Since Israel had demonstrated in 1967 for the second time in nineteen years that a small nation of 4 million surrounded by more than 100 million enemies could outfight those enemies by conventional means, terrorism had become the strategy of choice for the Palestinians who had lost their lands in the 1948 War of Independence, as it is known in Israel, or *naqba*, meaning 'the catastrophe', as the Palestinians call it.

In May 1964, with the state of Israel just 16 years old, an experienced Turkish-Palestinian politician named Ahmed Shuqairy had announced in Cairo the formation of the Palestine Liberation Organisation (PLO), an umbrella grouping of all the disaffected Palestinians. His reign as chairman was short-lived because a group of expat Palestinians working in Kuwait created el-Fatah – a reversed acronym of the words *Harakat al-Tahrir al-Watani al-Filastina*, or Movement for the National Liberation of Palestine. Their leader Yasser Arafat rapidly replaced Shuqairy and managed to remain head of the PLO for almost four decades. Two other Palestinians, living in Lebanon – Dr George Habash and Dr Wadi Haddadd – decided to focus on their 'true enemy' by re-naming their Arabic Nationalists' Movement to create the Popular Front for the Liberation of Palestine (PFLP) in 1967. Whereas the PLO recruited any man prepared to carry a gun or throw a grenade on a raid into Israel in the hope of dying a martyr for the cause, Habash and Haddad prioritised intelligence, education and motivation in their recruiting drive. The aim was the formation of a clandestine army that could wrest control of all the Arabic-speaking lands from the Persian Gulf to the shores of the Atlantic: a modern caliphate long before ISIL existed.

When first recruited, Ahmed Jibril seemed an ideal addition to their ranks. Born in 1937[4] in a small village just south of Tel Aviv, he had moved with his family to Jordan before the Israeli War of Independence in 1948. They then settled in Quneitra on the Golan Heights, which was at the time Syrian territory and seething with Palestinian refugees. At the age of 19 he joined the Syrian Army, overcoming its prejudice against non-Syrians to rise to the rank of captain in the engineering corps. Showing exceptional skill with explosives, he might have risen even higher, except for his loudly voiced pro-Communist criticisms of the government in Damascus. After the short-lived political union with Egypt known as the United Arab Republic (UAR), which folded up in 1961,[5] Jibril moved to Cairo, attracted by the large number of politically active Palestinian students at Cairo University. Unable to play second fiddle to anyone for long, he founded the Palestine Liberation Front (PLF), recruiting students of both sexes – the women joining their own section of the PLF headed by Jibril's wife Samira.

After returning to Damascus, Jibril re-joined the army to take command of PLF recruits from refugee camps in Lebanon and Syria for training under Syrian command and control for cross-border raids into Israel, usually via Jordan to avoid reprisals against their Syrian hosts. Once again, Jibril's insubordination saw the Syrian High Command getting rid of him by sending him and his followers off to Cairo, where they were to ferment anti-Nasser sentiment. Predictably, they were swiftly arrested, interrogated under torture by Nasser's Mukhabarat and expelled to Lebanon, Jibril nurturing a lifelong hatred of Egyptians for the way he had been treated while he was their prisoner. On the basis that 'my enemy's friend is also my enemy', the PLF then fell out with all the Cairo-supported Palestinian factions. His particular hatred, however, focused on Yasser Arafat's group, resulted in a spate of Mafia-style tit-for-tat assassinations.

Although regarded by the Syrian Mukhabarat al-Askariya or military intelligence as 'their man', Jibril also cultivated contact with Soviet intelligence officers and guerilla warfare experts in Syria. They, in turn, saw him as an efficient terrorist commander, who would stop at nothing to attack not only Israel but also its Western supporters – particularly the USA, which supplied most of Israel's armament. Able also to 'talk Marxism' when it suited him, Jibril allied himself with Habash and Haddadd's PFLP after the humiliation of the Six-Day War in October 1967. Secretly despising their brand of intellectual Marxism, which contrasted with his intention to conduct an undeclared war, he broke away from them a year later during a fundraising trip to Kuwait.

There was nothing unusual in this: Palestinian factions were constantly falling out with each other over real or imagined slights. But Jibril grabbed control of a new group calling itself *al-Jabha ash-Shabi le-Tahrir Filastin – al-Qiyada al'Amma*. Whether under its English title as the Popular Front for the Liberation of Palestine – General

Command or in Arabic, this was a mouthful. So the group was usually referred to as PFLP-GC. If asked what was the long-term policy or political philosophy of his new organisation, Jibril had no answer. Like most other leaders of Palestinian terrorist factions, he was focused on the destruction of the state of Israel by undeclared warfare – in Marxist talk, 'revolutionary violence'. For this, he needed uneducated *fedayeen* who were prepared to creep under the border wire into Israel and sacrifice themselves after killing as many men, women and children as they could find. But he also saw the importance of using the Palestinian diaspora in Europe and elsewhere to attack Israeli and pro-Israel targets abroad. Fittingly, he chose as his *nom de guerre* the title Abu Jihad – the father of the holy war.

This father needed fanatically loyal 'sons' – followers who had no conscience about killing innocent people. Among them was the plumpish, moustached 30-year-old Hafaz Mohammed Hussein Dalkamoni, a Sunni Muslim from the Christian Arab town of Nazareth in the hills of Galilee, Northern Israel. In October 1969 Jibril sent him and five other terrorists back to the Galilee region that Dalkamoni knew so well with orders to conduct 'massive sabotage' there.[6] The infiltration from Jordanian territory by wading under cover of night through the shallow and sluggish River Jordan went well, as did the long hike through difficult terrain to their first target, a pylon supporting a crucial power line. Then the IED they were planting against it detonated prematurely, killing most of the team and leaving Dalkamoni bleeding profusely from his right leg, which had to be amputated at the knee. Unable to flee, he was arrested by an Israel Defence Force (IDF) patrol investigating the explosion and tried in a military court, which handed him two consecutive life sentences for terrorism, to be served in a maximum-security prison at Ashkelon in Southern Israel, as far as possible from his birthplace in Galilee.

Another important figure in the early PFLP-GC was Jordanian explosives expert Marwan Khreesat.[7] It was never clear whether he had strong Palestinian sympathies, or simply enjoyed the technical challenge of constructing IEDs that would be difficult to detect and would explode at the right time and in the right circumstances. This fitted in with Jibril's obsession with blowing up aircraft belonging to pro-Israel states in mid-flight, rather than taking their passengers hostage as the other terror groups were doing. Brought to Damascus, allegedly as a highly paid mercenary,[8] Khreesat set to work in a PFLP-GC laboratory while Jibril's *Amaliyat Kharijiyya*, or external operations section, built up an impressive infrastructure of safe houses, documents and arms dumps in Europe, helped by East German and Bulgarian intelligence operatives. The Bulgarians also supplied arms and ammunition, some of which – including Czech-made Semtex – headed east to Damascus, while the rest was destined for the caches being built up in Europe. After the collapse of the USSR, Czech President Václav Havel stated that První Sprava of the Státní Bezpečnost – the Czechoslovakian external intelligence service under the Communist regime – also shipped 'more than 1,000 tonnes of Semtex' to Libya, which passed it on to the Provisional IRA, Palestinian and other terrorist groups.[9]

Semtex is a peculiarly nasty combination of two explosives, both invented before 1900: RDX or Research Department eXplosive, also known in various countries as cyclonite or hexogen, and PETN or pentaerithritol tetranitrate. Sometime in the late 1950s a Czech industrial chemist named Stanislav Brebera had the idea of combining them in a plastic, putty-like form, easily moulded and odourless, making it difficult to detect. It was relatively stable and safe to handle, and therefore became a favourite of amateur bomb-makers in the terrorist world. Small amounts were used in letter bombs; 3lb was reckoned to be enough to bring down a two-storey building. The Czech arms industry supplied Semtex to many states, much of which ended up in terrorist hands. The IRA used it both in Northern Ireland and mainland Britain. No one actually knows how much Semtex is in existence, or who holds substantial stocks of it.

But, back to summer of 1988: by then there were a whole slew of deniable Middle Eastern terror groups who could possibly execute the *qisas* for Tehran. Since terrorism is an expensive way of life, necessitating safe houses, secure training facilities with modern weapons, international travel, false documents, the purchase of illegal arms and explosives, frequent changes of vehicles and subsistence for members of each group, most of whom never earn a living in any normal way, they all had in common a desperate need for funds, mainly supplied by Arab governments, particularly those of Egypt, Syria, the Gulf states and Libya.

In March 1988, representatives of Iranian and Syrian intelligence organisations met with Libyan colleagues in the back room of a baker's shop owned by Abdul Salaam, head of the Malta cell of the PFLP-GC to discuss the possibilities of collaboration against Israeli and American targets, according to a witness who was at the meeting. So, when Iran Air 655 was shot down by USS *Vincennes* and the *qisas* pronounced, the job naturally fell to the only terrorist group in the unholy alliance. Thus, Iran could have its revenge, but not be directly guilty of an act of war against the USA.[10]

Libya's ruler, Muammar Gaddafi,[11] had carried out a bloodless coup in 1969 as a 27-year-old captain in the army of King Idris while his aged and ailing monarch – a protégé of Britain and France – was undergoing medical treatment in Turkey. Declaring that the name of the country was henceforth the Libyan Arab Jamahiriya, or Islamic Socialist Republic of Libya, Gaddafi set out to use the country's oil revenues to raise the standard of living and promote literacy in the largely illiterate population. He also founded a healthcare system and introduced non-Islamic measures to improve the lot of women.

Although selling them oil, Libyans had no reason to love Europeans or North Americans. During the early twentieth-century Italian conquest of the country that was only named Libya in 1934, half the civilian inhabitants had been wiped out 'to teach the natives a lesson they would not forget', as was normal in earlier colonial wars. During the Second World War, Allied and German armies had treated the country as an empty desert in their battles with each other, largely destroying its fragile infrastructure and causing many more civilian casualties, for whom there was little medical help at the time. The post-war foreign occupation lasted until 1953. Six years later, the discovery of significant oil reserves transformed the country from semi-desert poverty to riches. In September 1969 widespread discontent with the nepotistic distribution of the new wealth caused a group of army officers to overthrow the government of King Idris, making Muammar Mohammed al-Gaddafi the de facto ruler of Libya. This being the period of the Cold War, Washington initially approved the Gaddafi administration's apparently anti-Moscow stance, allowing it to purchase US weapons, 21 tons of C4 plastic explosive, delayed-action bomb timers, ten Lockheed C-130 Hercules aircraft and a Bell-121 helicopter. The CIA also warned the Tripoli government of several hostile factions identified in Libya and neighbouring countries.[12] But although it shared out much of the oil wealth to found a welfare state, this regime was not what Europeans would understand by the word 'democracy'. There was no parliamentary opposition. Gaddafi's principal foreign policy goals were Arab unity, the complete elimination of Israel and total support for Palestinians, the advancement of Islam, the elimination of Western influence in the Middle East and Africa, and support for a whole range of anti-Western terrorist groups, to which he gave generous subsidies, rivalling Syria's Baathist dictator Hafez el-Assad in this respect.

On 11 June 1972, Gaddafi announced that any Arab wishing to volunteer to fight in the Palestinian terror groups could register his name at any Libyan embassy and receive 'adequate training for combat'. In October 1972, Gaddafi praised the Japanese Red Army's massacre of passengers at Lod Airport. One way and another, he declared war on the West by supporting Fidel Castro in Cuba, Haile Mengistu in Ethiopia, the Polisario Front in Spanish Sahara, Jean-Bédel Bokassa in the so-called Central African Empire and Idi Amin in Uganda – the last being given asylum for a year in Libya. With Libyan conventional and other forces also fighting in neighbouring Chad, largely over the ownership of the mineral-rich Aouzou border strip, at the beginning of 1980, President Carter wrote:

There are few governments in the world with which we have more sharp and frequent policy differences than Libya. We have strongly differing attitudes toward the PLO and the support of terrorism.[13]

When the US Government of President Carter declared Libya 'a state sponsor of terrorism', the pattern of that primarily Middle Eastern terrorism had been clear for nearly a decade. On 26 December 1968 two members of Dr Habash's PFLP, who had just arrived on an Olympic Airways flight from Cairo, ran out of the transit lounge at Athens Airport to attack an El Al Boeing 707 which was about to take off for Paris and New York. One of the men sprayed automatic fire at the plane while the other threw two hand grenades at it, causing panic among the forty-one passengers, killing one man and injuring two women. Arrested by Greek security officers and awarded a long custodial sentence, the two were released after less than four months when another Palestinian group hijacked a Greek aircraft and demanded their liberation. Meanwhile Israeli paras from the Sayeret Mat'kal special forces unit landed in helicopters at Beirut Airport and destroyed thirteen aircraft of Lebanese national carrier, Middle East Airlines to prevent them being used for military purposes. On 18 February 1969 four members of PFLP attacked an El Al Boeing 720 on the ground at Zurich Airport. Before the watching armed Swiss Police had time to react, one of the El Al air marshals on board the Boeing burst open the door and sprayed the terrorists with automatic fire, killing one and wounding two others.

Back in Beirut, Jibril despised this sort of action, considering it a waste of talent for his followers who were properly drilled like regular soldiers, wore smart uniforms and saluted their officers. What he was planning was terror on a much bigger scale: a Semtex IED that could pass through airport luggage checks with a timer that would explode it during the flight, over water, completely destroying the aircraft, killing everyone on board and leaving no clues for forensic analysis. At a safe house in Sofia protected by Darzhavna Sigurnost – Bulgarian intelligence, which also facilitated the importation into Europe of arms, ammunition and explosives for PFLP-GC – Khreesat was working on two such devices, which were parcelled up and despatched by airmail to addresses in Israel. On 21 February 1970 a CV999 Coronado jetliner flying Swissair Flight 330 departed Zurich, bound for Tel Aviv and Hong Kong. Nine minutes into the flight,[14] at an altitude of 14,000ft, Khreesat's bomb exploded in the rear cargo hold. Captain Armand Etienne informed the tower at Zurich that he thought he could bring his damaged aircraft safely back to land there. With dense smoke on the flight deck making it impossible for the pilots to see their instruments, a few seconds later the Coronado jet crashed into thickly forested country in the German-speaking canton of Aargau. In the debris field spread over several miles lay the bodies of the forty-seven passengers and crew.

The parcel containing the second of Khreesat's IEDs was in the cargo hold of an Austrian Airlines Caravelle routed with thirty-eight passengers and crew Frankfurt–Vienna–Tel Aviv that afternoon. It exploded exactly as planned at 10,000 feet, blasting a 2ft-wide hole in the fuselage skin. With the vital controls intact, the captain managed to turn the Caravelle around and land safely at Frankfurt. Forensic investigators from several countries including Britain recovered the remains of the IED to analyse it and prepare a counter-strategy, which would not be easy.

Responsibility for the Swissair crash was claimed by a spokesman of Jibril's PFLP-GC, which was the first time most international aviation security experts had heard of it or him. Israel's intelligence service, Mossad, of course, had had him in its sights for years, but as a terrorist threatening Israel, which he reconfirmed on 20 May 1970 when a squad of his men used anti-tank rockets, hand grenades and automatic weapons to attack a packed school bus near the Lebanese frontier, killing eleven Israeli children and three teachers and maiming for life all the others aboard. As to where they obtained the armament, there were many reports of Soviet and Bulgarian cargo ships docking in Syrian and Lebanese ports to unload crates of AK47 assault rifles, rifle grenades and even 23mm anti-aircraft guns, 130mm artillery and North Korean multiple rocket launchers – allegedly paid for with Gaddafi's petro-dollars.[15] PFLP-GC militants were also flown to top-secret camps in the USSR, Poland, Czechoslovakia, Bulgaria and the German Democratic Republic, where anti-government irregulars from Latin America, Africa and Asia also received conventional military, guerilla warfare and terrorist training. Rather indiscreetly, the Palestinian 'students' were allowed into local towns at weekends, where unaccustomed alcohol and attractive women got many into trouble.[16] In case it be thought that all these terrorists-in-training sympathised with each other's aims, after the end of the USSR and the separation of Czech Republic and Slovakia, Czech President Václav Havel said that Czechoslovakian Army anti-terrorist units had spent much of their time protecting mutually hostile factions from one another.[17]

Less than four months later, on 6 September Habash's PFLP hijacked at gunpoint a TWA jet en route from Frankfurt to New York, then a Swissair flight from Zurich to New York, diverting them to Dawson's Field, a disused airstrip in the Jordanian desert. Only allowed to use the toilets after asking permission and with the doors open, the passengers soon found them unusable. Added to this, the intolerable heat, hunger and thirst made them fear even worse to come. That same afternoon, an El Al flight from Amsterdam to New York was targeted by another PFLP gang led by Leila Khalid, an attractive 25-year-old woman thought to be the mistress of Dr Wadi Haddadd.[18] She had already taken part in the hijacking and diversion to Damascus of a TWA Boeing 707 flying from Rome to Tel Aviv in August of the previous year, since when she had undergone several plastic surgery operations to make her face less recognisable.

What might have happened if all her team had arrived on time at Frankfurt Airport on her second hijack, we'll never know. The immediate response of the onboard Shin Bet[19] air marshals[20] riddled her single accomplice on board, Puerto Rican terrorist Patrick Argüello,[21] with bullets, from which he later died, but not before shooting a crew member in the stomach. Perhaps momentarily shocked by realising that she was now on her own facing a planeload of people who had every reason to want her dead, Leila Khalid was wrestled to the floor by a passenger and immobilised while air marshals relieved her of two hand grenades and a pistol. Also on board was an Israeli general, who had no wish to be flown to an Arab airport and tortured for his secrets, so it is possible that the normal quota of armed guards on that flight was augmented with the No. 1

team from Shin Bet. The aircraft landed without further incident at London, where Khalid was arrested.

The two members of her gang who arrived at the airport too late for check-in on the El Al flight at least showed initiative. Perhaps they were terrified of going home to explain to Dr Habash why they were late for the hijacking of the TWA Boeing. Was it because a woman was in command? At any rate, they immediately checked in on a Pan Am flight to New York and hijacked it shortly after take-off, forcing the pilot to divert to Cairo. That same week, another PFLP gang hijacked a BOAC airliner flying Bombay to London and diverted it also to Dawson's Field. On 1 October, Khalid was released in exchange for the Western hostages at Dawson's field, where the four hijacked planes were blown up in front of television cameras for all the world to see.

This flagrant involvement of his territory forced King Hussein to take the Palestinian bull by the horns or be tarred with the same brush by the whole world. To deflect international opprobrium, he gave his predominantly Bedouin army – who hated the arrogant Palestinians for openly carrying arms in what was not their country – carte blanche to rid Jordan of them by killing as many as possible and terrifying the rest into getting out while they were still alive. The atrocities practised by both sides in combat during the last two weeks of the month was labelled by the Palestinians *Ailul al-Aswad* – Black September.[22] Syrian forces intervened to support the Palestinians until severely damaged by the Jordanian Army and its tank-busters, flown by British-trained Jordanian pilots. In case the Syrians had thoughts of returning in greater strength, diplomats made it clear to Damascus that any repeat of this move would be a fatal error because the Israeli Army (IDF) and the US Sixth Fleet would join in on the Jordanian side and wipe out the invaders.

In Autumn 1987 the FBI, CIA and DEA collaborated with other international agencies to trick Fawaz Yunis, who had masterminded a 1985 hijacking in Beirut, into believing that he was being invited to participate in a very lucrative drug deal. Boarding a luxury yacht in international waters off the coast of Cyprus, Yunis had an unpleasant surprise when he was promptly handcuffed and arrested by FBI agents. He was flown to the USA on a USN aircraft – which was refuelled in mid-flight so that no European state was involved – and sentenced to thirty years' imprisonment. This was the first 'irregular rendition' in the war against terrorism. Although court-appointed lawyers did represent Yunis, he was convicted by his own words, spoken at a press conference for the world's media, videotaped on the tarmac at Beirut Airport. In February 2005, Yunis was released from prison and returned to Beirut shortly afterward.[23]

4

OF MULES AND MALTA

As a tool of terror, Ahmed Jibril rated hijacking and ransom of hostages far lower than his total *destruction* of Swissair 330. That success, however, was double-edged because packages sent by airmail to Israel that could contain a bomb were subsequently examined far more closely. Taking a leaf from the modus operandi of drug smugglers, he decided that one way round the increased airport security was to use 'mules' to carry the IEDs on board in their luggage. Preferably, they should be female, both because women were less likely to be suspected of terrorism in those days and also because the Palestinians regarded liberal Western women who would give them sex without marriage as disposable whores.

A suitably handsome member of PFLP-GC who could pass in Europe was given plenty of money to flash around and buy presents with which to seduce an unsuspecting European or North American girl. She would then do her generous boyfriend the favour of carrying onto a flight to Israel a 'present' for his invented family supposed to be living there, without her knowing she was carrying a bomb. On 28 July 1971 a young Dutch woman checked in for El Al Flight 426 from Rome to Tel Aviv with such a 'present' to deliver to the boyfriend's non-existent family. Concealed below the false bottom of her suitcase was a PFLP-GC bomb – which failed to explode.

However, when she told an Israeli woman in the next seat that her boyfriend had replaced her own case by another, smarter one for the trip, the fellow-passenger told a Shin Bet sky marshal on board. The Dutch girl was arrested on landing in Israel, where the bomb that had failed to explode was examined with extreme care. Five weeks later, on 1 September 1971 El Al found another bomb which had failed to explode on Flight 016 from London to Tel Aviv in the luggage of a 21-year-old Latin American beauty queen, who had been seduced by her charming and generous Palestinian lover.

On 9 September the two 'mules' were on display at a press conference, telling their stories to journalists, who were not allowed to question them or take photographs. The PFLP-GC was identified as the organisation responsible and the deactivated IEDs were also on display with the items of luggage in which they had been secreted. This was done in the hope that future potential 'mules' would read about it and be more prudent.

In February 1972 Jibril launched a letter bomb offensive against Israel. Essentially, the device was a small amount of explosive rolled paper-thin and flat with a fine spring trigger that was quite safe in transit. Only when the recipient opened the envelope and released the pressure on the spring, did it go off. The quantity of explosive that could be fitted into an ordinary envelope was too small to kill an adult, but would maim, disfigure and possibly blind him or her.

A year after the Dutch girl and the Latin American beauty queen were used as 'mules', on 16 August 1972 two young British women were allowed through the lax security at Rome Airport carrying a record player they had agreed to take as a present to the family of their Palestinian 'boyfriends'. The Semtex IED, designed by Khreesat to look on an X-ray screen like integral parts of the record-player, was not detected at the check-in but the prolonged El Al security procedure delayed take-off for some hours so that the timer started running before the Boeing had taken off. The explosion of the bomb in the cargo hold while it was still climbing at around 14,000ft, instead of after it reached its cruising height of more than twice that altitude, caused panic among the passengers and made a hole in the fuselage which fortunately at that height did not bring down the aircraft, as might have been the case in the far thinner air at over 30,000ft. The pilot was able to make an emergency landing back in Rome, with all 140 passengers and fourteen crew shocked but safe.

On being interrogated, the two girls produced a photobooth picture of the 'boyfriends', which enabled Interpol to identify them as known terrorists, one Jordanian and the other Iraqi. It seems incredible that they continued to enjoy their Roman holiday, assuming that the girls and the aircraft were at the bottom of the Mediterranean, but then no intelligent terrorist allows his unwitting accomplices to take and keep photographs of him, either. Three days after the incident a sharp-eyed Roman police patrolman saw the two 'boyfriends' strolling across a piazza, called reinforcements and had them under lock and key. Once behind bars, they sang like canaries, in turn identifying Khreesat as the man who had given them in Belgrade the bomb assembled by him at a safe house in Bulgaria protected by Darzhavna Sigurnost – the state security organisation cloned from the KGB.[1] Given lengthy prison sentences, they were quietly released in some kind of deal between the Italian Government and Jibril's organisation and promptly flown out of the country.[2]

Although collaborating from time to time, there was very little permanent unity among the various Palestinian factions and even Jibril's followers did not all approve his policy of avoiding embarrassment for their Syrian hosts. In 1977 another schism resulted in a new terror faction headed by fanatical Palestinian terrorist Sabri al-Banna, whose *nom de guerre* was Abu Nidal, meaning 'father of the struggle'. His Palestine Liberation Front (PLF) was financed by Iraq and supported by Yasser Arafat's PLO. When Abu Nidal lured away many of Jibril's lieutenants, Jibril sent assassination squads after them in one of the frequent internecine conflicts that characterised the Palestinian groups. The Iraqis also fielded their own 'Palestinian' group, labelled Arab Liberation Front, but it was Abu Nidal's PLF that Jibril could not forgive. On 13 August 1978 a huge IED constructed by Marwan Khreesat blew up a luxury high-rise building in West Beirut where Abu Nidal had concentrated all his senior followers. Over 200 of them lay dead in the smoking debris of the apartment block, but their leader was not present, having moved to Baghdad, where the government of Saddam Hussein announced he had committed suicide in August 2002. Later, it became known that he had bullet wounds to the back of his head from some unidentified professional assassin.

For some time Jibril concentrated on training his men under Soviet Spetsnaz troops[3] and North Korean, Cuban and East German instructors, who brought with them more weaponry than Jibril's men could possibly use. These included surface-to-air missiles, wire-guided anti-tank missiles and multiple rocket launchers.[4] Some of this was passed on to the Irish Republican Army and other international terror groups, whose members attended PFLP-GC training camps in Lebanon. Following instruction by the Soviets and others, one of Jibril's snatch squads managed to kidnap an Israeli reservist named Avraham Amran in Southern Lebanon. In March 1979 he was swapped for seventy-six imprisoned terrorists, including seven serving life sentences. Six of the released women and four of the men were allowed to return to their homes on the West Bank; the others were flown to Libya. Among them was Hafez el-Dalkamoni, for whom Jibril had another role in mind.[5]

Small groups of PFLP-GC members on cross-border raids from bases in Lebanon into Israel specialised in the planting of landmines near kibbutzim, where children playing would be maimed and killed. Letter bombs posted to Israeli addressees were much easier to make and despatch than bombs to bring down an aircraft, of which the earlier models suffered from two defects: simple timer fuses caused explosions on the ground if departure was delayed; barometric devices triggered the explosion soon after cruising height was reached, so that the crash might take place over land, where air accident investigators could analyse the IEDs. The solution seemed to lie in a barometric fuse that started a timer at or near cruising height, the timer being preset to ensure the aircraft crashed over the sea, where investigation of the bomb was impossible. But this double fusing was complicated, so Jibril tasked Hafez Dalkamoni and Marwan Khreesat with the manufacture of an improvised IED that could pass an airport check-in X-ray scanner.

Although passengers may not be aware of it, the air pressure in the cabin of a civil airliner is reduced to the comfortable equivalent of less than 8,000ft altitude and the difference between that pressure and ground level, which accounts for ear-popping on climbing and descending, is sufficient to activate IED barometric fuses. Airports in 1988 had decompression chambers, in which suspect baggage could be placed, the drop in pressure being sufficient to trigger an explosion. Aware of this, Khreesat introduced a delay system into his IEDs, consisting of a capacitor that began charging itself on the cue from the pressure sensor detecting the drop in cabin pressure and would not detonate the explosive until fully charged. This delay could be between twenty and forty-five minutes and would ensure totally destuctive detonation at cruising height, normally reached in seven or eight minutes.

Khreesat's technique was to secrete his new generation of IEDs inside apparently harmless electrical appliances like radio cassette players. The extra wires and opaque explosive charge of the bomb would show up on an airport security X-ray, but would appear to an inattentive or tired operator like normal components, without arousing suspicion in those days. Khreesat was thought to be a double agent, working also for the Jordanian security service General Intelligence Directorate (GID), which gave him the go-ahead to work again with PFLP-GC, making the bombs they wanted, but not arming them. If true, the GID's use of him in this way seems remarkably lacking in tradecraft, since Dalkamoni or someone else would have realised what he was doing and the PFLP-GC would have eliminated Khreesat as a traitor. When recalled by his old boss Ahmed Jibril in 1985 to make more modern aircraft bombs in Syria, Khreesat favoured, among other appliances, the Toshiba Bombeat 453 'ghetto-blaster' radio cassette player model. At 16.5in long by 5.5in high, it was designed to look big and had plenty of spare space inside the casing for his explosive charge and the timer/detonator.

Throughout all this time, the US Navy had been repeatedly trying to provoke Libyan response. A significant indentation in the North African littoral known as the Gulf of Sirte or Sidra was claimed as

Libyan territorial waters by Gaddafi in 1973 by drawing a line on the map from Benghazi on the eastern side of the gulf to Misrata on the western side, enclosing an area of roughly 270 miles east–west by 100 miles north–south. In the summer of 1981 a Sixth Fleet battle group centred on the aircraft carrier USS *Nimitz* sailed into the Gulf of Sirte, ostensibly as a Freedom of Navigation exercise, but actually with intent to provoke a Libyan reaction. On 19 August, two Libyan Soviet-supplied SU-22 bombers which were shadowing the American vessels without demonstrating any hostile intent were shot down by fighters from *Nimitz*. The US Navy's first account alleged that this took place 60 miles from the Libyan coast, although a spokesman later admitted it was more like 20 miles, thus well within the Libyan-claimed territorial zone.[6] Nor was that the only confrontation in the gulf.

On 10 March 1982 President Reagan declared an embargo on Libyan oil exports, one third of which had previously been sold to the USA. The US oil companies working in the Libyan oilfields obeyed reluctantly, bringing home some 3,000 technicians. Also embargoed by Reagan was the exporting to Libya of a wide range of goods, designed to weaken the Libyan economy. A kind of war in the shadows resulted in President Gaddafi convening on 15 March 1986 in Tripoli what might be called a terror summit meeting – one of several he chaired over the years. Twenty-two Palestinian groups were represented at this one. All attended in the hope of generous handouts from Libya's leader as reward for coming. Also present and hoping for cash or arms supplies were members of ETA, the Basque Independence group based in the Pyrenean area of south-western France and northern Spain, some Catalan separatists from north-eastern Spain, North American indigenous people, Latin Americans and Africans from south of the Sahara. It would be hard to count the number of deaths on the delegates' hands as they listened to Jibril announcing that no passenger would henceforth be safe on Israeli or American civil aircraft.

When the La Belle discotheque in West Berlin was blown up by an IED on 5 April 1986, killing one US serviceman and a Turkish woman, and injuring sixty-plus other Americans among the 200 wounded, unverified information from CIA sources implicated Libya. In misdirected revenge President Reagan approved the bombing of Libya on 15 April in Operation El Dorado Canyon – an illegal bombing raid on Libyan targets. Eighteen F-111F fighter-bombers, escorted by four EF-111A Ravens from RAF Upper Heyford, joined fifteen other American strike aircraft protected by three E2C carrier-based radar-jamming aircraft flying offshore and bombed Tripoli while eight USN A6 Intruders bombed Benghazi using cluster bombs on 15 April 1986. Carrier-based F/A 18 Hornets launched some fifty high-speed anti-radiation smart missiles against Libyan radar targets.[7]

The operation was facilitated by Britain's Prime Minister Margaret Thatcher authorising the F-111s to refuel and 'bomb up' on the outward leg in British airbases, including the headquarters of 48th Tactical Fighter Wing at Lakenheath. However, no other European power approved the raid, France and Spain refusing overflight permission and forcing a 2,700-mile round trip on the crews with mid-air refuelling on both legs. Altogether forty USAF KC10 and KC 135 tanker aircraft were required in the whole operation. Some military targets were hit, including the Bab Azizzia barracks in central Tripoli, where Gaddafi was normally based, but nearby buildings were also hit in error, including the French Embassy. Gaddafi was not at home during the raid, but his adopted infant daughter Hanna died shortly afterwards, her body covered in shrapnel wounds, although the cause of death was brain injuries. Both his sons were concussed by the explosions, the younger one lying in a coma for four days. An undisclosed number of other civilians were killed or wounded. The bombing of oilfield targets was rejected at the planning stage because that would have destroyed American-owned facilities.

Alleged cloud cover the following day was quoted as the alibi for the absence of the normal post-raid aerial reconnaissance photography that would have shown exactly which buildings were hit. In Washington, President Reagan's popularity rating soared to 77 per cent approval of his action when he called Operation El Dorado Canyon a way of 'contributing to an international environment of peace and progress within which our democracy, and other free nations, can flourish'. Other US spokespersons excused the bombing of the cities of Tripoli and Benghazi as 'self defence against future attack',[8] an argument worthy of Nazi Germany or the KGB in the Soviet Union. The US Congress offered Mrs Thatcher praise and thanks for supporting Operation El Dorado Canyon. In Britain, reaction of even loyal members of the Conservative Parliamentary Party was mixed. An all-night protest was held outside the US Embassy in Grosvenor Square and 2,000 people held a candlelit vigil outside Downing Street. At Lakenheath and three other US airbases in Britain demonstrations were held. Disapproval in most European countries ranged from protest marches to criticism by prominent politicians. Resentment of Western interference was furious in the Middle East

However, not even the most fertile imagination in Washington could blame on Libya the next attempt to destroy an international flight. It came on 17 April 1986 when a five-month-pregnant, 19-year-old Irish chamber maid from the Hilton Hotel on London's Park Lane named Anne-Marie Murphy was checking in to board on the London stopover of a Boeing 747-200 on El Al Flight 016 from New York to Tel Aviv. She had been driven to Heathrow Terminal One by the father of her unborn child Nezar Hindawi, a 32-year-old Palestinian with Jordanian nationality. He had been married for five years to a Polish woman, who had a 4-year-old daughter by him and believed his story that he was a journalist, to account for his frequent trips to Damascus and other Arab capitals. Hindawi had convinced Murphy, who knew nothing of his family life, that he was sending her to Israel in preparation for their supposed wedding in his parents' village there while he stayed behind 'to conclude some important business deals'. Murphy was besotted with her handsome Arab lover and, like all the other 'mules', had no idea of his true identity: a mercenary being paid to destroy the El Al aircraft for the Syrian Government.

Frequent travellers who flew El Al at the time recall that the airline's check-in at British airports was always at a distance from other airlines' desks, with a noticeable presence of alert, armed British

Police sporting Heckler and Koch 9mm machine pistols. Another difference from other airlines' check-in procedures was an apparently casual but shrewd questioning by young agents of Shin Bet. Kissing the pregnant Irish girl goodbye, Hindawi handed her an expensive overnight bag containing presents, so he said, for his non-existent family in Israel. She passed the first interrogation, but at the second one a different Shin Bet agent showed more curiosity as to why a pregnant Irish girl, who was not Jewish, would be travelling to Israel. After she innocently admitted she was going there to marry her 'Arab boyfriend', she was taken into custody and an IED with 1.5kg of Semtex and a pocket calculator as timer was discovered under the false bottom of the case. It was set to trigger the explosive when the Boeing jumbo was over the Alps.

Planning to leave on a later flight to Damascus, Hindawi was intercepted in the Royal Garden Hotel, where he had been staying, by an official from the Idarat Mukhabarat al-Quwwa al-Jawiya – Syrian Air Force intelligence, commanded by Brigadier General Muhammad Khouli, a spymaster well known to Israeli intelligence officers – with the news that the bomb had been discovered and removed from the aircraft. He was given a Syrian passport in a different name and had his hair cut and dyed in a safe house on the assumption that his pregnant 'mule' would have described the appearance of her lover to airport security officers. Promised that he would be put on a Syrian Airlines flight to Damascus the following day, Hindawi spent a sleepless night suspecting that he was about to be eliminated in order to destroy the link between the foiled bombing of El Al Flight 016 and his Syrian employers. En route to the Syrian Embassy next morning, he escaped from his escorting officers and – knowing London well from the years he had lived there with his wife and child and the months prepping Murphy for her intended rendezvous with death – rushed into a police station to give himself up. His false alibi that he was a victim of a plot by Mossad, setting an innocent man up as a terrorist, was disproven when forensic experts found his hair underneath the adhesive tape securing the bomb to the bottom of Murphy's overnight bag.

Trying to obtain the best deal for himself, Hindawi spilled the beans about the operation he had been hired for, and much else besides. Among all the information were some items that surprised Western intelligence agencies, for example that the bombing in April 1986 of the La Belle discotheque in West Berlin had been carried out not by Libya, as the CIA had 'proven', but by his own brother – a fellow Syrian agent – working out of a base in East Berlin in collusion with Hauptverwaltung Aufklärung, the East German external espionage branch of the infamous Stasi. At the time, Germany was still divided north–south into the mutually hostile Bundesrepublik on the western side and the so-called German Democratic Republic to the east of the internal frontier.

After the trial at the Old Bailey, where Murphy was the chief prosecution witness, she said, 'I was a naïve young Irish girl, who didn't think for a minute that he would harm me or the baby'. Hindawi was sentenced to forty-five years in prison, with appeals for earlier parole dismissed. More than once, Murphy offered to return to Britain from her home in Ireland and speak against Hindawi as a dangerous criminal at his appeal hearings. That Iron Lady, Margaret Thatcher broke off diplomatic relations with Syria, as did the US and Canada. Hindawi was eventually released in March 2013 and deported to Jordan. Is that the end of the story? As so often in terrorist operations, there is no clear answer. Jibril worked in close liaison with Khouli and the modus operandi, using an innocent young and emotionally involved woman as the 'mule', does suggest an involvement with PFLP-GC, but, unless it is in the inaccessible files of Mossad, the answer is unknown.

On 22 July 1986 Habash's PFLP emerged from the confusion of the other anti-Israel terrorist groups by hijacking El Al Flight 426 from Rome to Tel Aviv. In addition to thirty-five legitimate passengers, three smartly dressed Palestinians also boarded the Boeing 707, which took off just before midnight. Since thousands of Palestinians lived inside Israel, they attracted no particular attention. Shortly after the Boeing reached cruising altitude, the three headed fast for the flight deck and wrenched open the door. To show they meant business, one of them shot the first officer in the stomach with a 9mm bullet. Announcing to the terrified passengers that they were now hostages on the aircraft re-baptised *Liberation of Palestine*, the leader of the hijackers, Ali Shafik Ahmed, who called himself Captain Rifat, informed them that he had ordered a change of course to Houari Boumoudienne Airport, 10 miles outside Algiers, the capital of Algeria.

For three weeks, the Israeli Cabinet under Prime Minster Levi Eshkol debated how to deal with this unforseen event, for which the best organised and equipped army in the Middle East had no solution. After three weeks, the government in Jerusalem that had boasted it would never again negotiate with terrorists gave in and agreed to release sixteen jailed Palestinians in return for the safe return of the passengers on Flight 426.

Syria's generous subsidies for terrorism came from oil revenues. Although not a major oil-exporting country, the country needed its markets in Italy, Germany, France, the Netherlands and other European states, all of which, with the USA, imposed increased sanctions on the el-Assad regime for its role in fostering international terrorism. The Reagan administration even went so far as to advise US oil giants to think about withdrawing totally from the Syrian market. Unlike Yasser Arafat's PLO, which had built up a sizeable reserve in investments, Ahmed Jibril lived hand-to-mouth. He now needed another source of finance. Iran, bled dry by its war with Iraq, was not interested in financing anti-Israel activity and, in fact, *needed* the ransom money – or payment in kind, like weaponry – for the return of Western hostages repeatedly kidnapped by its associated terror groups in Syria and Lebanon.[9] Starting in 1976, PFLP-GC found itself in straitened circumstances, having lost Gaddafi's annual payments of over $20 million a year in return for the deployment in Chad and elsewhere of Jibril's special forces. As somebody once remarked, terrorism is an expensive luxury that creates no wealth, so if you succeed in cutting off the handouts, you solve the problem.

Jibril was reduced virtually to putting up a 'For Hire' notice, and was already in contact with Tehran through an envoy of Interior Minister Ali-Akbar Montashemi before the fateful morning of 3 July

1988. When news of the *Vincennes* shooting down Iran Air Flight 655 reached Lebanon, Jibril apparently grabbed the first telephone to hand in order to get in first, calling Montashemi in Tehran to offer his organisations for the execution of the *qisas* on the traditional eye-for-an-eye level. As he suggested, the best target was surely an American jumbo jet with approximately the same number of crew and passengers as the Iran Air 655 Airbus.

It is likely that NSA and Israeli interceptors monitored that unencrypted phone call. In any event the Middle East is as full of ears, electronic and human, as a bazaar. Other US agencies physically monitored movements of terrorists, as did Israel's Mossad, which had been keeping tabs on Jibril's meetings with the Iranian Interior Minister's envoy in the Hezbollah-controlled Beka'a valley. In addition, Saddam Hussein's Mukhabarat in Baghdad kept its collective ear to the ground, to pick up any vibrations from across the frontier with Iran, and may have passed some information to the CIA, Iraq being an ally of the USA at the time. At the meeting in Tehran, Jibril's born-again fundamentalism[10] went down well, as did the military record of Dalkamoni, who accompanied him on the trip. Nobody apparently *knows* what was the fee offered to Jibril for executing the *qisas*, but evidence exists that it was in the region of $10 million: $2 million on the handshake and the balance on completion. He was happy with the deal and MOIS was satisfied it had given the job to a deniable, non-Iranian group with a record of succeeding in similar operations.

Some agencies believe that the money may have passed from MOIS through Syrian hands. At any event, al-Assad's Mukhabarat in Damascus likewise did not want to be known as the state which hosted a gang that had brought down an American wide-bodied passenger jet and killed everyone on board. There is reason to believe that it was they who insisted on a red herring being injected into Jibril's plan of action, to deflect international sanctions away from Syria. There was little love lost between al-Assad and Hosni Moubarak, the current President of Egypt, but what would be a plausible motive for an Egyptian attack on an American aircraft when his country was largely dependent on American aid? Other fall guys may have been contemplated, but the personal hatred and rivalry between al-Assad and Gaddafi made Libya the candidate of choice for this unsought role. For the second time, Malta entered the story as being the customary port of call for Middle Eastern visitors like Jibril on his many visits to Gaddafi's Libya, since international sanctions had cut out direct flights from most other states.

5

AUTUMN LEAVES

Execution of a *qisas* is supposed to be rapid, in order to make the point that this is revenge. In September 1988 Dalkamoni, using the alias Hafez Hussein, moved to the PFLP-GC's European headquarters in the Serbian town of Kruševac, where weapons, explosives and other material were stored, to activate Jibril's several sleeper cells in the Bundesrepublik.[1] He arrived there on 5 October, travelling on a genuine Syrian passport in a false name, which was probably furnished by Syrian Air Force Intelligence. He took reasonable precautions in Europe, never using the same telephone twice and checking frequently for surveillance. One thing he could not conceal, of course, was the characteristic limp, due to the amputation of his leg in Israel, which made him easy to follow in a crowd. He also figured on the Interpol lists of known terrorists ever since his imprisonment in Israel. One would think that a man 'with previous form' would be wary of having contact in a well-policed country like Germany with a group of thirty-four obviously foreign single men of Arabic appearance, who were Jibril's sleepers, but that is what he did.

In addition, some of these men were in contact with members of Jabhat al-Nid'al el-Sha'abi el-Filastini, or the Palestinian Popular Struggle Front (PPSF), living undercover in Sweden. To have links to another terror group in Europe seems to be inviting attention from counterterrorist police, especially since the Swedish contingent included the Egyptian terrorist Abu Talb, granted Swedish citizenship after arriving in Sweden on a forged Moroccan passport with his wife and child in 1986. In July 1985 Abu Talb and three PPSF associates had committed three bombings in Copenhagen, killing one man and injuring seven at the Great Synagogue there, and also bombed the El Al office in Amsterdam.[2] In Sweden, his cover identity was running a shop in Uppsala selling Middle-Eastern food and videos.

In October 1988 Khreesat was despatched to Neuss on the west bank of the Rhine opposite Düsseldorf in northern Germany. There, PFLP-GC had an active duty cell based on the apartment at No. 16 Isarstrasse of Syrian terrorist Hashem Abbasi, a brother-in-law of Dalkamoni whose cover was managing a Middle-Eastern greengrocery. Khreesat arrived in Neuss on 13 October. By then the undercover surveillance teams of the Bundeskriminalamt (BKA) – a federal police force based in Wiesbaden – had already identified and photographed a stream of visitors to 16 Isarstrasse including Abassi's brother Ahmed, who was the liaison agent with PPSF in Sweden, and one of the Mograbi brothers, whose sister was married to Abu Talb. Also photographed were a known PFLP-GC courier and an unknown man – who may have brought the ingredients for Khreesat's IEDs. One did not need to be a trained counterterrorist officer to realise that all this activity was setting the stage for an exceptionally big terrorist attack somewhere in Europe.

Another address staked out by BKA was on the long Sandweg road in Frankfurt, a short distance from the Rhein-Main Airport and the important US base nearby. Here too, BKA surveillance teams observed several dozen Arab male visitors, some of whom were also photographed in Neuss and who arrived by circuitous routes obviously chosen to shake off followers. Suspicions grew that an attack on Frankfurt Airport was being planned, like the synchronised assaults in Rome Fiumicino and Vienna Schwechat Airports on 27 December 1985 when terrorists of the Abu Nidal group used assault rifles and hand grenades to kill sixteen and wound 100 waiting passengers in Rome Airport and kill three more and injure another thirty-nine in Vienna.

On 13 October Khreesat was identified by BKA watchers arriving in Neuss, which obviously meant that IEDs were going to be assembled there. On 16 October Dalkamoni's Ford Taunus was shadowed when he drove out of town to buy plastic bags and storage boxes. On 18 October two Ultrasound radios and a computer monitor were purchased in a second-hand electrical goods shop to house IEDs. On 19 October a telephone call made by Dalkamoni from Abassi's apartment in Neuss to a kebab restaurant in Cyprus, which functioned as a postbox for Jibril, was intercepted, but Arabic-speaking BKA officers could not make out what was said in some kind of code. Shortly afterwards, Dalkamoni broke his rule about never using the same phone twice to call Damascus, during which Khreesat picked up an extension phone to inform the man at the other end that he had made changes to 'the medicine', which was now 'stronger than before'.[3] On 20 October Khreesat was working on the IEDs, when he received a call from 47-year-old Palestinian Abdel Ghadanfar, using the name Masoud, informing him that he would shortly receive 'three black tins with lids, gloves and paste'. Dalkamoni also told him that he would personally bring 'at least seven white pointed buttons, four of which would be electric'.[4] Khreesat was working on a Toshiba Bombeat, which he later identified from a photograph as the F423 model. The modifications included a barometric switch to start a timer, so that the aircraft would be well into its flight when destroyed. In the not unusual opportunistic networking of terrorist groups, the timers available in Neuss had been made by a technician working for a Fatah group in Damascus, and were presumably brought to Germany by the unidentified courier, although Khreesat professed not to know how they got to Neuss, when later interviewed in Jordan by two American agents.

Dalkamoni and Khreesat had a strange shopping spree, buying batteries, insulated cable, digital and clockwork alarm clocks, electronic switches and small nuts and bolts. On 24 October, a call to Amman was intercepted, in which Khreesat said he would be done in a few days and would be back in Amman that Friday. Previous warnings from Mossad that an attack on a Western aircraft was being planned had been ignored but, acting reportedly on information from the CIA that a terror attack was imminent – the official version is perhaps designed to conceal and protect a source inside the PFLP-GC cell – the BKA launched Fall Herbstlaub, or Operation Autumn Leaves, in collaboration with Grenzschutzgruppe 9 (GSG-9), similar to Britain's SAS, the Bundesamt für Verfassungsschutz (BfV), counterpart of MI5, and the Bundesnachrichtendienst (BND), equivalent to MI6. A total of seventy officers were involved in this nationwide sweep to wrap up several Middle Eastern terrorist groups known to be based in the Bundesrepublik, including the Neuss gang. On 26 October BKA police with BfV agents and personnel from GSG-9 burst into a dozen or more apartments in several German cities, arresting seventeen Palestinians and other Arabic-speakers.

At the Sandweg address in Frankfurt they uncovered a mass murderer's treasure trove: assault rifles, automatic pistols, ammunition, mortar rounds, hand grenades, different kinds of explosive, night-vision goggles, one American anti-tank rocket – probably stolen from US stores in Germany – and 5kg of Semtex, the terrorists' explosive of choice for destroying aircraft. It is believed that some or all of this stash, which included many thousands of anti-personnel and anti-tank mines, was payment by the Sicilian Mafia for shipments of heroin from the Beka'a valley in Syria. Picked up in Sandweg was Abdel Ghadanfar, who made a point of insulting and irritating his captors, as though he was so important that they would swiftly be obliged to release him.[5] Khreesat and Dalkamoni were arrested while shopping in Neuss, a search of Dalkamoni's car revealing blasting caps and a mechanical alarm clock modified to serve as a timing device. Most incriminatingly, the boot of the Taunus contained a Toshiba Bombeat radio cassette player containing a charge of Semtex and a barometric firing device designed to blow up an aircraft at altitude. Both men denied knowing anything about it or how it came to be there. In Abassi's apartment, where they had been living, Spanish and Syrian passports bearing Dalkamoni's photograph were found, as was a Syrian driving licence, also with his photograph, in the name of Hafez Hussein – and a cache of British, German and Yugoslavian currency.[6]

A simultaneous search of 16 Isarstrasse and another apartment in the same street recovered stop watches, batteries, detonators and several other Syrian passports, including Dalkamoni's diplomatic passport issued by the Ministry of Religious Affairs in Damascus. There the BKA searchers found a Beretta pistol with 900 rounds of ammunition, plus six Kalashnikov assault rifles with nineteen loaded magazines and three silencers. Five kilos of Semtex were also taken away, with 5.7kg of another unidentified plastic explosive, 3kg of TNT and eighty-nine detonators.[7] Taken to Frankfurt for questioning, twelve of the men arrested that day were freed by a federal German judge on the grounds of insufficient evidence connecting them with the weapons and explosives! Two more two men, arrested in the car with Dalkamoni, were also released, leaving only three locked up.

A week after all the arrests, Khreesat asked to make a phone call to Jordan, as a result of which the West German Foreign Ministry was requested by GID in Amman to arrange his release. Four days later, a German judge released him on the grounds of insufficient evidence.[8] Immediately after release, he disappeared and was believed to have flown back to the Middle East. Some sources alleged that he had been working as a mole for the BKA inside the gang. Abu Talb was not picked up *because he was in Malta* at the time after a fortnight's stay in Cyprus, where he met Dalkamoni.[9] In a version of I-knew-nothing-about-it, Dalkamoni admitted after his arrest in Neuss that he was a member of PFLP-GC, but said that he was the group's finance officer and had nothing to do with terrorism. Ghadanfar claimed to be his assistant – a finance clerk. However, Dalkamoni was later charged with placing IEDs on American troop trains in August 1987 and April 1988 and possession of explosives. Convicted by a German court, he was sentenced to fifteen years' imprisonment, Ghadanfar receiving a sentence of twelve years for possession of explosives. Additional charges of belonging to a terrorist organisation were dropped by the prosecution so that the two men could be treated as criminals, rather than terrorists.[10]

For whatever reason, it was two days before the Bombeat found in Dalkamoni's car was examined by explosives experts and found, cunningly hidden inside it, an IED composed of 300g of Semtex with a thirty-minute timer that could only be primed by a barometric switch with thirty-five-minute delay to fool decompression chambers at airports where suspect baggage was placed for a few minutes as a precautionary measure. Dalkamoni repeatedly said he had no idea how it came to be in his car.

On 18 November the US Federal Aviation Authority issued a security bulletin advising airlines and airports of the haul accumulated by Autumn Leaves and warning of the need for extra vigilance to detect such IEDs in passengers' luggage.

The three modified second-hand devices were not found until much later. In April 1989, after Khreesat told an FBI officer in Jordan where they had been concealed in Abassi's apartment, the BKA conducted a more thorough search, and did find the two modified Ultrasounds and the computer monitor. *A fifth IED in a Bombeat was not found by BKA searchers.* Possibly as an alibi for himself, Khreesat later alleged that this one had been constructed by another terrorist in Neuss named Abu Elias, to whom he had taught his ghastly skills. In the BKA laboratory at Wiesbaden, where two explosives technicians were examining an Ultrasound radio recovered in Neuss, one technician was killed when it blew up and his colleague was blinded and permanently disabled – which suggests a sophisticated built-in booby-trap. A blonde, blue-eyed Lebanese Christian, who could easily pass in Europe and attracted no attention in airports, Abu Elias, aka Khaisar Haddad, was thought to be a nephew of Ahmed Jibril.

When interviewed for the 1994 television documentary *The Maltese Double Cross*, former Iranian President Abdulhassan Bani Sadr confirmed that MOIS settled on Jibril's PFLP-GC as the group most competent to plan and execute an attack on a suitable American airliner[11] and with nothing to lose for doing so. As to the target, since the bright blue, white and silver livery of Pan American was then as iconic a symbol of the USA as the Coca-Cola bottle, Pan Am was top of the hit list. When the CIA confirmed that Jibril had done some kind of deal with intelligence officers in Iran, this was passed to Interpol, which issued a warning to all European airports about the PFLP-GC bombs. Heathrow Airport issued an instruction to security staff to be 'extra vigilant' when finding radios, radio cassette players and other similar equipment in passengers' luggage. Photographs from the BKA of the Toshiba Bombeat IED were also circulated.

A hidden problem was that the responsibility for screening passengers' bags lay not with an airport's own staff, but with the airlines on which passengers were travelling. The airlines often chose the cheapest alternatives, to outsource this duty. As a result, although it was recommended that X-ray operators staring at screens should be relieved every twenty minutes to sustain concentration, the same person was often left to carry on throughout an eight-hour shift, with consequent eye strain and waning concentration. Although Pan American had imposed a $5 surcharge 'for security' on each ticket sold, checking baggage on its flights was outsourced to a wholly owned company called Alert Security. As to how 'alert' it was, the head of its Frankfurt operation was Ulrich Weber, a man with a criminal record who hired only attractive women whom he wanted to bed, and to whom precious little training for their important job was given.[12] In a classic example of shutting stable doors after the horse has bolted, a week after the Lockerbie crash, on 28 December 1988, Britain's Department of Transport issued a new directive tightening up security controls, particularly of baggage transferred at a British airport from an incoming flight, which in future was to be X-rayed and hand-searched if necessary.[13]

PART 2

THE FATAL LAST FLIGHT OF
MAID OF THE SEAS

At 12.10 p.m. on Wednesday, 21 December 1988 the Boeing 747 Clipper named *Maid of the Seas*, registration N739PA, landed at London Heathrow Airport from San Francisco. The aircraft was 18 years old, having been among the first of this model delivered to the airline brand new on 12 February 1970, and had logged 72,464 hours in the air, making 16,497 flight cycles of take-off and landing. All the requisite safety checks had been done, with all anomalies promptly corrected with fixes supplied by Boeing.

Passengers disembarked, the big jumbo jet was unloaded, cleaned and refuelled. During the latter part of the six-hour turnaround there was no luggage on board. At 4.45 p.m. westbound Captain James McQuarrie filed his flight plan for the return leg departing at 6 p.m. for New York and Detroit, designated Pan Am Flight 103. He was doing pre-flight checks when Flight 103A, the Pan Am feeder flight from Frankfurt, flown by a smaller Boeing 727, landed at 5.20 p.m. with 109 passengers, of whom sixty were ending their journey in London and forty-nine were to travel onward across the Atlantic on *Maid of the Seas*. They included American servicemen and their families heading home for Christmas. It was an easy transfer for them, the inbound flight from Frankfurt having parked at Stand 16 Kilo of Terminal 3, adjacent to the jumbo jet on Stand 14 Kilo. Offloading of baggage for passengers terminating at Heathrow and transfer of baggage belonging to people continuing to Kennedy Airport, New York, was routine. It was assumed that all the bags from Frankfurt had been properly inspected there, so they received no re-examination at Heathrow.

Another 194 passengers boarded at Heathrow, many of them having arrived there on nine other feeder flights. Hold baggage was not checked off against the passenger manifest, which is a basic security requirement today. Baggage handlers used the right-side forward cargo door of *Maid of the Seas* to place aluminium baggage container AVE4041PA in the forward hold of the jumbo jet, on the left side of the aircraft. This container also contained baggage from Pan Am's interline shed, where luggage from other airlines' feeder flights was scanned before loading.

The 243 transatlantic passengers settled back in their seats as *Maid of the Seas* pushed back from the pier at 6.04 p.m. and queued for take-off on Runway 27 Right (27R), finally lifting off at 6.25 p.m. McQuarrie brought the jumbo up through heavy cloud on a heading that would take it on the northern of the two most used corridors that follow the Great Circle geography to take advantage of the earth's curvature across the Atlantic, the choice being influenced by very strong westerly winds blowing that night. On a heading of 350 degrees the 747 flew below the Bovingdon holding point at 6,000ft. It was then cleared to climb initially to flight level 120 or approximately 12,000ft. It was subsequently cleared to climb to flight level 310 where it levelled off at 6.56 p.m. All was routine so far.

Since aircraft manufacturers and airlines have a tendency to blame what is called 'pilot error', or the human element, for crashes, it is worth noting that there could not have been a better flight deck crew. With 4,107 hours' experience flying 747s, McQuarrie spent much of his leisure time flying voluntarily with the Massachussets Air National Guard. His 52-year-old First Officer Ray Wagner had logged 5,517 hours on 747s and also flew both fixed-wing fighters and helicopters of the New Jersey National Guard. Sitting with them on the flight deck there was also Jerry Don Avritt, an experienced flight engineer.

The chosen flight path was to take Clipper *Maid of the Seas* over a small Scottish town, of which probably none of the passengers had ever heard, called Lockerbie.

Travelling several times a year to Scotland for business then, the author knew neighbouring Lachmaben and Lockerbie itself personally and had a tenuous family connection with the area, since in 1890-something his maternal grandmother, a pregnant actress from Newcastle-on-Tyne, married her lover at the smithy in Gretna Green, just across the border from England, to avoid the scandal of giving birth while unmarried, and became Mrs Adelaide Marie Branford. Lockerbie was then a quiet town of 3,500 people most famous for its sheep market. Although formerly written in Scots Gaelic spelling Locarbaidh, the name is actually derived from 'Loc-hard's by', meaning 'Lockart's town' in Old Norse. Even the Viking connection does not tell the whole story, for Roman remains to the west of the town indicate much earlier origins.

The reason why people have settled there, whether 2,000 years ago or now, is that Lockerbie lies athwart the best route from Carlisle and the south to Glasgow and the north. The town's main street was originally a stretch of the nineteenth-century main road that followed the line of north–south Roman roads. The King's Arms hotel was where stagecoaches carrying the mails changed horses before the London–Glasgow railway arrived in 1847–48, also following the ancient route. To the eye of the casual visitor, the place was like the people who lived there, clean, tidy and modest – the sort of small town where one wonders how everyone earns a living in a place where 'nothing ever happens'. Yet, in the past, clan warfare had claimed many lives, with Clan Johnstone taking on Clan Maxwell – no grand Highland names here – in December 1593, just outside the town. The Johnstones nearly exterminated the Maxwells in a bloody slaughter with sharp and blunt instruments, but little blood had been shed in anger locally since then.

The cabin crew of Pan Am 103 numbered thirteen. They were already serving drinks and giving out headphones to the passengers after the 747 reached cruising height when Ray Wagner contacted

Shanwick[1] air traffic control on 123.95 MHz at 6.58 p.m., giving his current position. With the 747's transponder squawking 0357 in Mode C, this code identified the small green blip on the radar screen in the ATC room at Prestwick Airport. Wagner requested westbound oceanic clearance at flight level 310, mach decimal eighty-four. Air Traffic Controller Alan Topp mentally translated this as a height of 31,000ft and speed of 540 miles an hour, and replied at 7.02 p.m., giving clearance. Providing the height and speed were maintained, Flight 103 represented no danger to any other aircraft in the skies over the Atlantic. All was perfectly routine with the aircraft approaching the Solway Firth, about 20 miles short of Lockerbie.

Then, suddenly, it wasn't.

Timers of the Toshiba cassette bombs seized by BKA were later tested and found to run for thirty minutes. To prevent the bomb exploding on the ground if the flight was delayed, a barometric switch did not start the timer running until the change in air pressure seven or eight minutes after the aircraft took off. It was thirty-eight minutes and some seconds after *Maid of the Seas* took off from Heathrow that Alan Topp blinked as the single green box on the screen in front of him bearing Pan Am 103's transponder identification disappeared and was briefly replaced by five undesignated boxes, representing the nose cone, the wings, the main fueslage in two pieces and the tailplane. These then vanished as they all fell below the radar horizon. He called across the control room to his shift manager Adrian Ford, but Ford was listening to the pilot of a London–Glasgow shuttle descending to 24,000ft who was reporting a fiery glow on the ground ahead of his aircraft.

It was later calculated that forward velocity of all the large pieces of the aircraft was lost in a descending curve from 31,000ft to 19,000ft, with a large part of the aircraft then falling more or less vertically from 19,000ft to 9,000ft. The needles of the recording apparatus at the Eskdalemuir Earthquake Monitoring Centre recorded a tremor of 1.9 on the Richter scale, timed at 7.03 p.m. and 20 seconds, when the wings crashed onto Lockerbie and all the aviation spirit for the transatlantic crossing ignited in a colossal explosion as a total of over

300 tonnes of metal and fuel and bodies at differing terminal velocities crashed to earth.

As would later be established, a small charge of Semtex had exploded inside baggage container AVE4041PA in the left forward cargo area beneath the first-class seating and the flight deck. In milliseconds, it stressed fuselage skin along the adjacent former or lateral strengthener, weakening the aircraft right around its body at this point, cutting control cables, damaging vital electronic equipment and blowing a hole, initially only 20in across, through the skin of the fuselage nearest to the explosion. This was referred to as 'the shatter zone' in the Air Accident Investigation Board report.[2]

Immediately after the primary shock wave, a secondary wave of high pressure followed, causing the fuselage skin to stretch and blister outwards before bursting and petalling back in a starburst pattern, with tear fractures propagating away from the shatter zone. The outflow of pressurised air through the aperture produced a characteristic curling of the skin 'petals' even against the slipstream. These strips of skin were torn from the frames and stringers, which also fractured and became separated from the rest of the aircraft's structure, producing a jagged hole 5ft horizontally by 17ft circumferentially, reaching up to just below the level of the windows and down almost to the centre line of the 747.[3] With the rivets that joined the panels to the airframe popping apart and the bond of adhesive reinforcing them at the lap joints giving way, whole panels just blew away with no further need for a second explosion.

The fuselage structure of N739PA was different from that of the majority of Boeing 747s since it formed part of the US Civil Reserve Air Fleet. The usual main deck supporting beams had been strengthened to carry the greater weight of military freight containers or vehicles in place of the seats in time of national emergency. A large side-loading door was added on the left side of the main deck aft of the wing. Neither of these modifications played any part in the disintegration of the aircraft.

Modern airliners like the Boeing 747 and the Iranian Airbus are, in physics terms, roughly cylindrical pressure vessels with the same internal air pressure throughout both the passenger deck or decks and the cargo space below, helping to keep the aircraft rigid. A catastrophic loss of pressure anywhere therefore entails a loss of airframe integrity. In milliseconds, the decompression of *Maid of the Seas'* cargo hold also decompressed the passenger decks and the flight deck, taking the 256 crew and passengers from the comfortable air pressure of less than 8,000ft notional height to a fraction of this. Although the comparison may be difficult to digest, given the size and initial rigidity of a jumbo jet, the effect was not dissimilar to a balloon being punctured: air, people and objects were expelled[4] through the rapidly widening hole at a speed calculated to be 600mph. It was not only the airframe that decompressed, but also the bodies of passengers and crew, as the pressure of the air in the soft tissue of their lungs and other organs in some burst in a phenomenon called 'explosive decompression'.

Since everything happened in milliseconds, it is difficult to say exactly the sequence of events. The aircraft lost rigidity, the entire nose cone consisting of flight deck, first-class seating and the space below separating almost entirely from the rest of the aircraft and briefly hinging back upside down on the roof of the fuselage until breaking free less than two seconds after the explosion, striking the tail of the aircaft before falling separately with passengers still strapped into their seats. By then, there was no light or oxygen in any part of the disintegrating aircraft and the temperature had dropped to around minus 60 degrees centigrade as the rest of *Maid of the Seas* broke into four pieces, spilling bodies, luggage and equipment into the dark void in a blizzard of thousands of separate items. Several passengers ejected from the fuselage were sucked into the still functioning engines. The jet stream of 120mph winds blowing at this height and the forward momentum of the aircraft at an airspeed of 540mph tore off clothing and wrenched bodies apart as they and other debris began a 6-mile plunge to earth, the wind decreasing in strength to 60mph at 10,000ft and 15–20mph at ground level.[5]

Depending on the direction in which they had been expelled from the disintegrating aircraft and other factors like drag and air currents, the falling bodies reached terminal velocity after twelve or so seconds, tossed like snowflakes in the jet stream winds until landing roughly two minutes later in the rain-sodden fields around Lockerbie or on the hard streets and roofs of the town. Lighter debris was blown away in two separate paths to the north-east, spread over 845 square miles. Some of it landed 80 miles away on the other side of Scotland, by the shore of the North Sea, and some lighter pieces were probably blown further still, to land in the sea.

There were indications that a few of the falling victims may have recovered consciousness to some degree on reaching a height of about 12,000ft above ground level, when their lungs, if not too damaged, managed to absorb some oxygen. A stewardess and a passenger were said to have briefly spoken to the first people who found them on the ground and another victim was thought to have had a faint pulse, but all were dead when the first would-be rescuers arrived on the scene. Another woman's body was found with grass and mud in her clenched hands, as though she had been scrabbling to get some purchase after landing, or maybe in the darkness trying to understand where she was.

The nose cone, with the bodies of the three flight deck crew and some first-class passengers still inside, landed 4½ miles south-east of the town, near the church of Tundergarth, an area that would eventually prove to be the last resting place of 160 people. The cone landed flat on its left side, crushing and mutilating the bodies seated there. Some early reports said the body of McQuarrie was thrown out and found some distance from it, but that may have been because he had been in the left-hand seat and his remains, entangled in the crushed metal, were unrecognisable as a human body.

The worst damage to people and structures in the town itself came from the wings, containing 20,000 gallons of aviation fuel for the 3,000-mile transatlantic flight, which ignited on landing in a huge explosion, gouging a crater 30ft wide, 100ft long and more than 30ft deep in Sherwood Crescent. The shock wave travelling through the ground also took a sizeable bite out of the southbound carriageway of the adjacent Lockerbie Bypass section of the A74 trunk road, for the repairs to which British Prime Minister John Major was still hoping to make Pan Am pay in 1994, by which date the airline had ceased to exist. The immediate effect of the damage was to reduce the two lanes in each direction to one and cause hour-long delays for emergency vehicles trying to reach the town.

As the fireball from all the aviation fuel in the wings rose to 300ft high, 1,500 tonnes of displaced earth, masonry and rock spread out in all directions, the lighter elements being blown miles downwind. Houses number 13 and 16 in the crescent vanished completely, together with every trace of their inhabitants except for the artificial knee joint that had belonged to 81-year-old Mary Lancaster – and, according to some accounts, one badly burned and unrecognisable corpse. The bodies of ten passengers were not recovered. Since eight of them had been sitting over the wing at the front of the economy section, it may be assumed they were completely vaporised in the fireball. What the official AAIB report called 'the fragmented remains' of thirteen passengers in seats around the eight missing bodies were found near the crater formed by the wing.[6]

In addition to the houses totally destroyed in Sherwood Crescent, more than a dozen others had their roofs completely torn off and walls severely damaged by the shock wave travelling through the air and the ground. In all, twenty-one houses were so damaged they had to be demolished; many others needed extensive repairs. A 14-year-old resident named Stephen Flannigan had taken his younger sister's bicycle from his home in the crescent to a nearby pal's house in order to mend a flat tyre for her. Taking shelter from the heat of the fireball behind the friend's house, he had no idea that he had just lost his parents, his sister and his home. Only he and an older brother, living away from the parental home, were left of what had been a large family. Both of them were later to die prematurely: the older brother when on holiday in Thailand and Stephen nineteen years after the crash, when killed outright by a train.[7]

From Sherwood Crescent damage continued in six major areas lying in a roughly north-easterly direction, right through the town. Earth and boulders from the crater, some large, were thrown considerable distances in all directions. Some abandoned cars on the A74 were at first thought to have been damaged *in situ*, until it was realised they could have been thrown there bodily by the explosion. In Rosebank Crescent, a street of pebble-dashed council housing, a 60ft section of fuselage had come down, leaving baggage and bodies littering the road surface and gardens. With much of the town deprived of electricity by the crash, most light outside was coming from the fireball in Sherwood Crescent. Perhaps mercifully, nobody on the ground yet had any idea how many were dead.

When the roar of the rapidly falling large parts of fuselage and the four engines was first heard, many people assumed that it was thunder – except that thunder came and went, while this was continuously getting louder. Mrs Ella Ramsden's house on the Park Plaza estate began to shake with the vibrations. Low-flying military jets were a common occurrence above Lockerbie. When she heard a tremendous explosion, her first thought was that one of them had crashed while carrying a bomb, which had exploded. Trying to get out of the house, she went to the kitchen door, but found it jammed tight. A loud whooshing noise and a huge draught that dragged her backwards made her look up – and see, instead of the kitchen ceiling, stars. Using a pan to smash the kitchen door open, she staggered out and called for help. Her immediate neighbours were looking for her at the front of the house, but concluded from the damage – the gable end had been blown completely away and little of the roof was left – that she must be dead. Hearing her calls, three of them ran to the back, and found a large portion of fuselage sitting in her vegetable garden. A body lay in the street, another was spreadeagled across what remained of the roof. Eventually some seventy bodies, many horribly mutilated, were dug out of the ruin of her house and the garden. Yet, as she soon realised, she was one of the lucky residents of Lockerbie. Her grandson had left with his parents only a few hours before. Had he stayed, he would have died in his bedroom, which no longer existed.

Overlooking the ruin of the Ramsden house, Margaret Cameron's kitchen windows had been blown in by the hail of earth and stones displaced by the section of fuselage crashing to the ground. Among the rubble on her kitchen floor were hundreds of plastic airline knives and forks with two half-written postcards and a pot of face cream. Her garden was covered in pieces of paper, among which were thousands of dollars in cash.

Only a few yards from the base of the fireball, pensioner John Smith and his wife were alerted by the roar of the wings incoming. They heard and felt metal hit the roof of their house a glancing blow. Flames erupted everywhere. Fighting his way outside, Smith went back for his wife and dragged her out into the front garden. The house was blazing and they had to pick their way between patches of burning fuel in the garden until meeting neighbours who came looking for them. The radiated heat from the fireball was now so intense that lawns, hedges, garden sheds, and even houses at first untouched, burst into flame. A pile of old tyres behind the nearby filling station ignited, adding the stench of burning rubber to the all-pervading smell of kerosene. This in turn ignited the underground storage tanks of petrol and diesel motor fuel.

Hearing the explosion and seeing the fireball, retired doctor Alistair Cameron was unsure exactly what had happened. Assuming that his medical knowledge would be needed, he drove into town until debris on the road forced him to stop his car and walk the rest of the way to Rosebank Crescent on the eastern side of the town. In the darkness, he missed a sight that made many stare in daylight: an empty aircraft seat half in and half out of a shattered window in the crescent. Uncertain what he was stumbling over in the darkness, he turned on a pocket torch and recognised what he was standing on, and surrounded by, as dismembered body parts. He hurried on to give first aid to the injured, but found surprisingly few needing his professional attention. The psychological damage to traumatised residents would take many years to disappear; in some cases, it never did.

A NIGHT IN HELL

At 7 p.m. that night there had been one policeman in Lockerbie. Off-duty Superintendent John Carpenter and his wife were peacefully watching television. *This is your Life* presenter Mike Aspel was hosting that night's guests, Harry Corbett and Sooty. Carpenter's boss John Boyd, Chief Constable of the Dumfries and Galloway force, the smallest force in Britain with one of the largest 'parishes' to police, was also off duty. At home in Dumfries, 12 miles to the south-west, he saw an ITN newsflash about the crash almost at the same time as a call from his headquarters gave him a slightly fuller picture. Putting on his uniform, he drove to work, pretty certain he would not be returning home for some time.

There was coincidentally a regional emergency plan that had not been envisaged for a plane crash, but for a possible accident at the nearby Chapelcross nuclear power station. Setting it in motion, Boyd called his opposite numbers in neighbouring police forces, who ordered hundreds of their personnel to make their way to Lockerbie. Among them was Detective Stuart Henderson, whose first reaction on arrival in the town was that it was more like a war zone than a disaster area. Fire and ambulance services from all over southern Scotland and northern England were heading for the disaster zone already at 7.07 p.m. Three minutes later, one rapid-response vehicle was already in attendance in the Rosebank area. Once multiple fires had been identified the Fire Brigade Major Incident Plan was implemented, and the initial fifteen pumping appliances from various brigades were augmented by three more. Three hours after the crash, the Firemaster reported that there were numerous fires in the town and that water and electricity supplies were interrupted. Water for the fire hoses had to be brought into the town by tankers. It took a further four hours before the main fires had been extinguished and the firemen turned to damping down the debris. At 4.42 a.m. small outbreaks of fire were still being attended in the Sherwood Crescent area.[1] In the initial stages of the emergency plan, hospitals for miles around had been put on standby for a large influx of injured people – which never materialised, since all the crew and passengers in *Maid of the Seas* were beyond help. An appeal for blood donors over the radio thus turned out to be unnecessary and before midnight many of the medically trained first responders at Lockerbie had been sent away, as there was nothing they could do.

Three hours after the crash, names of survivors and dead residents of Lockerbie were already being listed at the town hall, which became a focus for local people wanting to know what had become of relatives and friends. The first floor of the building was also pressed into service at the initial mortuary until the body count passed eighty corpses, at which point Lockerbie's ice rink was used for this purpose. It is hard today to remember that in 1988, although the police and emergency services did have some radio links, there were very few mobile phones in private hands. In addition, many homes in and around Lockerbie had lost both power and phone services and the telephone lines not damaged were swamped with calls from Lockerbie back to their bases made by the arriving media teams. Strathclyde Police set up a special hotline for relatives to call and another was manned at Heathrow Airport. On the other side of the Atlantic a hotline was announced by Pan Am, but soon appeared to be ignoring relatives' attempts to get the latest news. There was, of course, no news except that all the passengers on Flight 103 were dead. The airline detailed available ground staff to liaise with individual families of passengers, but these employees were not grief counsellors and many were plainly doing the harrowing job under protest. More in total incomprehension at what had happened than anything else, some relatives drove to John F. Kennedy Airport, there to become prey to intrusive television cameras recording their uncontrollable desperation and grief.

Raymond Pratt, a young police officer based in Glasgow, was among the first to be drafted to Lockerbie after the crash. Sent to Sherwood Crescent to search for survivors, all he and his team could find by the light of their hand-held torches were bodies and body parts lying on the scorched ground, many so burned that they were hardly recognisable as such. It was months before he could close his eyes without seeing these horrific images. When eventually released to return to Glasgow, Pratt's fellow Glaswegian police officers were too numbed with shock to speak on the journey home.

BBC Scotland researcher Alan Clements and his presenter girl-friend returned to his office just after 7 p.m. from a rather alcoholic pre-Christmas party, to be press-ganged by the BBC Scotland Controller into jumping into the boss's chauffeur-driven car as the fastest way of getting them to Lockerbie. Talking their way through the police cordon, they found a town apparently on fire with twisted pieces of aluminium everywhere and the stink of aviation fuel heavy in the air. The later to be married couple worked through the night putting together a live transmission at 6 a.m. Although then childless, seeing American television coverage from Kennedy Airport which included Nicole Boulanger, whose daughter had been on Pan Am 103, collapsing in anguish, Clements reflected that the death of a child is a life sentence without parole.

At the search-and-rescue training base in RAF Valley on Anglesey, acting Station Commander Squadron Leader Geoffrey Leeming had been recalled from leave shortly after the news of the disaster reached the base just after 7 p.m., to fly one of two Wessex helicopters tasked with making the 130-mile trip to Lockerbie and liaising there with other emergency services. Held on the ground awaiting clarification of the mission – such as number and type of casualties – they eventually took off anyway at 9 p.m. with only a sketchy idea of what lay ahead. All the crews had been told was that a large airliner had crashed in the hills near Lockerbie, so it was assumed they would be searching for survivors. Diverted to Manchester Ringway Airport to pick up a ground rescue team, Leeming continued north. Warily approaching the town above a darkened landscape in which some power lines had not been cut and only flashing blue lights indicated where roads lay, a red glow appeared in the distance and grew rapidly more intense until, in his own words, the view 'resembled looking down into the crater of an active volcano near the heart of the town'.[2]

Having no common frequency with anyone on the ground, the two RAF search-and-rescue helicopters tentatively felt their way to a safe landing place with their searchlights picking up potentially fatal obstacles like power and telegraph lines, trees, unlit buildings – and also scores of bodies lying on the ground. Dropping off the ground rescue team as near as possible to the fires, Leeming lifted off again and picked up the flashing anti-collision lights of the other helicopter from RAF Valley, parked on the sports field of Lockerbie Academy – the town's secondary school. A Royal Navy Sea King helicopter was also parked there. Reporting to a police officer in a mobile incident room parked at the school, he was told that a large aircraft had been circling the town in some sort of emergency before crashing on high ground to the east of the town – which seemed improbable to the RAF personnel.

In gusting wind and persistent downpour, Leeming, as the senior RAF pilot, wanted to get the two crews from Valley into shelter to check maps of the area and concert a plan of action. His request to have the school opened up was denied, as the caretaker was not present and no one else had a key. Search-and-rescue personnel being accustomed to solving for themselves any problem standing in the way of their urgent missions, he suggested they could break a single windowpane to get in, only to be threatened by police with an accusation of 'criminal damage'. Similarly, his request for large-scale local maps was refused because the local bookshop was closed for the night. The arrival of politician Malcolm Rifkind, Secretary of State for Scotland, was no help. He too declined to authorise breaking a single pane of glass to get inside the school. With other RAF helicopters landing on the sports field, contact was established with Rescue Coordination Centre at another school in the centre of town via a helpful RAC breakdown patrolman's radio.

Reporting there after walking along streets littered with debris ranging from masonry to pieces of fuselage and a Pratt and Witney engine, which had dug itself in on impact 15ft deep into a street between a football field and a row of town houses, Leeming and his men realised they could do nothing useful until daylight. Kipping down in a school corridor, they were roused and told that local inhabitants wanted to give them more comfortable accommodation. Typical of the locals' warm and practical hospitality throughout the emergency, their hosts fed them a hot meal, and gave up their own bed, where the search-and-rescue men lay down fully clothed, to get what rest they could.

In addition to the ambulances and police vehicles clogging the streets of Lockerbie, a media onslaught was already beginning before midnight, causing such congestion that many print reporters and radio and television crews had to abandon their cars miles from Lockerbie and continue to the town on foot. One of them was David Johnston, an Edinburgh-based reporter for local radio station Radio Forth, who filed reports at the time and wrote one of the earliest books chronicling the events following the crash.[3] He arrived in the town by using back roads, to find some houses still burning and flashing blue lights in all directions. A yellow-painted Sea King helicopter was lifting off from an open space, although it was soon obvious that there was little search-and-rescue activity for the crew to carry out, so they were tasked instead with using the Sea King's powerful spotlights to try and find bodies on the ground and map how far the debris had spread.

A BBC news bulletin broadcast at 10.45 p.m. showed pictures of houses on fire in Lockerbie and flames still rising from the crater in Sherwood Crescent. A broadcast of a Pan Am spokesman in New York included wrong information and eyewitness accounts filmed in Lockerbie were also confused and confusing, some people being certain that the plane had been on fire as it came down. This was due to No. 3 engine still burning fuel on its descent. The broadcast included a plea from Pan Am to relatives of passengers on Flight 103 not to come to Heathrow but to stay at home, where they would be given any news as soon as it became available. The avenues to be explored were noted in the newsflash as catastrophic structural failure, mid-air collision and sabotage. Two previous 747 crashes were mentioned: in June 1985, 329 people had been killed when an Air India flight was brought down in mid-Atlantic by a bomb; two months later a Japan Airlines 747 on an internal flight crashed with the loss of 520 lives after the airtight bulkhead between the pressurised cabin and the unpressurised tail unit was badly repaired and ruptured in flight. An expert from *Flight* magazine mentioned problems of stress, corrosion and metal fatigue which had beset 747s in the past, some as a result of severe turbulence in flight, but said that Boeing had warned all users of the aircraft in each case and made available fixes for these problems. With mid-air collision being ruled out on the evidence of ATC radar, that left a sudden technical emergency or sabotage as the cause of the crash.

Having already decided in his own mind that there was a possibility it had been caused by foul play, which would result in a prosecution for mass murder, Chief Constable Boyd instructed all the uniformed officers to return to the six main crash sites and cordon them off to prevent members of the public contaminating them or removing souvenirs. They were also to ensure that the exact position and circumstances of each body, or possible murder victim, be precisely noted. Dr Keith Little of Edinburgh Royal Infirmary, with extensive experience of road accident victims, was at Sherwood Crescent when he decided that trying to identify body parts in the pouring rain and driving wind using pocket torches was a waste of energy. The police agreed to cordon off that area completely and wait until daybreak. So far, only one badly burned body had been recovered from the remains of the destroyed houses. Amazingly, when all the on-ground casualties were totted up, there were only eleven deaths, two serious injuries and three less than serious. Added to the 243 passengers and sixteen crew members, that brought the total number of dead to 270 lives lost in the space of a few minutes, although Pan Am's first announcement of casualties was slewed by someone counting the crew twice. It was, as one elderly inhabitant of Lockerbie remarked, like the war all over again. An analysis of crew and passengers' nationalities later revealed that the 170 American and thirty-three British victims predominated, with the other victims coming from thirty other countries.

Hidden within the overall tragedy there was a tragedy of young lives cut cruelly short. Of the 243 passengers, 137 were less than 30 years old; some were infants; some children; but most were American students returning home for the holidays and others heading across the Atlantic to spend Christmas with their girl- or boyfriends, like 23-year-old Flora Margaret Swire, a medical student from London, who would have been 24 the next day. The explanation of why the fatal flight was a sort of 'student special' lies in the telephoned warning to the US Embassy in Helsinki, which was forwarded to the State Department and passed to all its European embassies. That resulted in many pre-booked US diplomats going home for Christmas cancelling their reservations on Pan Am 103, just in case. As a result, student travel agencies offered cheap rates for late bookings in an endeavour to fill the empty seats. Many of their young clients taking advantage of this called their parents excitedly, saying how lucky they had been to get a cheap seat just before Christmas, which is how Dr Herbert 'Jim' Swire, a GP practising in Worcestershire, and his wife Jane learned that Flora was going to be on the flight.

Air accident investigators have to be quick off the mark because vital clues can be misplaced in hours, removed by souvenir hunters or even washed away by wind and weather, particularly the sort of weather at Lockerbie. Among those directly concerned heading for Lockerbie were ten experts from the Air Accident Investigation Branch of the British Department of Transport, who touched down at Carlisle at 2 a.m. in a Pan Am 727 after an unpleasantly bumpy ride from London in the continuing rough weather. Their job was to investigate what exactly had happened to the aircraft, not to interfere with the police and other agencies whose duty it would be to identify the perpetrators of any criminal act. Also on board that flight with the AAIB investigators were Pan Am ground staff and, interestingly, at least three men from the CIA's London station, in a hurry to get to the scene for reasons no one else knew. These spooks were incognito, carrying identification stating they were Pan Am staff members. Nor were they apparently the first Americans to arrive in Lockerbie: a south Scotland mountain rescue team reported to the police station at 9 p.m. to offer their services and found themselves unwelcome intruders when they stumbled into a room where several Americans were studying maps, and were told to leave.[4]

Officers from the Metropolitan Police arrived to give advice, which was politely listened to, but no more. The Scottish Police were quite sure this was their case, and some Scottish officers were despatched to Whitehall to liaise there with Scotland Yard's inquiry, and stayed there for some considerable time in a mutually useful exchange of information. Senior police officers in Lockerbie at first based themselves in the town's little police station, which was far too small, but later moved the Lockerbie Incident Control Centre (LICC) to Lockerbie Academy, where there was more space. The school's dinner ladies turned up to provide refreshments and meals for people working there and the tuck shop opened to hand out sweets and chocolate. Many searchers on the ground had not been given waterproof boots. Squelching through boggy fields with wet feet, even those with walkie-talkies found they were useless as the frequencies were jammed by other traffic. It was often quicker to send one man from a team on foot to deliver a report back at base – quicker, that is, unless like many other helpers strange to the area, he became disorientated and lost.

At 2 a.m. Chief Constable Boyd called in all the second-rank officers to lay down the procedures to be followed, if bodies were to be recovered as respectfully as possible and all the debris conserved and logged geographically as possible evidence. The last requirement meant that, in those times when even the police had few computers, and those with limited memories, there would be thousands of handwritten reports compiled in the effort of preserving every scrap of evidence for a possible trial in a Scottish court, where the procedures were, in the words of reporter David Johnston, 'so laborious to the point of numbing the minds of any jury'.[5] Dumfries and Galloway Constabulary did not have the integrated computer system that was currently being assessed by UK police forces under the title Home Office Large Major Enquiry System, abbreviated to HOLMES. So the Strathclyde force sent its HOLMES computer by helicopter with a senior officer to instruct local officers how to operate it. What seemed like police delay and obstruction to relatives who made it to Lockerbie, desperate for news of their loved ones and to give the bodies a decent burial, was simply the inevitable result of this meticulous and multifaceted approach.

8

THE MORNING AFTER

Hugh McMullen was an air traffic controller at Carlisle Airport, recalled from sick leave to do what turned out to be a twenty-three-hour shift handling 196 'aircraft movements', including several Pan Am aircraft, a USAF C130 and search-and-rescue helicopters as well as media traffic. There were eventually twenty-eight FBI personnel at Lockerbie under a young agent named Hal Hendershot, described as 'an affable Kentuckiyan', who had been chosen because his easygoing manner was thought least likely to ruffle Scottish feathers.[1] In addition, there were the CIA officers flown to Lockerbie by Pan Am. This did not especially surprise the Scottish Police officers, since most of the passengers were US citizens and it was rapidly becoming obvious that the cause of the crash might be a terrorist bomb.

On the morning of 22 December, Squadron Leader Leeming's men roused themselves and tucked into a cooked breakfast of bacon and eggs kindly provided by their hosts before a police car arrived at dawn to drive them to a different school, where an old flying colleague, Squadron Leader Bill Gault, had brought some order into the prevailing chaos by setting up overnight a combined operations room for both ground and airborne search teams, with radio links and what appeared to be the entire stock of the town's large-scale local maps. After the search area had been divided into numbered sectors, so that the position of every find could be methodically plotted, Leeming returned to Lockerbie Academy and got airborne. A second wave of uniformed and plainclothes police officers arrived to relieve those who had been working all night. They were immediately sent out to search surrounding fields and woodland, after being briefed that their priorities were firstly to find and tag all bodies and identifiable body parts, secondly to log all passengers' effects and thirdly to mark for recovery all pieces of the aircraft scattered no one knew how far away. No one then knew that debris was spread over hundreds of square miles.

From the air in the grey light of a Scottish winter morning, Squadron Leader Leeming was able to formulate an even more horrifying appreciation of the situation than could be seen from the ground. The largest single piece of debris in his designated search area was the nose cone by Tundergarth parish church. Nearer and lower, it became apparent that the whole field in which it lay and several adjacent ones were littered with bodies and body parts, strewn on the ground and lying draped across the drystone walls, each corpse guarded by a policeman in black rainwear. Again in Leeming's own words, they resembled 'dark, grim-visaged effigies, standing their silent motionless vigils for the blanket-shrouded corpses at their feet'.[2] He noticed that the bodies lying in the open fields had each gouged a shallow scrape in the turf when first landing before bouncing back into the air and coming to rest a few feet further to the east. This suggested that any passengers or crew members still clinically alive would have been killed by the impact when their bodies hit the ground at roughly 120 mph.

Suitcases had burst open on landing, with their contents of clothing and other personal belongings blown by the gale far and wide. Marking on the map everything found as far out as 30 miles from Lockerbie, his radioed reports of the extent of the debris trail were at first not believed back in the town, but were later all verified. There were in fact two debris trails that separated a few miles outside Lockerbie. The shorter northern trail was made of debris released from the aircraft in its vertical dive of 10,000ft over Lockerbie. The southern trail appeared to have been created by wreckage scattered right across Scotland from the initial disintegration at cruising height.

Leeming and his crewman were unaware that they had flown over some of the most horrific human remains. A policeman on the ground at Tundergarth noticed a hand sticking out of a boggy area of waterlogged peat. Aproaching cautiously, not to get sucked down, he found a woman's face staring up at him through several inches of brownish peaty water. A squad of Royal Fusiliers was detailed to get the woman's body out, and discovered nine other corpses under the surface of the water, one of which had burst open on hitting something solid. This sight reduced the young soldiers to uncontrollable vomiting.[3] Diverted to Glasgow Airport to collect a team of FBI officers – presumably based as 'legats' or legal attachés at the American Embassy in London – and bring them to Lockerbie, Leeming found on his return that recovery of bodies and their placing inside body bags was now being more efficiently conducted by police working with much larger Chinook helicopters from RAF Odiham.

Conversation outdoors in the town was made difficult by the clattering of helicopter blades overhead and the wail of police sirens. After recovery, the bodies were flown to Lockerbie's ice rink, serving as a ready-made mortuary. While some bodies seemed untouched, as though just asleep, it was harrowing work handling the badly mangled corpses – especially those of children – and fitting them into body bags. This traumatised many of the officers involved. At the ice rink, Professor Anthony Busuttil, head of the faculty of forensic medicine at the University of Edinburgh and an experienced police pathologist, had the daunting task of carrying out hundreds of post-mortem examinations and, in the case of bodies whose faces were unrecognisable, comparing the results with medical and dental records supplied by the victims' families. By a strange coincidence that only later became evident, Professor Busuttil had qualified as a medical professional on his native island of Malta.

After lifting a few corpses from places too awkward for the much larger Chinooks to reach, since there were no lives to save at Lockerbie the search-and-rescue teams from RAF Valley were recalled to standby at base near dusk on this shortest day of the year[4] in case they were needed for a mountain rescue or to save persons in peril at sea. By the time they left Lockerbie, the normal population had already swollen to an estimated figure of 10,000 with the influx of 1,100 police officers and another 1,000 soldiers, plus more than 4,000 media reporters, cameramen and others. For the local people, standing in hushed groups on street corners trying to come to terms with the drama, these newcomers were like aliens, with their cameras, microphones and, most surprisingly of all, cell phones, which had not previously been seen in the town. The insensitivity of reporters who were trying to prise out 'human interest' stories they could use caused many Lockerbie people to scream or shout at them to go away.

The 'black box' recorders – the digital flight recorder with its record of the aircraft's performance and the cockpit voice recorder (CVR) with its second-by-second record of everything said or heard on the flight deck were discovered by two boys at 10 a.m., lying in a field near Tundergarth. On subsequent examination at the Air Accident Investigation Branch laboratory at Farnbrough, speech on the CVR was found to be somewhat garbled by previous recordings not having been completely erased – but neither black box indicated anything untoward except for a millisecond of loud noise on the CVR at precisely the time Pan Am 103 disappeared from the Shanwick radar, followed by blank tape. In addition, exploration of the nose cone proved that the controls were in their normal positions, indicating that the pilots had no advance warning of the cause of the crash. This seemed to prove that Boeing and Pan Am could reasonably expect to be exonerated and that sabotage was the cause. Also at noon on 22 December an Iranian group calling itself 'Guardians of the Islamic Revolution' informed the Associated Press news agency that it was responsible for the destruction of *Maid of the Seas* in revenge for the downing of IR655 by USS *Vincennes* in July. Complicating things, the Ulster Defence League and several less credible callers also claimed responsibility.[5]

As the grey Scottish midwinter day wore on, the full extent of the tragedy became more obvious. Mrs Ramsden's house and garden were one mass grave. Among the seventy bodies there, the youthful faces of a party of thirty-five students from Syracuse University stared sightlessly at those who came to dig them out of the garden and the rubble of the house. The residents of Rosebank Crescent found thousands of sodden banknotes and travellers' cheques lying where they had been blown in the gale, trapped against garden fences, or on window ledges. Where windows had been shattered, money carpeted kitchen floors. Two teenage farmer's sons illicitly exploring near the nose cone at Tundergarth picked up in a short while something like half a million dollars' worth of travellers' cheques.

In London, Queen Elizabeth II decided that the quickest way of expressing the royal family's sympathy with the bereaved was to have her second son, 28-year-old Prince Andrew, a naval officer currently serving on HMS *Edinburgh*, which was in dock on the other side of Scotland, travel by car to Lockerbie. The usual red tape and protocol governing royal visits was cut to the minimum and a tour of the area laid on for him. Unfortunately he lacked the charm and diplomatic skills called for. Although a serving naval officer, he was overwhelmed by the mutilation of bodies in the partly crushed nose cone, many of which were unrecognisable and inextricably mixed in with the tangled metal of the aircraft. Trying to say the right thing both for the town and those who died in the 747, he then said within hearing of the media microphones, 'Statistically, something like this has to happen on a town. It is most sad and unfortunate that it happened to Lockerbie and so close to Christmas, but my deepest feelings and sympathy go out to ... the families of those Americans that died in the crash.'[6] This tactless remark under the stress of the moment had some media outlets dub him, 'the second Lockerbie disaster'. It was rumoured that Her Majesty was not best pleased with his performance either. A second politically unfortunate event that day was the departure on holiday to the Caribbean of Transport Secretary Paul Channon, who left it to junior minister Michael Portillo to reply to a question from Shadow Transport Minister John Prescott by saying that the government considered terrorist action was only one of the possible explanations for the Lockerbie crash – and that all necessary security measures had been taken on British soil. This last contention, as will become obvious, was not true.

Outside the party political in-fighting at Westminster, already on 22 December rumours circulated. One was that Flight 103's delayed departure was due to late arrival at Heathrow of a mysterious party of American scientists. Ignoring the existence of diplomatic couriers, another was that 'important documents' had been given to pilot McQuarrie to deliver personally in New York. Later, an even more bizarre *and true* story surfaced. But that day the international news agencies focused on reports about the man with an Arabic accent who had telephoned the US Embassy in Helsinki shortly before the crash. Special Agent Ken Luzzi had taken the call, in which the caller warned that a bomb would be carried onto an American aircraft by an unwitting passenger before its transatlantic departure from Frankfurt – and that this would happen before Christmas. The Abu Nidal terrorist group was alleged to be responsible. Subsequently, advice had been posted on notice boards of the US Embassy in Moscow for personnel with reservations to travel home for Christmas on Pan Am from Frankfurt, where Flight 103's main feeder flight originated, to change their bookings to another American airline. They had to 'fly American' or pay their own way. The State Department alleged that a similar warning had been passed to the British Embassy in Helsinki. If it was, that did not apparently reach British Airports Authority, although the State Department did warn several American intelligence services and the Federal Aviation Authority was instructed to pass on the warning to US carriers with international routes.

It took several days, while police and forensic workers photographed and tagged all the bodies, checking where they had been seated in the 747, before the last one was lifted, to be taken to the skating rink. At last a list of victims could be drawn up, although it was some time before it was complete, due to some remains never being found or identified. Until then, the residents of Lockerbie had to walk past corpses in their gardens and in the streets. A lady named

Bunty Galloway later recalled the scene when she ran out of her damaged house shortly after the crash:

> There were spoons, underwear, headsquares, everything on the ground. A boy was lying at the bottom of the steps [leading from the garden down] to the road. A young laddie with brown socks and blue trousers on. Later that evening, my son-in-law asked for a blanket to cover him. I didn't know he was dead. I gave him a lambswool travelling rug, thinking I'd keep him warm. Two more girls were lying dead across the road, one of them bent over garden railings. It was as though they were just sleeping.[7]

The idea that the dead boy needed a warm blanket expresses better than anything else the sheer incredulity of the inhabitants of Lockerbie at what had just happened. The boy's body was still there the next day and the next. Not until the Saturday – three days after the crash – was it taken away. Unwilling to think of another child as a corpse, another Lockerbie resident referred to the body as 'the little girl in the red dress'.

More than fifty families of American victims living in the New York area set up their own support group and thirty-two relatives took advantage of Pan Am's offer to fly them to Britain overnight on 22 December. On arrival in London, they discovered that the airline wanted to keep them there incomunicado in Kensington's Royal Garden Hotel, with regular updates from US Embassy staff and airline personnel, who tried to persuade them that it was too early to go Lockerbie. Elizabeth Dix, the wife of a British passenger on Flight 103, learned that the American relatives were there and invited herself to join them. Told that she would not be allowed to see her husband's body until it had been 'reconstructed', her grief turned to anger. With no idea how badly some bodies had been mutilated and even dismembered, she wanted her husband's remains released into her care, so she could give him a decent burial. Seven of the Americans present also moved from helpless grief to determined anger and insisted on being taken to the scene of the crash. Flown to Glasgow, they were taken by minibus to LICC at Lockerbie Academy. Walking from the minibus into the school, they were bombarded with questions by waiting reporters, eager for a more 'human interest' story than the crash itself, which was already 'yesterday's news'. Other relatives stayed at home in the States, replying to Pan Am's telephoned offer of a free trip to Britain that Lockerbie was the last place on earth they ever wanted to visit. Relatives who did travel to Lockerbie were deeply moved by the town's open-hearted generosity in providing accommodation and advice. Practical sympathy included local women volunteering to take in soiled items of the victims' clothing for washing and ironing before return to the grieving families with other personal effects. Someone even cleaned up a child's damp and mud-stained diary and ironed the crumpled pages so that it could be treasured by the family.

Impatient with Pan Am's efforts to control her and the grieving American relatives, Mrs Dix rented a car at Glasgow Airport so that she could be independent. At Tundergarth near the nose cone, where she felt her husband may have died, she was not hysterical but just quietly grieving. Repeatedly taken aside by police – whose numbers she thought excessive, as though they were expecting a riot – she insisted on her right to be there. Grasping at straws, trying to find out her husband's seat number, she was told by a Pan Am official that this was confidential information. A US diplomat in Lockerbie actually lost his temper with her persistent questions. From shock and loss of sleep, many designated contact personnel were on short fuses.

Given that parts of the aircraft landed several miles apart, it seems strange that the BBC website reported on 26 December:

> Investigators cannot establish if the plane disintegrated before it came to ground, suggesting a bomb, or if it was destroyed by impact on the ground after severe structural failure led to its descent. Aviation experts have said they believe the most likely cause is structural failure after an initial inspection of the black box flight recorders did not disclose anything.[8]

After a piece of the fuselage skin bordering the small initial hole was recovered on Boxing Day, American Federal Aviation Authority explosions expert Walter Korsgaard, who was working with the AAIB team, recognised the signs of melted metal and characteristic pitting and sooting, from which he calculated that the explosion had reached a temperature of between 2,760°C and 4,426°C (in the range 5,000–8,000°F). From there, Mick Charles of the British Airports Authority announced that the cause of the crash was a bomb – and the hunt began to find the perpetrator.

It was natural for the British investigators to be wary of their American colleagues trying to take over the search, and for the Americans of the task force designated 'Scotbom' to suspect that Scottish police officers, who had never had to deal with such a crime before, might be less than assiduous in their hunt for clues – until Walter Korsgaard lost his miniature hearing aid in the fields around Lockerbie. Unsure of exactly where, he was pleasantly amazed when it was returned to him, proving that 'no stone was being left unturned'.

On 28 December the AAIB announced that examination of some luggage from the crash indicated proximity to an explosion. Traces of a licorice-like substance was determined to be the residue typically left by Semtex after exploding. The debris of aluminium baggage container AVE4041PA also indicated an explosion, probably within the container.

Although almost all of the bodies had been recovered from the hills and fields around Lockerbie and lay in the skating rink, police, soldiers and civilian volunteers were scouring hundreds of square miles to the north-east of Lockerbie for items that had been blown there by the winds on the evening of 21 December. Problems included the continuing bad weather, wreckage trapped in treetops that was visible from the air but impossible for searchers on the ground to see – and human emotion. The leader of the Upper Teasdale and Weardale Fell Rescue Team, Ian Findlay picked up a South African passport in some woodland, opened it and was confronted with the photograph of a pretty 23-year-old girl, who must have been the last person before him to touch it when she packed it away in her hand luggage. Finding children's clothing, torn from their bodies by the high-altitude winds during the descent was also deeply disturbing.[9]

Among the FBI personnel was Tom Thurman, employed as an explosives expert. He returned to Washington on 9 January and gave a briefing to colleagues seeking clues on American soil. The briefing was, as the FBI task force supervisor Richard Marquise recorded, reassuring with both verbal and photographic evidence of the search for every possible fragment of the aircraft. In view of Thurman's past performance, it is interesting that he was regarded at the time as a competent and trustworthy officer of the FBI.

By 1 March 1989 the bodies of 236 of the 259 passengers and crew of *Maid of the Seas* had been identified and thirteen other victims had been identified by body parts. Of the inhabitants of Lockerbie killed in the crash, only three could be positively identified by their corpses and one other by a body part, leaving seven unaccounted for. Twenty-eight bags of body parts were eventually buried in a mass grave at the Dryfesdale cemetery; 607 items of luggage had been recovered, of which 415 were matched with their owners; most surprisingly, considering their proximity to the explosion, twenty-three bags from AVE4041 had been matched.

DRUGS AND DOLLARS
IN THE DEBRIS

The anger of American and British relatives of victims at what they saw as unreasonable delay in releasing their loved ones' bodies for burial was increased to flashpoint on 16 March 1989 when they learned that FAA had circulated a warning about the Neuss arrests to airlines, in which specific mention was made of the barometric fuse in the Bombeat radio cassette player found there, indicating its intended use to destroy an aircraft in flight. Someone at the top of the investigation must have sympathised with the relatives' feelings, because in that same month four senior Scottish Police officers flew to America to meet relatives and explain that bodies had not been released by LICC because further examination might give important clues to what had happened. They took with them colour slides of Lockerbie and the surrounding countryside, to show how difficult it had been to conduct the widespread searches. The visit was a success, almost all the relatives accepting that what had before seemed unfeeling delay was no more or less than meticulous investigative procedure, necessary to track down whoever had killed their loved ones.

At Lockerbie, the problem of finding a secure area to store all the passengers' belongings was solved by taking over a disused chemical factory, the ice rink being obviously the best place to keep so many bodies. Eventually more than 10,000 items of debris were recovered, including a plastic bag containing some marijuana belonging to one of the Syracuse students and a 2lb block of cannabis resin which, it was thought, was being smuggled home by a US serviceman who was counting on being waved through customs because he was travelling in uniform.[1]

Parts of the aircraft itself were transported to the Army Central Ammunition Depot at Longtown, across the Scottish border in Cumbria, where there was a large enough hangar for it to be re-assembled. Approximately 90 per cent of the 747's hull was successfully recovered, identified, and laid out on the floor in a two-dimensional reconstruction. The remains of baggage container AVE4041 were sent to Royal Armaments Research and Development Establishment (RARDE), together with the remains of the dual-speaker Toshiba Bombeat radio cassette player. The charge of Semtex was there calculated to have been only about 300–400g or 10–14oz.[2]

Five months after the crash, on 18 May 1989 Säkerhetspolisen SWAT teams raided several apartments in Stockholm, Göteborg and Uppsala, arresting fifteen members of PPSF. Among the reasons was the warning after Autumn Leaves that BKA had passed to its colleagues in Stockholm about the number of Palestinian terrorists observed driving Swedish-registered Volvos in Germany, but Säkerhetspolisen investigators had slowly been closing in on the gang in any case. A month later, in June 1989 the Scottish Police inquiry into the Lockerbie crash was working on the theory that one of two 'mules' had brought the bomb on board Flight 103 concealed within a 'Christmas present' they were to post after return to the USA.[3] The suspects were two 20-year-old American students named Patricia Coyle and Karen Noonan, who had been studying in Vienna. Items of the clothing in their cases in the hold showed traces of burning that indicated they had been close to the explosion. This hypothesis caused great anguish for the families of the two girls until it was realised that their cases had simply been close to the one containing the bomb at the moment of explosion. Another possible 'mule' or suicide bomber on Flight 103 was Khalid Ja'afar, a 20-year-old Lebanese-American who had been studying in Germany. It was at first thought he had checked in two items of luggage, but his father, a former lawyer in Lebanon who had moved to the USA to escape the violence there and was employed as manager of a filling station in Detroit, received a photograph taken by a family friend of his son arriving at the airport with only one small item of cabin baggage. Ja'afar was also cleared, to the relief of his family.[4]

Travellers in a wide-bodied jet aircraft who look around do not usually ask themselves why all the others on board are travelling. But for what reason did all those CIA and FBI men arrive in Lockerbie so soon after the crash? The FBI even set up a permanent office in the academy with a secure computer link back to Washington. Here, we trip over several subplots, which might or might not have had anything to do with the destruction of *Maid of the Seas*. Farmer Innes Graham's land lay about 5 miles east of Lockerbie town near the village of Waterbeck. Instinctively saving debris and personal belongings that had fallen into a watercourse on his property, he had been warned off by police and told to leave everything where it had landed. On Christmas Eve – some reports say earlier – a white helicopter landed near his farmhouse. This time, it was an American in civilian clothes who emerged and told Graham to keep away from one of his own fields on Torbeck Hill that day. The CIA was about to recover a shattered suitcase belonging to US Army Major Charles McKee, an exceptionally tough Special Forces expert in what Winston Churchill used to call 'ungentlemanly warfare' and now referred to as 'black ops'.

McKee was officially on secondment to the ultra-secret Defense Intelligence Agency as a military attaché in Beirut, but actually conducting clandestine negotiations for the release of American hostages held by the pro-Iranian Hezbollah Shi'ite terrorist group in the Lebanese capital. He was returning on his own initiative to the States with two or more colleagues. Among the CIA's finds on Torbeck Hill was said to be the detailed plan of a building in Beirut where at least two of the nine current American hostages were being held under armed guard, together with a summary of how the building might be stormed by a rescue team. Covert enquiries by Interfor, a private security company retained by Pan Am or its insurers, discovered that McKee had been travelling back from Beirut via Cyprus to expose a regular drug-running operation conducted by the US Drugs Enforcement Agency (DEA) under the code name Corea[5] in order to trace traffickers' distribution systems in America, because McKee considered this was jeopardising his own mission.[6] Although the rule of the Lockerbie search was that the geographical location of *all* passengers' belongings must be logged and the items handed in, the white helicopter flew away with what it had recovered, no one was told where. The suitcase was eventually returned empty by CIA officers to the place where it had been found on Torbeck Hill. After two or three Scottish detectives refused to play their part and 'discover' it there, two Ministry of Transport searchers later signed for 'finding it' on the hill. Bearing traces of having been near the explosion, it was therefore an important piece of forensic evidence.[7] It is thought that the half a million dollars found by the two boys had come from this suitcase after it burst open.

Also on board Flight 103 were three other US officials associated with McKee. Daniel Emmet O'Connor was a State Department 'regional security officer' based in Cyprus. Ronald LaRivière was also a 'regional security officer', but based in Beirut. Matthew K. Gannon was a CIA officer, also based in Beirut. There was evidence to suggest that all three men and McKee were working to secure the release of American hostages by a team of US Navy SEALs, using what means of infiltration and execution was never made public. In the 8 a.m. news on 1 February 1989 Edinburgh-based Radio Forth broadcast a news item about the presence on Pan Am 103 of McKee and his team, mentioning a theory that the bomb had been placed in their luggage. The source of the story was reporter David Johnston, who, although not involved in the broadcast, was visited within the hour by two senior Lothian and Borders Police officers. They demanded he divulge his source within the force. He refused. They then threatened him with jail, and tried to break his resolve by a promise to take him to Prime Minister Margaret Thatcher, so he could tell her in confidence. He still refused and the case was forwarded immediately to Lord Advocate Lord Fraser of Carmyllie. Where this might have led is unknown because colleagues in the media reported Johnston's problem and the Lord Advocate dropped the matter on 3 February.[8]

One of the wilder hypotheses explored in the months following the crash was that Flight 103 had been brought down by Iranian intelligence in order to protect its Hezbollah proxies. An even wilder theory was that *Maid of the Seas* had been destroyed by the CIA, forfeiting a few of its own personnel in order to cast suspicion on Tehran. Someone even came up with an apparent link with the IRA. As late as April 1992, *Time* magazine published a story about a Syrian drug lord named Monzer al-Kassar, whose wife was related to Syrian President Hafez al-Assad, and whose brother-in-law was Ali Issa Duba, the head of a Syrian intelligence service. According to this theory, al-Kassar had engineered the sabotage of Flight 103 to double-cross the DEA.[9] As with the Kennedy assassination, the numerous conspiracy theories all had to be considered by the investigators, adding to their workload.

Jim Wilson, another Scottish farmer with land near Graham's, found among the debris in his fields a suitcase filled with cellophane packets containing white powder. This suitcase, too, was taken away by some American civilians with no explanation given. It was later established that the name Mr Wilson saw on the suitcase's name tag did not correspond with any name on the Pan Am 103 passenger list. Israeli-American Juval Aviv, who was the boss of the New York security company Interfor, alleged that the DEA's method of shipping Syrian heroin from Frankfurt to Detroit was by checking in an innocent piece of baggage that passed through Frankfurt Airport's security control and was afterwards switched by a complicit baggage handler with an identical bag in which the heroin was packed. The inference from Aviv was that a drug suitcase which bypassed security controls with the help of Frankfurt security personnel collaborating with the DEA *could* have subsequently been replaced by the Samsonite suitcase containing the bomb.[10] In that case, where did the heroin come from that landed on Mr Wilson's land?

Much of the world's heroin was at the time produced from opium obtained from extensive poppy fields in the Hezbollah-controlled Beka'a Valley of Eastern Lebanon and converted there or in Europe for the US market. After six months' investigation, Aviv was definite that Flight 103 had been used in this way on 21 December. The DEA denied it, for obvious reasons.[11] Roy Rowan, a respected and highly experienced correspondent and bureau chief for *Time* magazine, also reported that McKee was travelling back to the States to denounce the DEA collaboration with al-Kassar. Under one of the several identities he used, al-Kassar had allegedly been the Syrian contact for Oliver North's Iran–Contra drugs-for-arms deal in 1986 that financed the US-sponsored guerillas fighting the democratically elected government of Nicaragua from the proceeds of arms smuggling to Iran. Although tried as a criminal, facing a 10-year jail sentence and a fine of $750,000, Vietnam veteran North was regarded as a hero by President Reagan.[12] Al-Kassar was in one transaction given $1.5 million to purchase weapons. What his markup was, no one knows. In this curious sequence of events, the USA was clandestinely supplying weapons including anti-tank and anti-aircraft missiles to Iran for use against Saddam Hussein's armed forces in the Iran–Iraq War. To avoid the necessity for fake end-user certificates, in some cases, Israeli intelligence organisation, Mossad arranged to supply weapons from Israeli stocks to the Iranians. These were then replaced by the USA, Israel being a legitimate destination for American arms exports.

Once other possible bomb-carrying mules had been discarded, Ahmed Jibril's 500-member PFLP-GC seemed the likely cause of the crash, but with the initial assumption that the IED's position so near to the skin of the fuselage was sheer chance. This belies the knowledge of aircraft and methods of sabotaging them which the PFLP-GC terrorists possessed. Would experienced bomb-makers who planned the attack so meticulously have used such a carefully calculated small charge on the off-chance of the Samsonite case being placed by a random baggage handler in *exactly* the right place to effect critical damage to the aircraft? The condition of the baggage recovered at Lockerbie showed a collossal difference between items that had been adjacent to the explosion and others hardly damaged at all, except in their fall to earth. So, if the Samsonite case had been at the other end of the baggage container, more or less on the centre line of the jumbo and possibly sitting on several other cases, with all that damping the explosion would certainly have caused damage and casualties to passengers sitting above or near it but the Boeing 747 could probably have made an emergency landing at a Scottish airport with no vital controls damaged. Mr Walter Korsgaard, the FAA aircraft bombing expert who came to Lockerbie, made a point of saying that pilots of three out of four aircraft on which IEDs exploded had managed to make emergency landings that saved the lives of most people on board.

Despite the fact that the angled overhang of the baggage container was customarily used for soft luggage like holdalls, which could better fit into it, with hard cases stowed in the main cube, that is exactly where the Samsonite case was loaded: partly in the overhang and close to the bottom of the container, placing the IED as near as possible to the skin of the fuselage. Yet no one, it seems, reasoned that a vital member of the terrorist group responsible for the attack *must* have been present at some point in the interline shed at Heathrow to ensure the positioning of the suitcase in container AVE4041 exactly where the small charge of Semtex could destroy the whole aircraft and kill everyone aboard, as required by the *qisas*. As to why that line of enquiry was not pursued, it was presumably because it would have placed blame on the British Airports Authority and the management at Heathrow for inadequate security arrangements there. For eight months after the crash, British investigators persisted in maintaining that the bomb suitcase had been placed on Pan Am feeder flight 103A in Frankfurt, in the face of the BKA arguing that it had not. Spreading the blame far and wide by implication, British Foreign Secretary Sir Geoffrey Howe called on governments all over the Middle East for help in tracking down those responsible for destroying *Maid of the Seas*.[13]

Among non-governmental factions, even the Palestine Liberation Organisation offered help on this aspect of the case as part of its endeavour to ingratiate itself with the international community as a political, but no longer terrorist, organisation, at the same time embarrassing the rival group headed by Ahmad Jibril. It was the PLO that published an eighty-page report on how Iran had paid Jibril's organisation $10 million for the Lockerbie bombing. A prime suspect for breaking into the Pan Am baggage store on the night before Flight 103, cutting his way through a chain with bolt cutters, was Abu Elias, the wily second bomb-maker and expert on airport security who was missed when the PFLP-GC Neuss cell was arrested in Autumn Leaves.

Although it is likely that American intelligence agencies and Britain's MI6 with sources in the Middle East may have obtained relevant information on this aspect of the Lockerbie bombing, those organisations are notoriously reluctant to divulge what they know, on the grounds that they must protect their sources. Israel's Mossad also never gives anything away publicly. Was the Israeli Air Force strafing of the PFLP-GC training camp in the Lebanon's Beka'a Valley on 20 March 1989[14] in some way connected with the Lockerbie bombing? Nobody will say.

The Senior Investigating Officer of the team at Lockerbie was Detective Chief Superintendent John Orr from the CID of the neighbouring Strathclyde force, an officer with very relevant experience and qualifications who had even spent some time studying policing methods in Kansas and Oklahoma. He was, exceptionally, given security clearance to see intelligence from MI6, but that does not mean he received much before he was promoted to Deputy Chief Constable in mid-1989 and replaced by his former deputy, Stuart Henderson. By pure coincidence, his superior, Scotland's Lord Advocate Peter Fraser of Carmylie had both personal and professional reasons for taking a close interest in the Lockerbie investigation. His aunt and uncle, living at No. 11 Sherwood Crescent, had not been injured although their house had suffered damage.

The two-dimensional reconstruction of *Maid of the Seas* fuselage at Longtown established exactly where the explosion had occurred. However, the amount of specialist attention to detail in the AAIB investigation of the way in which the 747 broke up is illustrated by the transportation of a 65ft section of the fuselage – approximately 30ft each side of the explosion – to AAIB in Farnborough. There, it was attached to a purpose-built metal framework to form a three-dimensional reconstruction of that part of the fuselage with access to each fragment both internally and externally. The two reconstructed baggage containers closest to the explosion were also brought there to allow correlation of evidence with, and partial incorporation into, the fuselage reconstruction. The tailplane structure was also rebuilt at AAIB in Farnborough, proving that its leading edges had been damaged by collision with metallic debris from further forward in the aircraft. Gruesomely, the presence of smear marks on the metal indicated that some 'unidentified soft debris' had also collided with the tailplane in the moments when the aircraft was breaking up.[15]

Charred material said to have been found some weeks after the bombing in woods near Lockerbie under rather unclear circumstances was sent for analysis to RARDE at Fort Halstead in Kent. Strangely, the note of its original discovery had labelled it as 'cloth', but this had been rubbed out and replaced with 'debris'. At RARDE, according to his later testimony, Senior Scientific Officer Thomas Hayes identified the piece of cloth as the neckband of a grey Slalom-brand shirt found near Castleton, from which he recovered bits of black plastic, a small piece of metal and some wire mesh. All were subsequently declared to be parts of a Toshiba RT-SF16 radio cassette player. Fragments of white paper also recovered were said to be from the owner's manual belonging to it. Compounding the mystery of this piece of 'debris', Hayes testified that he also found in the shirt collar a half-inch fragment of circuit board. His colleague Alan Feraday sent a Polaroid photograph of that to Detective Chief Inspector William Williamson at Lockerbie, asking for help in identification.

The record of RARDE was far from being unblemished. Fourteen years before the Lockerbie crash, its staff were important witnesses against 25-year-old Judith Ward, jailed for the M62 coach bomb that killed nine soldiers, one woman and two children. The critical testimony by Douglas Higgs of RARDE that she had handled nitroglycerine was based on chemical analysis of a swab by a test that was known to give the same result for many other substances. After spending seventeen years in jail for a crime she did not commit, whatever else this IRA sympathiser may have done, Ward was cleared of the M62 coach bombing on appeal, the judge saying that the RARDE staff had 'knowingly placed a false and distorted scientific picture before the jury'.[16] And this was not the only case where RARDE-produced 'evidence' was distorted in favour of the prosecution.

In June 1990, Feraday and DCI Williamson visited FBI Headquarters in Washington to consult Thomas Thurman, who had been at Lockerbie early in the investigation and afterwards interviewed Marwan Khreesat in Jordan. Reputedly an explosives expert, Thurman identified the fragment as being part of an electronic timer after showing it to an anonymous CIA agent, who compared it with detonating devices seized by the CIA in Togo,[17] which had been made by Swiss company MEBO for the Libyan armed forces, but these were not the same design as the one used to bring down Pan Am 130. MEBO co-owner Edwin Bollier said later that he declined to accept a $4 million bribe from an unnamed FBI officer to testify that the fragment was indeed from an MST-13 timer. Bollier's partner Erwin Meister said that MST-13 timers had been sold to the Libyans. An employee of MEBO named Ulrich Lumpert contradicted him at the trial, but later admitted he had lied, presumably for some financial reward.

Thurman's identification of the fragment later proved to be flawed, after examination under electron microscopy, when technical experts in the business of making such appliances were able to say that the copper used on the fragment produced in evidence was of a type that had not been manufactured until some time *after* the crash.[18] It subsequently became known that Thurman had a degree in politics but no scientific training. How he came to be employed as an expert in the FBI laboratory is not known, but US Inspector General Michael Bromwich issued a report in 1997 stating that in thirty of fifty-two cases signed off by Thurman he had altered laboratory reports to bias them in favour of the prosecution. In other cases Thurman had circumvented procedures and had testified in court to areas of expertise in which he had no qualifications; he had also fabricated evidence. Although several people convicted on his testimony had to be released from prison, Thurman was fired but not prosecuted because this would have been embarassing for the FBI. He was banned from acting as an expert witness in any other court case.[19]

In Britain, Thomas Hayes' career as an expert witness also ended before the Lockerbie trial after a British Parliamentary inquiry conducted by leading appeals judge, the Right Honourable Sir John May concluded that he was not a reliable expert witness, having conspired to withhold evidence in the notorious trial of the Maguire family, seven members of which were wrongly sent to jail for years on the grounds of their involvement in the IRA bombing of two pubs in Guildford during 1974 which killed twenty-one people and maimed 220 others. Sir John May discovered that the notebooks of the three scientific expert witnesses had been deliberately concealed from the court. In his report to Parliament dated 9 July 1990, he wrote, 'The whole scientific basis on which the prosecution [of Anne Maguire and six members of her family] was founded was in truth so vitiated that on this basis alone the Court of Appeal should be invited to set aside the convictions'. By that time Hayes had seen the writing on the wall and resigned from RARDE, to work as a self-employed chiropodist.

Four other men were also accused of carrying out the 1974 IRA bombing of the two pubs in Guildford. They were convicted on the basis of confessions extracted after physical abuse and threats by Surrey Police while the suspects were detained under anti-terrorism laws. Among the coerced confessions was a statement that the house of Anne Maguire was a bomb factory. Police found no evidence of bomb-making there, but took swabs from under the fingernails of all the family. Forensic tests that were later discredited and banned appeared to show the whole family had handled nitroglycerine, but would have shown the same results for the presence of domestic soap. Seven members of the Maguire family having been jailed on this evidence, in 1991 the Court of Appeal quashed their convictions after it ruled that the 'scientific' evidence proving their guilt was entirely discredited.[20]

In 2005 Prime Minister Tony Blair made a public apology to all eleven of these wrongly convicted people for the gross miscarriages of justice they had suffered.

10

THE FATAL ACCIDENT INQUIRY

A fatal accident inquiry (FAI) – similar to an English coroner's court – must be held to determine the cause of any case of sudden death in Scotland. A secondary function of the FAI in the case of workplace deaths – and the flight deck and cabin crews of Flight 103 were working at the time of the crash – is to recommend procedures that may prevent a recurrence of the fatal event. The FAI for the Lockerbie crash began on 1 October 1990 and lasted until March 1991, the court sitting through sixty-one days, presided over by Sheriff Principal John S. Mowat QC. In the first fifty-five days, he heard evidence from 131 witnesses and submissions from the Crown, from counsel for Pan American Corporation and its associated companies, the British Airports Authority and from next of kin of the victims or their representatives. He was throughout under some pressure from the Lord Advocate's office to tread a delicate path, establishing the truth without apportioning blame or identifying the bomber or bombers – which was the duty of the continuing police investigation. In the expectation that there would be considerable public interest and that next of kin would exercise their right to appear or be represented at the FAI and also that many members of the public would attend, he ruled out a normal courtroom as being too small. Easterbrook Hall, formerly the largest psychiatric hospital in Europe, a few miles south of Dumfries, was chosen instead as the venue. The arrangements for the FAI there were to cost £3 million.

Kenneth Roy, editor of the *Scottish Review*, arrived at the press centre there towards the end of the inquiry and was given a badge, a desk and a telephone. Seeing the rows of empty desks labelled with the names of famous newspapers and broadcasting organisations, he asked where were the other media representatives, and was told there was so little interest that most of the phones had never even been connected. A security man advised him to stay in the press centre and listen to an audio feed of the proceedings as it was warmer there than in the 400-seat theatre being used as the courtroom. Entering the courtroom anyway after a body search and passing through a metal detector arch, Roy found not one of the 400 seats occupied. In an interval, he asked an usher whether this was usual and was told that the highest attendance had been ten people on one day at the beginning of the FAI, and that he was the first person to use the press facilities in several weeks. Looking around the rows of empty theatre seats, Roy's attention was caught by the attractive, stylishly dressed woman sitting with the American and Scottish lawyers and busily taking notes of what each witness said. This was Spanish-born New York resident Marina Larracoechea. Like Dr Swire, she had abandoned her former busy professional life as an interior designer to pursue the truth about the death of her beloved younger sister, a member of the cabin crew of Pan Am 103.[1]

So, there were perhaps ten observers spread out among the 400 seats on the first day of the FAI to hear the hour-long reading of the names and domiciles of all the crew and passengers, who had 'died from multiple injuries at about 1905 hours on Wednesday 21 December 1988 at or near Lockerbie, Dumfriesshire' and listing also the eleven fatalities on the ground, who had 'all died from multiple injuries and/or severe burning at about 1905 hours on Wednesday 21 December 1988 at Sherwood Crescent, Lockerbie, Dumfriesshire'.[2] Point 6 of Sherrif Mowat's Preamble stated that the primary cause of all the deaths was a 'criminal act of murder'.

Passengers checking in at Heathrow for Pan Am 103 on the afternoon of 21 December saw their hold baggage disappear on a conveyor belt into the bowels of the Departures building. However, what looked to them like a fully automated baggage handling system was anything but that. Confirming that the IED had been in a Samsonite suitcase in baggage container AVE4041, Point 5 of the Preamble stated that this was one of the pieces of baggage placed in 'the said luggage container' by employees of Pan American World Airways at Heathrow Airport, London. It emerged in evidence that the baggage handling system at Heathrow was at the time rather primitive. Luggage received at the check-in desks did disappear into the bowels of the airport on a network of conveyor belts, but was then driven in vans of an outside company, Whytes Airport Services, to one of several buildings known as 'interline sheds'. The Whytes drivers did not enter this area, but placed the baggage on a conveyor belt that carried it into the shed. Inside the shed at the end of this conveyor belt, baggage was tipped onto a carousel similar to those in passenger baggage reclaim halls. The bags were removed from the carousel by security personnel of the airline for which they were ticketed, or of a subcontractor working for that airline, and taken to that airline's area in the shed for processing.

Pan Am's fully owned security subcontractor was a company called AlertSecurity. On 21 December 1988, after a busy morning clearing baggage for several flights, most of the shift workers went off duty at 2 p.m., leaving three AlertSecurity male employees to deal with the evening flight to New York and Detroit. That afternoon, the man on duty at the carousel was Harjot Parmar. He took the bags checked in at Heathrow to the X-ray machine manned by his AlertSecurity colleague, Sulkash Kamboj. Kamboj then passed each bag through the scanner and affixed a label to it, confirming it had been scanned. It was then taken by Parmar to Pan Am loader-driver John Bedford, who placed it in one of the baggage containers prepared for *Maid of the Seas*.

In the case of baggage that had been checked in at another airport and arrived on a feeder flight, on the assumption that it had already been X-rayed at the first airport, he gave it directly to loader/driver John Bedford, who placed it in a Pan Am baggage container without any further check, ready to be driven out to the aircraft. These containers were cuboid and roughly 5ft in each direction, with the end that would face the outside of the aircraft extended and the bottom cut away at an angle of 45 degrees, the overhang, as it was termed, accommodating the curvature of the fuselage skin.

Since personnel from several airlines worked in this interline shed, it was confirmed in evidence that anyone suitably dressed and sporting an airside badge could come and go there without arousing suspicion. At 4.15 p.m. activity in the Pan Am area was quiet, so Bedford went off for his tea break and spent half an hour chatting with his supervisor, returning to the interline shed at roughly 4.45 p.m. Interviewed by police on 3 January 1989,[3] he said that Kamboj informed him on his return that two other suitcases for Flight 103 had arrived during his absence and been placed in the baggage container by Kamboj. Laid almost flat with the hinged side of the cases resting on the overhang and the handles pointing to the rear of the container, the bottom one was – as he told police on 9 January 1989 – a brownish Samsonite hardshell case. When Kamboj was interviewed by police, he denied placing these cases in the container, as did Parmar – whose name, despite being properly spelled on his badge, was written down as 'Palmer' by police. At the FAI, Alan Feraday of RARDE, giving evidence *before* Bedford, insisted that the case containing the bomb was not on the bottom layer in the baggage container, but Bedford was certain the brown Samsonite case was the lower one of the two placed in the overhang of AVE4041 during his absence. According to Morag C. Kerr, an astute veterinarian from Peebleshire who had been driving along the M74 on 21 December, and wrote a critical book pointing out inconsistencies in procedure and evidence at the FAI and the trial at Camp Zeist,[4] apparently no one at the FAI queried the inconsistency.[5] Since both these cases had X-ray security stickers on them, Bedford quite properly left them where they were, hooked the trailer bearing AVE4041 to his tractor, drove it to the supervisor's office and left it there. He then clocked off and went home for the day.

For whatever reason, Andrew Hardie, the lead QC for the Crown at the FAI, undermined Bedford's evidence, using this witness's admission that he could not be 100 per cent certain of the case's exact colour, two *years* after the event, although he had been completely certain when talking to the police two *weeks* after it. In fact, the forensic scientists examining the fragments of the bomb case described the colour at various times as 'brown', 'maroon', 'bronze' and even 'burgundy'. Having a metallic finish, its appearance would have been different in the fluorescent lighting of the interline shed and outside in the grey daylight of the overcast afternoon of 21 December. Even Samsonite's trade description of the finish as 'antique copper' is open to several interpretations.[6]

Back to the events of 21 December 1988, when baggage container AVE4041 stood on the tarmac outside the supervisor's office. It was unattended for forty-five minutes after Bedford left it there until another loader/driver, named Amarjit Sidhu,[7] was asked whether there was enough room in it for the luggage that had just arrived on Flight 103A from Frankfurt, twenty minutes late and leaving very little time for New York-bound baggage to be unloaded, placed in AVE4041 and loaded onto the jumbo for the flight to New York. It was a rush job for one man. Sidhu estimated that there was enough room, and thirty-five pieces of baggage from Frankfurt, labelled for airports in the USA including JFK Airport New York and Detroit, were hurriedly loaded in on top of the bags already in the container, according to Sidhu's evidence to police on 10 January 1989.[8] This turned out not to be the case, since later examination found that between seven and nine bags were loaded into AVE4041 before the Frankfurt feeder flight arrived. A number of the Frankfurt bags were indeed later also loaded into AVE4041, but when it was full, the others were placed in a baggage container loaded towards the rear of the Boeing 747.[9] In view of the crucial positioning of the Samsonite case containing the IED, this detail was not given the importance it merited; in fact, it appears to have been totally ignored by the investigators at the FAI and at the trial and appeal. In fact, Points 8–11 of the FAI Preamble stated:

[8] That the bags transferred from Pan American Flight 103A were taken directly from that aircraft in the said baggage container to Pan American Flight 103. They were not counted or weighed so as to check that they corresponded to the baggage checked in at Frankfurt by passengers proceeding to New York or reconciled in any other way with such passengers. They were not x-rayed at Heathrow.

[9] That the suitcase containing the said explosive device was among the said pieces of baggage transferred from Pan American Flight 103A and was unaccompanied on the flight from Frankfurt to Heathrow and on the flight from Heathrow, destination New York.

[10] That the said suitcase *probably* [author's italics] arrived at Frankfurt on a flight or an airline other than Pan American and so was interlined to Pan American there. It was loaded on to and allowed to fly on Flight 103 without being identified as an unaccompanied bag.

[11] That bags interlined to Pan American at Heathrow were subjected to x-ray screening but there was no reconciliation procedure there to ensure that passengers and their baggage travelled on the same aircraft. The same procedure probably applied at Frankfurt.

Points 13 – 19 of the Preamble pursued the same theme:

[13] That in 1988 it was accepted [a] that there was a danger of an explosive device being concealed in a piece of baggage and loaded on to an aircraft; [b] that such a piece of baggage was likely to be unaccompanied; and [c] that such a bag was likely to be introduced by being interlined at a particular airport from another airline and that the person introducing it would not check in as a passenger at that airport.

[14] That positive passenger/baggage reconciliation was recognised as an important element in any system designed to prevent the carriage of an unaccompanied bag on an aircraft.

[15] That the limitations of x-ray screening as a means of detecting plastic explosives contained in electronic equipment were generally recognised as at December 1988.

[16] That in all the circumstances the procedure of transferring baggage from Flight 103A to Flight 103 without any security check involved a substantial risk that an unaccompanied bag containing an explosive device would be so transferred.

[17] That it would have been a reasonable precaution to have instituted or reverted to a positive passenger/baggage reconciliation procedure in relation to interline baggage at Frankfurt designed to detect the presence of any unaccompanied bag. Such a precaution might have avoided the deaths.

[18] That in the absence of such a procedure at Frankfurt, it would have been a reasonable precaution to have instituted a positive passenger/baggage reconciliation procedure in relation to bags transferred from Flight 103A to Flight 103 [at Heathrow], either by counting the bags so transferred or by a physical match. Such a precaution might have prevented the deaths.

[19] That reliance on x-ray screening alone in relation to interline baggage at Heathrow and Frankfurt was a defect in a system of working which contributed to the deaths.[10]

In his written determination, Sheriff Mowat made a point of noting that he had allowed Dr Herbert 'Jim' Swire, whose daughter Flora died in the crash, to 'elicit in cross-examination and to lead evidence in relation to the part which the Government should be expected to play in promoting aviation security'. This, Sheriff Mowat noted, was 'tenuously linked to the state of technology in relation to the detection of explosive devices at the time of the disaster and how far the Government was responsible, through the Department of Transport, for the lack of research and development in that field'. However, Sheriff Mowat made a point of *not* having allowed Dr Swire 'to lead evidence … into the state of airport security at Heathrow'. As events would later prove, Dr Swire – a self-described small town GP – had been on the right track. It happened that this modest Old Etonian, born in Windsor Castle, where his father was a colonel in the Royal Engineers, had some knowledge of explosives, having himself taken a short-service commission in the Royal Engineers before deciding on medicine as a career. He it was who set up UK Families Flight 103 (UKFF103), a group of British relatives of those killed on Pan Am 103, who wanted to know the truth about the destruction of *Maid of the Seas* and the murder of their loved ones. Across the Atlantic, families of the 189 US victims of the crash formed Victims of Pan Am Flight 103 (VPAF103). As events would prove, the two support groups were to have very different agendas.

Under the section of the FAI determination headed SUBMISSIONS, the sheriff noted that:

> Andrew Hardie QC, appearing for the Crown, submitted: that Pan American Airways had failed to comply with Section 15 of the Air Carrier Standard Security Program [ACSSP] which set out the requirements of the Federal Aviation Administration in relation to special risk airports such as Frankfurt and Heathrow and, in particular, with Section 15C[1][a] which required baggage/passenger reconciliation. Pan American had used x-ray [examination] in place of reconciliation in respect of interline baggage.[11]

The airline had stopped using manual searches of check-in baggage in 1987 at both Frankfurt and London, claiming that the US Federal Aviation Authority (FAA) had given it permission to scan unaccompanied baggage by X-ray rather than carry out time-consuming physical searches. The determination continued:

[Pan American] suggested that they had been allowed to do so by a waiver from Mr Salazar of [the] FAA but Sheriff Mowat insisted that, had the requirements of Section 15C[1][a] been complied with in relation to interline baggage, the unaccompanied bag containing the device should have been detected and the accident might have been prevented. He then submitted that Pan American Airways had failed to comply with the requirements of the [British] Department of Transport in relation to the arrival of Flight 103A from Frankfurt and the departure of Flight 103 from Heathrow.

Mr Hardie had also observed that a circular issued by the [British] Department of Transport in September 1985 *recommended* [author's italics] that a reconciliation be effected between the baggage to be loaded aboard Flight 103 and the passengers who boarded the aircraft. Had Pan American sought to make such a reconciliation in relation to the baggage being transferred, the unaccompanied bag containing the device might have been identified.[12]

Counsel representing a group of bereaved relatives known as the Lockerbie Air Disaster Group, Mr Gill QC submitted that:

Pan American Airways had risked the lives of their passengers and crew by abandoning passenger/baggage reconciliation procedures in relation to interline baggage for reasons of commercial advantage.[13]

By 'commercial advantage', he was touching on the reputation of an airline for punctuality. It is a perennial problem for all airlines that increased security introduces delays in take-off, with the security-conscious pilot being penalised by losing his take-off slot and being relegated to the rear of the queue for take-off. Even quite short delays can lose custom by irritating passengers seemingly unaware of the overriding need for security. Mr Gill also blamed the Department of Transport for:

failing effectively to inspect and supervise the operation of the airline, to implement and enforce their own security requirements and to appreciate the risks involved in Pan American's continuation of an X-ray-only policy in regard to interline baggage and the tarmac transfer procedure.[14]

He went further by labelling:

Pan American's decision to rely on x-ray alone in relation to interline baggage reckless and dangerous as was the failure to review it in the latter half of 1988. In the absence of any waiver it clearly breached Section 15C[1][a] of the ACSSP. He submitted that the evidence in support of a waiver which effectively excluded the provisions of Section 15 was virtually non-existent. In any event, if x-ray only was a dangerous procedure the airline was not entitled to rely on any such waiver, which was overtaken by subsequent events. The tarmac transfer procedure at Heathrow was in breach of the Department of Transport's requirement that hold baggage be reconciled with passengers. In these circumstances, Mr Gill submitted that [Sheriff Mowat] should make a finding ... that the deaths might have been avoided had Pan American implemented a proper system of passenger/baggage reconciliation at Frankfurt and Heathrow and if they had not followed the practice of x-ray only of interline baggage at these stations and the practice at Heathrow of tarmac transfer of hold baggage without any security checks.

... Mr Gill submitted that [Sheriff Mowat] should consider ... finding ... that the deaths might have been avoided if [a] the Department [of Transport] had carried out an effective system of inspection of Pan America's operations at Heathrow; [b] the Department had enforced the security principles set out in its own circulars and directions; [3] the Department had stopped the practice of tarmac transfer of baggage between flights such as 103A and 103; and [d] the Department had taken effective action to enforce passenger/baggage reconciliation of all hold baggage on Heathrow-originating flights in response to the warnings they received in November and December 1988.[15]

Sheriff Mowat also noted that:

> There were serious inadequacies in record-keeping in that the operators did not know how many passengers, crew or bags were aboard Flight 103 and AlertSecurity failed to realise its aim of providing enhanced security *because of poor staff and under-funding* [author's italics].[16]

Among the submissions by relatives of the victims, we find:

> Ms Larracoechea, appearing for her brother-in-law, who is the husband of one of the crew members who died in the disaster, submitted that [the Samsonite suitcase] could have been substituted in the [baggage] container when it was in the baggage build-up area [at Heathrow]. If so, it was necessary to look more closely at the role of Heathrow [in the tragedy].[17]

As events would later prove, it was a pity that Dr Swire and Señora Larracochea had no official role in the investigation. They were on the right track, connecting the IED on board with the Syrian-based PFLP-GC and Iran, but the investigative line being currently followed was that the suitcase containing 'the said explosive device' must have arrived at Frankfurt on a flight of an airline other than Pan American and so was interlined to Pan Am there, being loaded onto Flight 103A without being identified as an unaccompanied bag either on the flight from Frankfurt to Heathrow or the flight from Heathrow. Allowed to sit with the lawyers at the FAI as an 'official representative' of the victims, Larracoechea had asked Amarjit Sidhu whether he was aware of at least three security breaches at Heathrow after the crash, but the question was disallowed by Sherrif Mowat, saying he was not concerned with events after the disaster, but only with what led up to it. She also asked Sidhu if he recognised staff entitled to be in the interline shed by badges or their uniforms. He replied that this was the job of airport security personnel, but other staff on duty would have known if a stranger was in the shed, and none had been noticed on 21 December. Loader-driver Terence Crabtree agreed that he had closed baggage container AVE4041 when it was full and driven it to Clipper *Maid of the Seas* for loading.

Señora Larracoechea had spent much time studying legal aspects of the flight and the crash. Her questioning of Michael Sullivan, Pan Am's Director of Flight Services at Heathrow, revealed a minor tragedy within the greater one. Since the Boeing 747 was only two-thirds full, the requisite cabin crew numbered twelve, but thirteen stewards and stewardesses were listed among the fatalities. Why was this, she wanted to know. It appeared that the unlucky thirteenth person had requested unofficially to travel on that flight and been allowed by the purser to join the scheduled crew. Asked whether he knew who was the thirteenth person, Sullivan replied that he thought so but was not going to give a name.

As to why she and her bereaved brother-in-law were at the FAI, Larracoechea replied that they wanted to raise issues in a personal way – not how lawyers would have done it. For example, what about the advance warnings to US diplomats, not to travel on that flight? The public was not warned, nor was the crew. She maintained that responsibility for the death of her sister, known as Nieves or Snow to other Pan Am colleagues, and the 269 other victims lay not just with the bombers but also with what she called 'the passive accomplices' in the US State Department, the counter-intelligence agencies and Pan Am management who had, for whatever reasons, blocked dissemination of the warning. Mowat's note of her submission ended:

Finally, [Ms Larracoechea] submitted that the Inquiry had been too limited in its consideration of [a] The role of international intelligence and its attitude in countering terrorism; [2] The assessment of the Helsinki threat; [3] The publication of threats to a privileged few and [4] The extent, if any, to which Pan American's bookings had been affected by publication of the Helsinki threat in the US

Embassy at Moscow. There should, [she submitted] be a further judicial inquiry into these matters.[18]

Appearing for Pan American and AlertSecurity, Mr Anderson denied any lack of funds or staffing on the security side in an attempt to minimise his clients' responsibility for the bomb being placed on *Maid of the Seas* and:

> argued quite reasonably that it was not possible to say how the Samsonite case got into the Pan American system and that it had not been proved that it arrived at Frankfurt as an interline bag.[19]
>
> Confusingly, he also argued that ... It was reasonable to assume that, as the transferred baggage came from another Pan American flight, proper checks had been made at Frankfurt.[20]

Another QC, Colin MacEachran, representing some of the families, made a point that must have surprised many people:

> He accepted that passenger manifests should be as accurate as possible, but there was no statutory obligation to have completely accurate manifests.[21]

Under the heading CAUSE OF THE DEATHS, Sheriff Mowat noted:

> The main task of the presiding Sheriff in a Fatal Accident Inquiry is to determine the time and place of the death or deaths and their cause. The other matters in respect of which he is entitled to issue a determination are secondary. In this case, although the evidence on the central matters of the case was necessarily protracted, only Sra Larracoechea suggested that she was not satisfied with the general thrust of my suggested findings. Accordingly, there was no difficulty in the end of the day in reaching the determination set out in the first five findings above. It was abundantly clear that the cause of all the deaths was the detonation of an improvised

explosive device which was in a particular luggage container situated in the forward cargo hold of the aircraft and the disintegration of the aircraft which followed. ... The clear inference to be drawn from these findings is that the primary cause of the deaths was a criminal act of mass murder and I have made a finding to that effect.[22]

Sheriff Mowat's determination stressed that it was not his place to attribute responsibility for the deaths but it did include a witness's submission that:

Pan Am's priorities had been shown to be financial economy, punctuality and facilitation rather than security and that the adoption of an x-ray-only policy for interline baggage was to avoid the dislocation caused if interline bags had to be offloaded [for individual examination].

The Alert programme [*sic*] had never fulfilled its ambitious image because Pan American had withheld the necessary funds and support. [Pan American's counsel] denied that funds and support were withheld by [the corporation, adding that] there was no evidence that anybody at Heathrow or Frankfurt was not doing his job. The pay rates [of Alert] were [he said] higher than those in similar security companies.

[As to the alleged waiver of passenger/baggage reconciliation given by the FAA] it had been argued at the Inquiry that there was virtually no evidence that the waiver was given. [Despite evidence that Mr Sonesen, Systems Director of Corporate Security of Pan American had been given an oral waiver at a meeting with a Mr Salazar of the FAA in Miami], it was improbable that the FAA would, in the course of a conversation, have relaxed their [security] requirements in respect of two airports where extraordinary security applied, and not confirmed this in writing. [And further,] if x-ray-only was a dangerous procedure, the airline was not entitled to rely on any waiver, particularly after they received the FAA bulletin which demanded rigorous application of [the standing unamended FAA security requirements. Whether or not the waiver was given, it] did not relieve US carriers in the United Kingdom from fulfilling the directions [of the Department of Transport] requiring a check that passengers had boarded the aircraft [and] Mr Salazar [had stated that] where host state requirements were spelled out, they were 'paramount' to FAA requirements.[23]

INVESTIGATING MASS MURDER

Police enquiries at Heathrow determined that baggage container AVE4041 had first been loaded at Terminal Three interline shed with checked-in luggage from feeder flights of other airlines by loader-driver John Bedford, an employee of Pan Am. He told police that he had placed a number of cases in this container in the afternoon of 21 December before leaving on his thirty-minute tea break. When he returned he found two more cases had been placed in AVE4041. One of them was a distinctive brown Samsonite case lying flat on the floor of the container at the front, where the cutaway angle would be closest to the skin of the fuselage.

When interviewed by police on 9 January 1989 – less than two weeks after the crash – Bedford declared that the X-ray operator employed by Pan Am subcontractor Alert Security that afternoon was Sulkash Kamboj, and his assistant was Harjot Parmar. According to Bedford, Kamboj told him that, after running them through the X-ray scanner, he had placed the two bags there during Bedford's tea break. Although admitting that X-ray operators might sometimes help out baggage handlers by doing this, Kamboj repeatedly told police he had not done so on this occasion. He did remember that a Pan Am flight to New York was due to leave that afternoon, but he did not recall Bedford working in the interline shed that day.

If the two suitcases bore security tags[1] confirming passage through the X-ray scanner, Bedford might not have bothered to ask Kamboj about them, but Bedford was apparently never asked whether the two cases in question bore X-ray tags or not when he noticed them in AVE4041 after returning from his tea break. Since, on 21 December 1988 the BKA's Autumn Leaves warning about Toshiba radio cassette players used by PFLP-GC had not been communicated to Heathrow interline shed staff, Kamboj would not have paid any particular attention to the Toshiba radio cassette player showing up on his screen, if indeed he had noticed it.

A crucially important question was, and remains, who placed the two suitcases in the very front of AVE4041 in such a way that the IED would cause the maximum damage to the structure of Pan Am 103? As noted by investigative reporter Paul Foot at the time, it was of critical importance that analysis by the AAIB experts established that the bomb suitcase ended up *in the precise position where it would cause maximum damage* – that is, closest to the fuselage skin, in the overhang section of AVE4041. It was also lying flat with its handle facing inboard and the bottom of the case facing outwards. The IED was not packed in the centre of the case, where the explosion would have been to some extent damped down by clothing all round, but tight up against the bottom, indicating that whoever did the packing was counting on the suitcase being placed in the container by someone who would ensure it went in the 'wrong' way round, i.e. with the handle down and the bottom of the case higher in the overhang, which was not normal.

There was evidence that the padlock on the interline baggage shed had been cut with bolt cutters about midnight on 20 December, and the damage discovered by an airport security guard named Ray Manly.[2] Had an accomplice of the bomber, wearing an airside pass, done this so he could deposit the Samsonite case in the shed? If so, he could just as easily have attached a 'passed X-ray' tag to the bag from the stock of them kept in the unlocked drawer beside the X-ray scanner. Interestingly, the US President's Commission on Aircraft Security and Terrorism, whose report was published in December 1989 does mention the possibility that 'tampering ... may have occurred with baggage left in a partially filled, unguarded baggage container that was later loaded on [Flight 103] at Heathrow'.[3]

Whether baggage documentation is faultless now, with all the computers that were not available in 1988, is unknown. However, one suitcase found on the ground at Lockerbie *was* unaccompanied and unaccounted for. It belonged to a Pan Am pilot in Berlin, who needed to send two suitcases back to his home in Seattle after being posted to Karachi. Following normal procedure for Pan Am staff, he booked the two cases with 'rush tags' on Pan Am 103A Berlin to Heathrow via Frankfurt on 21 December, there to await the London–Seattle flight the following day. One case duly arrived in Seattle on that flight; the other was somehow loaded onto Flight 103 and recovered in Scotland after the crash.[4]

Also recovered there was property of a female Pan Am flight attendant, who was at the time visiting her boyfriend, the son of a Syrian diplomat in post at Moscow. Given the alias of 'Sally Vincent' to protect her true identity, she had mentioned to other Pan Am girls how her thoughtful Syrian boyfriend packed her bag for her at the end of each visit. There was in 1989 no liaison channel between the FBI and the KGB, each of which regarded the other as 'the main enemy'. Through the Department of State and the American Embassy in Moscow, the Bureau requested help from the KGB, which made available one of its best surveillance teams. Ten days of close surveillance revealed only that 'Sally' and the boyfriend were just having fun together. However, when she checked in for her flight home, she was body-searched at the airport and her baggage confiscated by the KGB. On arrival at Frankfurt, she was again body-searched before being allowed to board her onward flight. Arriving eventually in New York, she was met by FBI agents, to whom she complained of her treatment in Moscow and Frankfurt before being interrogated at length.[5] The interesting aspect of this incident is how ready the KGB was to cooperate with its perceived enemy the FBI in an investigation of aircraft sabotage at the height of the Cold War.

The Lockerbie investigators knew that in October 1988 the BKA's Autumn Leaves operation against the PFLP-GC cell in Neuss had recovered a Toshiba radio cassette player which had been modified to form an improvised explosive device. Mr Feraday therefore visited West Germany to examine this device, and ascertained that the fragments in his possession did not originate from the same model of Bombeat. However, he considered that there was a sufficient similarity to make it worth investigating other models of Toshiba radio cassette players. It was found that there were seven models in which the printed circuit board bore the same markings as his fragment. Subsequently, when the blast-damaged clothing found in the debris trails was examined in detail, minute bits of paper were found embedded in two different Slalom brand shirts, a Babygro, and a pair of tartan checked trousers. These proved on examination to be from an owner's manual for a Toshiba RT-SF16 Bombeat radio cassette player. All the other fragments thought to have originated from the radio containing the explosive were consistent with having come from an RT-SF16.

In a letter addressed to Detective Chief Superintendent Orr at LICC on 3 February 1989, Feraday wrote:

> I have compared some fragments of electronic circuit board recovered at Lockerbie [stored at Longtown] and marked as item AG/145 with various radio/cassette tape recorders. I am completely satisfied that these fragments originate from a Toshiba brand radio stereo cassette recorder types RT-8016 or RT-8026. These fragments are shattered in a manner consistent with their intimate involvement in a violent explosion, and I therefore conclude that the bomb was concealed in the aforementioned Toshiba type portable radio/cassette player. The Toshiba RT-8016 and RT-8026 are visually similar and differ only in that the 8026 has a 3-band graphics equaliser on its front panel. Both sets measure 16 and a half inches [wide] by 5 and a half inches [high] by 4 inches [deep].

Meanwhile the investigation continued overseas. In Amman, the Jordanian capital, Marwan Khreesat admitted to his GID case officer that he had used both mono and stereo Toshiba radio cassette players, which information was passed on to the CIA early in 1989. By the time FBI special agents Edward Marshman and William Chornyak interviewed Khreesat in Amman in November 1989 for a total of ten hours, he had changed his story, and told Marshman that he had never used a stereo model and was therefore not responsible for building the IED that destroyed *Maid of the Seas*. Yet, when the BKA raided 16 Isarstrasse, the address in Neuss where Khreesat had been making his bombs, they had found twelve unmodified stereo radio cassette players, purchased by the PFLP-GC cell for him to modify for use as IEDs. So, his statement to Marshman sounds like nothing more than a way of absolving himself from making the particular IED which had brought down Pan Am 103.

Khreesat told Marshman that he been working undercover for Jordan's GID or Mukhabarat, which has been taken to mean that he was a proxy asset of the CIA, to which Jordanian intelligence had historically been close. He declared he had been ordered by GID to infiltrate the PFLP-GC in Germany, using his known bomb-making skills, and gave Marshman a detailed account of his activities in Germany which tallied with the BKA report of Autumn Leaves. The division of responsibilities was this: Khreesat was to design and make improvised bombs with which the PFLP-GC's German cell would attempt to destroy civil aircraft in flight while Abu Elias, an expert in airport security, would smuggle the bombs on to aircraft, although Khreesat was not told how. Khreesat stressed that his Jordanian controllers ordered him to ensure that his IEDs would not explode! If that is true, it was a suicide mission, since someone else in the PFLP-GC cell would have noticed, resulting in his elimination. According to his debriefing in Amman, on 24 October 1988 he started constructing five IEDs in modified Bombeat radio cassette players, but broke off to take a shower. While he was in the shower Dalkamoni knocked on the door and told him he was leaving for Frankfurt. On resuming work on the Bombeats, Khreesat saw that one of them was missing. Next day he telephoned his case officer in Jordan with the news that it had been given to Abu Elias.

On 14 September 1989 Swedish Säkerhetspolisen (security police) officers at a counterterrorism conference in Meckenheim, Germany, reported the arrest at long last of Mohammed Abu Talb, the Swedish-domiciled Egyptian-born member of PPSF, guilty of acts of terrorism involving explosives in Denmark, Sweden and Holland. It was known that he had visited Malta in October and November 1988. Clothing bought in Malta was found in his apartment by Säkerhetspolisen searchers on 1 November 1988, as was a calendar belonging to Abu Talb's wife Jamila with the fatal date of 21 December highlighted. Also found under a bed were fourteen wristwatches, some of them missing parts, a partly dismantled barometer and various electrical miscellanea. Abu Talb's only legitimate income was from a small café and video rental business in Uppsala, yet Säkerhetspolisen checks revealed that five large payments had been made into his bank account in 1988 and 16,000 kronor in cash was found in his home.[6]

Ten days after the Meckenheim news, the US Defense Intelligence Agency (DIA) issued the following notice dated 24 September 1989:

> The bombing of the Pan Am flight was conceived, authorised and financed by Ali-Akbar Mohtashemi-Pur, Iran's former interior minister. The execution of the operation was contracted to Ahmad Jibril, leader of the Popular Front for the Liberation of Palestine – General Command for a sum of $1m [*sic*]. Of this, $100,000 was given to Jibril up front in Damascus by the Iranian ambassador to Syria, Muhammad Hussan Akhari, for initial expenses. The remainder of the money was to be paid after successful execution of the mission.

At a briefing on the Lockerbie bombing in December 1989 the DIA confirmed its belief that Iran was the state sponsor untimately responsible for the Lockerbie bombing. It claimed that the PFLP-GC was a proxy doing Iran's dirty work and that the destruction of Pan Am Flight 103 to avenge the shooting down of Iran Air 655 was the result of close Iranian and PFLP-GC cooperation. Planning the execution of the *qisas* close to Christmas Day in order to mirror the closeness of the *Vincennes* shoot-down to the Muslim feast of Eid al-Fitr at the end of the month of Ramadan seemed to bear this out.

In an article published by *Jewish News Online* on 28 July 2017, London barrister David Wolchover referred to a warning given before the Lockerbie crash to MI6 by Israeli intelligence organisation Mossad that Heathrow was the most likely place where Ahmed Jibril's PFLP-GC, tasked to execute the *qisas* by Iran, would plant a bomb on a US-registered aircraft. Wolchover's investigation indicated that the bomb was probably transported to Heathrow on an Iran Air cargo flight that docked seemingly only 200 yards from the Pan Am interline shed and was carried there in the Samsonite suitcase – possibly by Jibril's nephew, Marwad Bushnaq aka Abu Elias – during the night of 20–21 December. That would have enabled him, wearing a genuine airside pass purchased in a local bar, to stroll in the following afternoon and position the suitcase in baggage container AVE4041 precisely as required during Bedford's tea break.

Why was no attention paid at the time to such a warning from Mossad, the world experts in keeping tabs on Islamic terror groups? In the summer of 1988, British Special Branch officers arrested a suspected Palestinian Fatah terrorist. Mossad requested his release because he was one of their undercover agents. Angry that Mossad was running its own undercover operations to infiltrate Fatah and PFLP cells in Britain, on 17 June the British authorities expelled the Mossad station chief in London and four members of his staff – all five holding diplomatic status. In late November 1988 Mossad alerted MI6 that a Middle-Eastern terrorist group, probably Syrian-based, would try to sabotage an airliner departing from Heathrow as it was the airport of choice for a terrorist to place a bomb on a wide-bodied American airliner in the busy pre-Christmas period. It seems that MI6 dismissed this warning as a trick by which Mossad thought it could make amends. At this point, Mossad seems to have let matters take their course.[7]

It was no secret to counterterrorist officers that the pro-Iranian PFLP-GC was known to be based in Syria, and was not just tolerated by the country's al-Assad regime but supported by it. The shaky alliance of the USA and Iraq's dictator Saddam Hussein was already showing signs of cracking up and the Pentagon was planning to invade Iraq in the not too distant future and force a regime change. When that happened, the US Combined Chiefs did not want to have enemies on both flanks in Syria and Iran, who might intervene against the Western coalition forces and turn the entire Muslim Middle East into a hostile environment.

In August 1990 Saddam Hussein invaded Kuwait on the pretext that it was a province of Iraq – for which there was no historic justification. The real reason was to grab Kuwaiti oil wells and write off the $14 billion borrowed from Kuwait by Saddam Hussein to finance his war with Iran. Washington and London, together with several client Gulf oil states, immediately declared him an outlaw. In planning to repulse Iraqi forces in Kuwait followed by a punitive invasion of Iraq, neighbouring Iran to the east and Syria to the west had to be let off the hook. At a meeting to agree the basis for this, US Secretary of State James Baker III showed al-Assad confidential evidence provided by Mossad which tied PFLP-GC to the Lockerbie bombing. This had been supplied to the CIA on the understanding that its source would not be revealed. Thanks to Baker's flouting of this golden rule of intelligence, two, or possibly three, Mossad moles among the 500 members of Ahmed Jibril's PFLP-GC were exposed and tortured to death later that month.[8]

If Syria and Iran were removed from the list of suspects, a plausible new prime suspect had to be found for the downing of Pan Am 103. Egypt was considered as a possible candidate, but since its government depended on generous subsidies from the USA, it made no sense to involve itself in sabotaging an American airliner. However, Egypt's western neighbour was Muammur Gaddafi's Libya, which was known to have supported terrorism in the past. Conveniently, in June 1991 rumours surfaced which could have been borrowed from the script of the 1975 Robert Redford/Faye Dunaway film *Three Days of the Condor*. It was said that a brilliant lone wolf CIA officer had 'had a hunch' that the Iran–PFLP-GC link was a false lead. Instead, he saw similarities between the Lockerbie modus operandi and the arrest at

Dakar Airport in Senegal of two Libyans carrying 20lb of explosives and triggering devices like the one from which the Lockerbie fragments had apparently come.[9] A person's ability to commit a crime is not proof that he did it. Yet Thomas Hayes, then still working in RARDE at Fort Halstead in Kent, became convinced that a fingernail sized fragment of a circuit board, said to have been recovered in Scottish woodland months after the crash, was a remnant of the IED, hidden in a radio cassette player that had brought down Pan Am 103.

As identified by FBI officer Thomas Thurman, the circuit board had been made by the Swiss company MEBO of Zürich, owned by Erwin Meister and Edwin Bollier. MEBO made circuit boards for domestic appliances and had made about twenty that *could* have been used to detonate a bomb. Several of these had been sold to Izzel Din al-Hinshiri, assistant director of a Libyan intelligence service. Bollier said that the ones sold to Libya were not of the same type as the fragment, and also stated that he had declined an offer from the FBI of several million dollars for a circuit board to be used in evidence and for testifying that the fragment produced in court was part of one specifically supplied to Libya.[10]

One of MEBO's technicians named Ulrich Lumpert said he had actually hand-made this particular board, and was willing to testify against his employer. Yet, in 2007 he gave a sworn affidavit[11] in which he later admitted he had lied.[12] He also admitted stealing in June 1989 from MEBO's workshop a part of a non-functioning timing device of the type referred to, which he handed over to an 'official person investigating the Lockerbie case', during that person's visit to Zürich in June 1991.[13] Elsewhere, Bollier avers that Lumpert gave it to Swiss Federal Police, who passed it on to Scottish Police. Lumpert's expressed excuse for not coming clean earlier was that he had been living in 'an indescribable condition of depression and fear since [his] second examination by the police in 1991' after realising that he was the 'bearer of secrets' that could get him killed.[14] He recognised the fragment because one relay soldering point was 'flat and clean', and had never been soldered. As to why Lumpert made his affidavit in July 2007, he said it was because he could no longer be prosecuted under

Swiss law due to the applicable statute of limitations.[15] It seems that his former employer Edwin Bollier had something to do with the making of the affidavit – presumably to clear the name of his company, if that was possible, after it had supplied similar timing devices to the Libyan military and to the East German Stasi. In a separate document, Bollier mentioned a desire to file a claim for $200 million against the Scottish authorities, of which 50 per cent would be given to charity!

Overnight, Libya became prime suspect for the Lockerbie bombing. It seemed plausible because the Gaddafi regime's past support for terrorism in many countries included even supplying arms to the IRA and reportedly giving the PFLP-GC one handout of $4 million.[16] Britain and America had had no diplomatic relations with Libya since the murder at an anti-Gaddafi demonstration in London of a London policewoman in April 1984. PC Yvonne Fletcher was shot by an automatic weapon fired by someone inside the Libyan People's Bureau in Knightsbridge when it was occupied by pro-Gaddafi 'students', the murderer escaping through a rear door before the building was surrounded by police. Consequently, British and American oil installations in Libya had been shut down and sanctions were in place both on exports of Libyan petroleum products and imports to Libya of everything except medicine and food.

But you cannot prosecute a country for murder. Accepting that he was between a rock and a hard place, Gaddafi asked his intelligence service to find a *plausible* scapegoat or two, who could be prosecuted, in the hope of getting the sanctions lifted. Unfortunately for a 47-year-old Libyan citizen named Abdelbaset al-Megrahi, he filled the bill, having been abroad on business and travelled back to Libya on 20 and 21 December 1988, passing though Luqa Airport on both days. A friend and former subordinate of al-Megrahi, Lamin Khalifah Fhimah, was also at the airport on 21 December.

THE PLOT THICKENS

Fortunately for the new strategy, the CIA had, in addition to its brilliant lone wolf with the hunch, a very low-level Libyan 'asset' in the person of Abdul Majid Giaka, originally employed as a motor mechanic by the Jamarahiya el-Mukhabarat, Gaddafi's intelligence service. In 1985 Giaka was posted to Malta on secondment to the staff of Libyan Arab Airlines at Luqa Airport. To make himself sound more important, when walking into the US Embassy in Valetta on 10 August 1988 to offer his services as an agent in place, he claimed to have been employed in the Mukhabarat's secret archives. Taken onto the books as a source of intelligence for the CIA in Malta, he assured his case officers that the Libyan Arab Airlines office in Valetta was 'a primary launching point' for Libyan intelligence officers and terrorists flying to Europe. In October he alleged that 8kg of orange explosive was stored in a locked drawer in the desk of Lamin Fhimah, Libyan Arab Airlines assistant station manager at Luqa Airport until September 1988. Fhimah also ran a private business – not unusual in Middle Eastern or North African countries – as did his boss, the Libyan Arab Airlines Security Director, Abdelbaset al-Megrahi.

Giaka had been throughout his relationship with his CIA handlers in Malta a frustratingly intermittent source of unimportant bits and pieces, some of which were genuine, but were apparently hearsay with confusion over dates and other details. It was clear to his handlers that he was desperate to have himself and his wife flown away to live in the USA. On the vague understanding that this might be arranged if he came up with enough genuine material, he agreed to stay in post and meet his CIA handlers once a month, to pass on inside information and receive payments of $1,000 or $1,500 each time for his services. This stopped in 1990 when he was patently not giving value for money. Giaka had to return to Libya, but managed in July 1991 to sneak into neighbouring Tunisia with his Maltese wife Cynthia and fly from there to Malta. His CIA handlers – understandably trying to prove they had not been wasting time and money on a useless contact – arranged for the couple to be smuggled aboard USS *Butte*, a warship lying some 27 miles off the Libyan coast, where Giaka was debriefed for three weeks.

Under the threat of being dumped back ashore if he could not give his CIA interrogators something useful, Giaka now declared himself ready to testify on oath to something that he had never mentioned to his handlers before: that on the evening of 20 December 1988 he had seen Fhimah and al-Megrahi collect a brown Samsonite suitcase from the Arrivals carousel in Luqa Airport and depart with two other people. On the following morning, he alleged, Fhimah had personally carried the suitcase through security and placed it with other baggage to be loaded onto the morning flight from Malta to Frankfurt designated KM 180. As to why he gave this important information only now, Giaka maintained that he had told his handlers this at the time, but no one in the CIA could find any evidence of that.

Given his previous abysmal record as a source, his compelling reasons to say whatever his case officers wanted to hear, and the fact that he had never mentioned this before he heard there was a substantial reward for information leading to the conviction of the saboteurs of Pan Am 103, Giaka's new allegation should have been treated with extreme scepticism. Instead, it was treated as important evidence that merited him being spirited away to the USA and placed with his pregnant wife in a witness protection programme with a regular salary and the expectation of receiving the $4 million reward offered for information leading to the arrest of the Lockerbie bomber,[1] plus an additional $50,000 from the FBI.

When the BKA requested the computerised baggage manifest for the Pan Am 103A feeder flight on 21 December 1988, they were told by Frankfurt Airport security personnel that the hard drive file for that day had routinely been wiped. However, a 57-year-old Slovenian IT specialist named Bogomira Erac employed by a sub-contractor at Frankfurt Airport, surprised them with the news that she had preserved a copy of the day's work on a floppy disc 'from personal curiosity' after she heard that *Maid of the Seas* had crashed at Lockerbie. According to her copy of the manifest, an unaccom-panied suitcase had arrived in Frankfurt on Air Malta Flight KM180 on 21 December 1988 and been transferred as an interline bag to Flight Pan Am 103A, eventual destination New York. This fortui-tous information seemed to corroborate Giaka's allegation. Now began an international game of buck-passing between Heathrow and Frankfurt airports, London arguing that the Samsonite bag had origi-nated on Malta and been interlined to Pan Am 103A from Frankfurt to London and Frankfurt Airport security equally convinced that the bag had entered the system when loaded at Heathrow onto Flight Pan Am 103 for New York.

When investigators from LICC visited Malta to check the records at Luqa Airport, they found no evidence of any unaccompanied bag on KM180. That could have meant, as senior CIA officer Vincent Cannistraro alleged, that 'the entire Luqa Airport operation had been suborned by Libya, with wholesale forgery of the flight documenta-tion'. It could also have meant, very simply, that no such suitcase left Luqa on Libyan Air flight KM180 to Frankfurt in the morning of 21 December 1988, no matter what the conveniently discov-ered unofficial copy of the Frankfurt hard drive data and Giaka's testimony appeared to indicate. The harrassment by British and American investigators attempting to prove allegations of Air Malta's inefficiency or Luqa Airport employees' complicity resulted in the investigators twice being requested to leave the island because the publicity they were causing was thought to be damaging for the Maltese tourist industry.

With the bit between their teeth, the American and British investigators do not appear to have asked themselves why experienced aircraft saboteurs would choose to prime the detonator mechanism of the IED in Luqa Airport before the take-off of flight KM 180 at 9 a.m. in the morning of 21 December. If there was a barometric trigger for the timer, how would that have coped with two take-offs – from Luqa and Frankfurt airports – and two landings – at Frankfurt and Heathrow airports - before being loaded onto *Maid of the Seas*? Even if there was only a simple timer mechanism, it would have had to be set only minutes before take-off, which made it likely that someone would have noticed unusual activity on the tarmac at Luqa Airport – and that was still nine hours before Pan Am 103 was scheduled to lift off from Heathrow Airport.

Aircraft departures are frequently delayed for all sorts of reasons, so KM180 could have been late arriving at Frankfurt, completely missing the connection to London. In the event, Pan Am 103A *was* late taking off and could easily have landed in London after the departure of Pan Am 103. In either of those cases the IED would never have been on *Maid of the Seas*. The evidence of Heathrow loader/driver Amarjit Sidhu, in charge of AVE4041 after John Bedford clocked off, was that baggage from Pan Am 103A was loaded into the hold of *Maid of the Seas* within minutes of the delayed Pan Am feeder flight parking at an adjacent bay, but the Samsonite case was already in AVE4041 *before the arrival of Flight 103A*.

Among the thousands of pieces of cloth recovered from the debris trails in Scotland were several traced to garments manufactured in Malta. While on the island, detectives from Scottish Police, Scotland Yard, the BKA and FBI questioned the manufacturers and determined that the garments had been sold retail by Mary's House, a shop in the Maltese town of Sliema, about 3 miles from Luqa Airport. It was owned by Edward Gauci, whose son Tony claimed to have sold these garments in early December 1988 to an Arabic-speaking customer. He was, Gauci said, probably a Libyan, many of whom took advantage of the brief 200-mile flight to visit the island for business or pleasure. Alcohol and prostitution were big draws, but so were feminine hygeine products, medicines, disposable nappies, fresh fruit and other goods that were unobtainable or in short supply in Gaddafi's sanctions-deprived Libya. At any one time there were an estimated 15,000 Libyans on Malta. It has to be noted that, apart from Tunisians who have French as their second language, pretty much all Arabic-speakers are called *libyano* by the Maltese. The problem was that, on being shown photographs of a number of Arabic men in October 1989 Tony Gauci picked out a photograph of Mohammed Abu Talb as being the purchaser of the clothing ten months earlier, shortly before Christmas 1988. Being in the business of selling clothes, he described the purchaser as a dark-skinned, 50-year-old man over 6ft tall, with a 36in waist and broad chest – which fitted Abu Talb – and gave from memory a list of clothing sold to this client that sounded like the blast-damaged clothes found at Lockerbie.

Rather conveniently, over the course of *eighteen* further statements to police by Tony Gauci, the purchaser of the clothes in his shop in Sliema changed from a tall, well-built, dark-skinned, 50-year-old Arab to a slightly built Libyan 5ft 7in tall, fair-complexioned and less than 40 years old – a description that fitted Abdelbaset al-Megrahi like a glove.

On 21 February 1991 Scottish detective Harry Bell wrote a memorandum to his superior Detective Superintendent Gilchrist entitled *Security of Witness Anthony Gauci*, in which he mentioned this witness's interest in the large financial reward being offered by the CIA. This was not disclosed at the trial as Gauci's motive for testifying. The CCRC also had a confidential report dated 10 June 1999 regarding the desire of Gauci for inclusion in a witness protection programme run by Strathclyde Police. Of the brothers, it was believed that Tony Gauci had even been taken on expenses-paid fishing trips in Scotland by police, trying to bring him fully on-side. His brother Paul, had also been considered for inclusion in the programme. The following passage in Mr Bell's report contains this:

It is apparent from speaking to [Tony Gauci] for any length of time that he has a clear desire to gain financial benefit from the position he and his brother are in relative to the case. As a consequence he exaggerates his own importance as a witness and clearly inflates the fears that he and his brother have ... Although demanding, Paul Gauci remains an asset to the case but will continue to explore any means he can to identify where financial advantage can be gained.[2]

The report makes it clear that the Gauci brothers had not then received any money. But a note in Mr Bell's diary for 28 September 1989 read:

He [Agent Murray of the FBI] had authority to arrange unlimited money for Tony Gauci and relocation is available. Murray states that he could arrange $10,000 immediately.[3]

On 14 November 1991 al-Megrahi and Fhimah were formally accused at simultaneous press conferences in Edinburgh and Washington by the Scottish Lord Advocate and the US Attorney General of the 'bombing' of Pan Am Flight 103. They heard the news that day over the BBC Arabic service, al-Megrahi at home in Libya and Fhima in neighbouring Tunisia. London and Washington ordered Gaddafi to extradite al-Megrahi and Fhimah for trial, despite neither Britain nor the USA having an extradition treaty with Libya. Since the two accused men were unlikely to get a fair trial in either country, President Gaddafi quite reasonably refused to hand them over, but did offer to place them on trial in Libya, the accused being entitled to stand trial in their own country. This solution was completely in accordance with the 1971 Montreal Convention governing prosecution of aircraft saboteurs. As confirmed by a formal memorandum prepared in April 1992 by Professor Francis A. Boyle of the University of Illinois:

There is no obligation for Libya to extradite its two nationals to either the United States or the United Kingdom. The United States government has purposely and illegally made it impossible for there to be a pacific settlement of the dispute.[4]

Marc Weller, Research Fellow in International Law at St Catherine's College, Cambridge also analysed the US–Libyan dispute and concluded that Libya had fulfilled its international legal requirements by offering to try the two men, and that, to secure the UN resolutions on the Libyan embargoes the USA had to expend considerable political capital and goodwill in the Security Council, bullying fellow members to obtain the necessary votes and enraging many UN member governments who were non-members of the Council and who keenly observed this spectacle. The US and UK governments may well have contributed to, or brought about, an abuse of rights by the Security Council.[5]

After Giaka's allegations of poor security at Luqa Airport in Malta, where the Samsonite suitcase was supposed to have originated as unaccompanied luggage, were repeated in a Granada TV documentary on Lockerbie, Air Malta received a considerable out-of-court settlement in 1993. When a similar allegation was screened in Scottish Television's Lockerbie programme in August 2010, Dr Swire wrote to BAFTA pleading with it not to give an award to STV because he and the other relatives of the victims wanted the truth about the responsibility for the destruction of Flight 103 and the murder of all the passengers and crew to be clearly established.

A trial in Libya was rendered impossible by the refusal of the British and American governments to hand over their alleged evidence against the two men. Although initially refusing to extradite Fhimah and al-Megrahi, Gaddafi ordered them to be given a tough grilling by Libyan intelligence. They had their passports confiscated, as well as their driving licences and identity cards, and were held under house arrest in Tripoli, reporting each week to a police station. This state of affairs lasted seven years, during which al-Megrahi depended on his Libyan Arab Airlines pension and also worked as a teacher. On 23 March 1995, over six years after the bombing of Pan Am 103, al-Megrahi and Fhimah were designated as fugitives from US justice and their names became Nos 441 and 442 on the FBI's Most Wanted Fugitives list.

13

A UNIQUE SOLUTION

The stalemate was not resolved until almost ten years after the Lockerbie crash when, at the suggestion of Edinburgh University professor of Scots law, Robert Black QC, a former courtroom lawyer who had grown up in Lockerbie, a formula was agreed for the two accused Libyans to be tried in a neutral country, and the Dutch Government agreed to cooperate. The trial was arranged at Kamp van Zeist, a disused American Air Force base in the province of Utrecht, where a school building was converted into a courtroom for a special sitting of the Scottish High Court of Justiciary. Another building in what was generally referred to as Camp Zeist was converted into a prison, where the suspects could be held. Under a bilateral treaty between the United Kingdom and the Kingdom of the Netherlands, the premises were stated to be under the authority and control of the Scottish court for the duration of the trial *and any subsequent appeal*. Barring an emergency, the Dutch authorities were banned from entering the premises and the court had the authority to enact regulations that superseded Dutch law when necessary for the execution of the trial, and also to jail people for contempt of court. The court personnel and all others involved in the trial, whether as witnesses or otherwise, were granted immunity from Dutch law.

On 27 August 1998 UN Security Council Resolution 1192 welcomed the initiative for the trial of the two Libyans charged with the bombing of Pan Am flight 103 before a Scottish court sitting in the Netherlands and the British Government asked the Secretary General of the United Nations by a letter dated 28 October 1997 to nominate international observers to attend the trial, as agreed with the Permanent Representative of the United Kingdom at the UN. At a UN press conference on 5 April 1999, Secretary General Kofi Annan promised that there would be an effective international presence during the trial. Five international observers were named. Of these, Dr Hans Köchler, a professor of law at the University of Innsbrück in Austria, was the only one to submit comprehensive reports on the Lockerbie trial and appeal proceedings to the Secretary General of the United Nations in accordance with his role under Security Council Resolution 1192.

Although guilt or innocence of the accused was to be decided by three Scottish judges without any jury, Gaddafi gave his consent. The absence of a jury was publicly justified by the virtual impossibility of finding in Scotland fifteen men and women who would come to hear the case with no previous opinion about the crime, as required by Scottish law. There was perhaps a more sinister reasoning at work, with judges being paid servants of the state. Among those who sought to persuade the Libyan President to agree to this unique proposal was Dr Swire, who paid his own fares to travel to Tripoli, where he personally appealed to President Gaddafi to allow the two suspects to be tried under Scottish law in a neutral country. Dr Swire, having ceased medical practice to devote himself to the pursuit of justice for the murder of Flora and the other victims of the sabotage of Pan Am 103, made a second visit to Tripoli with Professor Robert Black. This was arranged with the help of a sympathetic Egyptian journalist and the backing of Esmat Abdel-Meguid, Secretary General of the Arab League.[1] According to Dr Swire, his visit to Libya led to his partners in the group practice to 'kick me out because they said I was making them a terrorist target'.[2] His campaign for the truth about the Lockerbie bombing also put a strain on his marriage, not least because giving up his job and forfeiting pension rights cost the couple their comfortable home in Worcestershire.

Gaddafi's acceptance of Professor Black's solution of holding the trial in neutral Holland was taken by many people in the West as an admission of Libya's guilt in the bombing of *Maid of the Seas*, but is easily seen as his way of ending the UN and American sanctions that were crippling the Libyan economy in return for handing over two scapegoats named by two witnesses of doubtful veracity in the belief that no court would credit their assertions, so that the two Libyans would be acquitted. Nearly ten years after the crash of Pan Am 103, on the day of the UN press conference, al-Megrahi and Fhimah landed in an Italian aircraft bearing UN insignia at Valkenberg Airbase near The Hague. On disembarking, they were formally arrested by Dutch police. Several hours later, they were made to sign permissions for extradition to Scottish territory, i.e. Camp Zeist.

Then, as al-Megrahi rightly put it, 'it all became ludicrous'.[3] Despite having voluntarily surrendered themselves, both men were hand-cuffed by Dutch security officers, the handcuffs were padlocked to chains around the waist and they were shackled with ankle chains so short that they could only walk in a shuffle. Next, they were chained to Dutch officers and blindfolded. They had to be helped to walk to waiting helicopters and lifted inside. On arrival at Camp Zeist, they were driven to what al-Megrahi described as a Scottish Police station, where Senior Investigating Officer Thomas McCulloch was horrified and told the Dutch to remove the restraints immediately, after which he cautioned and arrested the two Libyans anew.[4] McCulloch's reaction was typical, the Libyans found, of most Scottish Prison Service officers, but security at Camp Zeist was provided by 200 prison service, police and private security personnel, not all of whom were as correct in their treatment of the detainees.

The Sherrif having left for the night by the time the formalities were completed, al-Megrahi and Fhimah had to try and get some sleep in the small cells of the police station. In this highly disconcerting manner they commenced their confinement under strict remand conditions, which included regular body searches and searches of the cells they were occupying. Scottish law had what was called 'the 110-day rule', which was meant to limit the time during which the accused could be held before the start of their trial. The trial should therefore have commenced in October 1999, but the prosecution was not ready then. The defence team could have insisted on the application of the 110-day rule, and taken advantage of the prosecution's unreadiness, but took the safe course and conceded more time for the preparation of the Crown's case. For that reason, it was over a year before the trial started on 3 May 2000.[5] If the long delay was hard on al-Megrahi, conditions were even more difficult for Fhimah, who needed twice-daily injections of insulin and had both eye and kidney problems too. Even the family visits they were permitted were uncomfortable, with both adults and children being searched, officers even poking into the nappy of al-Megrahi's 5-month-old baby and the other children understandably terrified of the attack dogs surrounding them.

Under Scottish criminal law defending lawyers are allowed to interview witnesses before the trial. In this case, the list ran to 1,100 names of people in many different countries, so this was largely impracticable. When interviewing Gauci in October 1990 they received a startling answer to the question whether he could recall the date the clothes were purchased: 'I remember it was the twenty-ninth of the month. I think it was November. All I can say is, that is what I think.' Since al-Megrahi was alleged to have purchased the clothes on 7 December, if Gauci had repeated this statement in court, al-Megrahi would have been acquitted. There were a number of other significant discrepancies with his earlier statements.

In addition, the defence team had to read 3,000 Crown, i.e. prosecution, documents – many running to several hundred pages – plus the BKA Autumn Leaves report, which totalled 169 volumes in German that required translation. What they did not have to read was the pile of notebooks kept by the police investigators of the original PFLP-GC connection, because these had been destroyed. The Crown also initially failed to reveal many documents and names of other witnesses, which were disclosed in November 1999 and February and April 2000. One unexpected development was the resignation, just two months before the scheduled date for the trial to open, of the chief prosecutor, Lord Advocate Andrew Hardie QC. Rightly or wrongly, his resignation was taken by many in the legal profession as a refusal to drink from a poisoned chalice.[6]

All was far from being well otherwise in the lead-up to the trial. Lawyers defending the two accused were about to cite Article 6 of the European Convention on Human Rights at the High Court in Edinburgh at a preliminary hearing in the legitimate challenge over alleged delays by the Crown Office in disclosing prosecution evidence which, they said, was making it difficult to prepare the defence case. The principle involved was that the defence should have access to all the evidence the Crown intended using at the trial. Unbelievably, given the eleven years which had elapsed since the crash, it was thought by many that this was not a deliberate attempt to delay proceedings but in order to give the investigators time to gather more evidence!

In fact, officers of Dumfries and Galloway Police force had recently travelled to Libya, Sweden and Cyprus seeking evidence for the prosecution, which indicates someone's doubts over the strength of the prosecution case.[7] In Sweden, the CID officers and a representative of the prosecution attended two closed court hearings, the local press being told they were making enquiries into a murder in Scotland. As to what the detectives were doing during a five-day stay on Cyprus, local police officer Galafkos Xenos refused to identify the person under investigation, except for saying that he was 'currently in prison in Scandinavia following his conviction on a terrorist bombing charge. All I can say is that he used various names while he was in Cyprus.' Although described at the time as a Lebanese businessman, this was former Egyptian army officer Mohammed Abu Talb, who, at the time of the detectives' visit, was serving a life sentence in Sweden for terrorist offences in Scandinavia. The Scottish CID officers obtained a court order to examine a bank account he had used on the island in 1992, and were trying to trace records of his telephone calls. Although they requested Mr Xenos to keep their visit to Cyprus secret, their presence on the island was revealed by a detailed front-page report in the Greek Cypriot newspaper *Phileleftheros*.[8]

In April 1999 Tony Gauci was brought to Camp Zeist for an identity parade. His brother Paul had been collecting press photographs and other material on al-Megrahi, and shown this to Tony, to help him come up with the 'right' answer at the ID parade. This should absolutely *not* have been allowed. The most recent material included a two-page photo spread from the Maltese magazine *It Torca* of 28 February 1999, which Tony Gauci had seen as recently as four days before the crucial identification. In it, al-Megrahi's appearance was virtually identical to his appearance at Camp Zeist, whereas Gauci was supposed to be identifying the man who had bought the clothing eleven years earlier. Given his original statement that the purchaser had then been about 50 years old at the time he bought the clothes in Mary's House, the suspect he was to pick out in the identity parade should have been 60 or older. Al-Megrahi was 47 and looked nowhere near 60, but he was the second-oldest man in the identity line-up and the only man older than him was much shorter and should not have been present, since the original description Gauci had given police was of a man about 6ft tall. Since his business was selling clothes to mainly male customers, this was not a wild guess, but a professional estimate.

Nor were these the only blatant irregularities in the ID parade, to which al-Megrahi's solicitor Alastair Duff objected: one man removed from the line-up would have been only 15 at the time of the clothes' purchase and four others would have been only in their 20s when the clothes were bought in 1988. Four men were eventually rejected, leaving seven men in identical orange tracksuits. However, al-Megrahi was made to wear polished brown leather shoes while all the other, visibly younger, men in the line-up wore trainers, which made him look immediately different. Witnesses present at the ID parade also said that he alone looked nervous, which is understandable. Apart from all that, al-Megrahi did not resemble Gauci's original description of the clothes purchaser in height, age, physical build or skin colour. After examining the line-up through a one-way mirror,

Gauci said to Inspector Brian Wilson of Dumfries and Galloway Police, 'Not exactly the man I saw in the shop ten years ago. I saw him, but the man who look a little bit like exactly is Number Five.' Duff informed al-Megrahi of the exact wording because it fell a long way short of a positive identification. He also made clear to the police supervising the process that, despite Tony Gauci supposedly recognising a man casually seen for less than half an hour eleven years before, it was police experience that a delay of eleven *months* is sufficient to reduce the reliability of ID parade identification to no better than sheer chance. The 1982 Scottish Police guidelines on identification of suspects was clearly breached in several particulars, one of which was that the only man in the line-up of approximately the same age as al-Megrahi was a Dutch police officer of very European appearance.

A tale of two aircraft: *Above* is the ill-fated Iran Air Airbus 300 EP-IBU that was operating Flight IR655 on 3 July 1988 when it was blown out of the sky while in Iranian airspace over the Strait of Hormuz by two surface-to-air missiles launched from USS *Vincennes* with the loss of 290 lives. *Below* is Pan American Boeing 747-121 N739, blown out of the sky above Lockerbie, Dumfriesshire, Scotland on 21 December 1988 with the loss of 270 lives in the aircraft and on the ground. (*Top:* by kind permission of Werner Fischdick Collection; *bottom:* by kind permission of Arno Jansen/Werner Fischdick Collection)

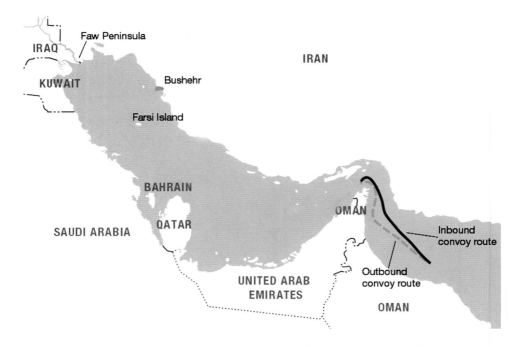

The dual tragedy began at sea level, in the Persian Gulf (*above*). During the eight-year Iran–Iraq War the US Navy stationed warships (*below*) in the Gulf under Operation Ernest, to protect tankers carrying Iraqi oil from Iranian harassment. (Both author's collection)

On 3 July 1988 the missile cruiser USS *Vincennes* (*above*) was on patrol. It was among the most advanced warships in the world. Its state-of-the-art Aegis computers fed to the screens in the darkened Combat Information Centre (*below*) the real-time situation, tracking up to 100 simultaneously attacking air and surface craft. (Both author's collection)

Captain Will Rogers, commanding *Vincennes*, mistook the Iranian civilian jumbo jet climbing in a recognised civilian flight corridor at 7,000ft after take-off from Bandar Abbas for a smaller, faster F-14A Tomcat (*above*) attacking his ship at 2,000ft. He launched two supersonic SM-2MR missiles (*below, left*) that blew the Airbus out of the sky, killing all 290 people on board. (Both author's collection)

A CIA map of the event.

At the press conference in Washington after the shoot-down (*above*), the body language of Secretary of Defense Frank Carlucci and Admiral William J. Crowe says it all. On return to San Diego, Captain Rogers (*below*) was awarded the Legion of Honour and all his crew received medals for valorous service in combat. (Both author's collection)

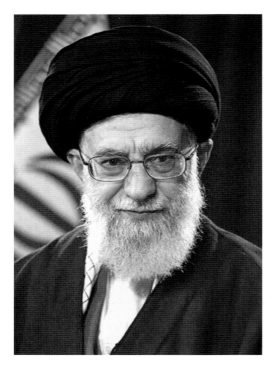

With no apology from Washington, the government of President Ayatollah Ali Khomeini of Iran (*left*) ordained a *qisas* or legal revenge under sharia law. The execution of the *qisas* was outsourced to Palestinian terrorist group PFLP-GC, whose usual activities included destroying this Israeli school bus (*below*) with anti-tank weapons, killing or maiming all on board. (Both author's collection)

Ahmed Jibril (*left*) was head of the PFLP-GC group. He called on experienced Jordanian bomb-maker Marwan Khreesat (*below*) to build an IED that would crash an American jumbo jet and kill all on board. (Both author's collection)

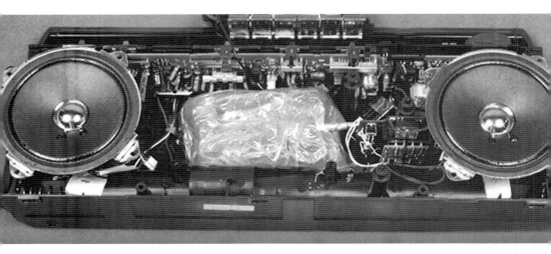

At a PFLP-GC safe house in Germany, Khreesat concealed inside a Toshiba Bombeat radio cassette player a small charge of Semtex, with battery, timer and detonator (*reconstruction above*). This was to be packed in a suitcase to be checked in on the chosen aircraft (*reconstruction below*). (Both ©Crown)

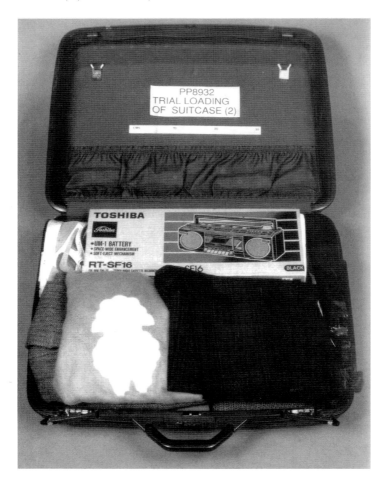

Above is a cross section of an Airbus A300. Its construction is similar to that of the Pan Am Boeing that was the target. By placing the suitcase in the overhang of the baggage container (*below*), Khreesat's IED was as close as possible to the skin of the aircraft's fuselage. (Both ©Crown)

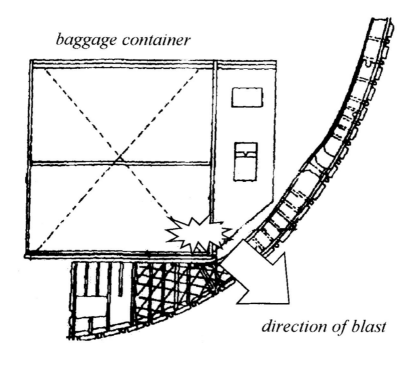

baggage container

direction of blast

On 21 December 1988 the suitcase was carefully placed in the overhang of baggage container AVE4041 exactly like this (*above*). Just south of Lockerbie, the explosion ripped a hole in the fuselage of the Pan Am jumbo jet. Within seconds, the aircraft depressurised and broke up into thousands of pieces, killing 270 people. One of the larger pieces was the crushed nose cone that landed near Tundergarth church (*below*). (Both ©Crown)

Lockerbie's Victorian town hall (*above*) was used as a morgue for the first bodies found. When the tens of corpses became hundreds, the town's ice rink (*below*) was the most logical place to keep them. (Both author's collection)

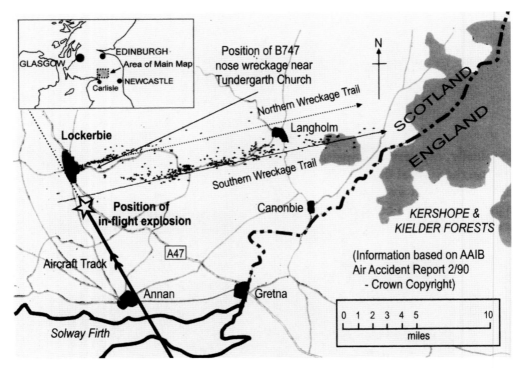

Because Pan Am 103 disintegrated 6 miles up, bodies, body parts, belongings and bits of the aircraft were blown downwind right across Scotland to the North Sea in two major trails (*above*). Among the thousands of pieces of debris recovered, clothing that had been very close to the explosion was traced to a small shop in Malta (*below*). (*Top:* ©Crown; *bottom:* author's collection)

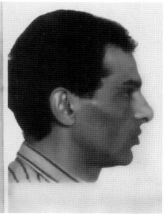

Shopkeeper Tony Gauci (*above, left*) sold the clothes. He identified Egyptian terrorist Mohammed Abu Talb (*above, right*) as the purchaser. After thousands of man-hours spent pursuing the trail of the Syria-based PFLP-GC group, President Reagan and Margaret Thatcher decided that Libya was the guilty country. Two Libyan airline officials, Abdelbaset Ali al-Megrahi (on wanted poster, *below*) and Lamin Fhima, were accused of the murders of all the Lockerbie victims. (Both author's collection)

$4,000,000
REWARD

On 12/21/88, Pan Am Flight 103 from London to New York exploded over Lockerbie, Scotland killing all 259 on board and 11 more people on the ground. A massive investigation over the next three years culminated in the indictments of two suspects, who are both Libyan nationals and intelligence officers.

Abdel Basset Ali Al-Megrahi, one of the two suspects, is believed to be in Libya. The Libyan Government, against which the United Nations has invoked resolutions and sanctions, has been unwilling to turn Al-Megrahi over to the United Kingdom or United States for trial.

The United States Department of State and the U.S. airline industry are offering a reward of up to $4,000,000 for information leading to the apprehension and prosecution of Al-Megrahi. The U.S. Government also can provide for the protection of identity and the possibility of relocation for persons and their families furnishing such information. If you have information about Al-Megrahi or the Pan Am 103 bombing, contact authorities or the nearest U.S. Embassy or consulate. In the United States, call your local office of the Federal Bureau of Investigation or 1-800-HEROES-1, or write to:

HEROES
Post Office Box 96781
Washington, D.C. 20090-6781
U.S.A.

ABDEL BASSET ALI AL-MEGRAHI

DESCRIPTION

Date of birth:	April 1, 1952
Place of birth:	Tripoli, Libya
Height:	Approximately 5'8"
Weight:	Approximately 190 lbs
Hair:	Black curly, clean shaven
Eyes:	Dark brown
Complexion:	Light brown
Sex:	Male
Nationality:	Libyan
Occupation:	Formerly Chief of Airline Security, Libyan Arab Airlines, in Malta
Aliases:	Abd Al Basset Al Megrahi, Abdelbaset Ali Mohmed Al Megrahi, Mr. Baset, Ahmed Khalifa Abdusamad

Program developed and funded by Air Line Pilots
Association and Air Transport Association in coordination
with U.S. Department of State

Libya refused to send al-Megrahi (*left*) and Fhimah to trial in Britain or the USA, so a Scottish court was set up in neutral Holland. With no jury present to decide the accused's guilt, four senior Scottish judges (*below*) decided that Fhimah was innocent and that al-Megrahi alone was guilty of mass murder. They sentenced him to life imprisonment. (*Top:* author's collection; *bottom:* ©Crown)

ALIVE IN CHRIST

21ST SEPTEMBER 1969
21ST DECEMBER 1988
PAN AM FLIGHT 103
DEATH WHERE IS YOUR VICTORY

With most traffic bypassing Lockerbie on the A74(M) motorway, there are few traffic jams (*below*). Casual visitors might write the town off as 'a place where nothing ever happens', unless they wander into the cemetery. There, they wonder why so many gravestones commemorate young lives cut tragically short on the same awful night (*left*). (Both author's collection)

But many visitors are pilgrims. They go to Tundergarth Church (*above*), where so many died. In Lockerbie's garden of remembrance (*below*), the names of all who died here on 21 December 1988 are graven in stone. (Both author's collection)

PART 3

THE TRIAL

As if this trial needed further complication, it was likely to last as long as two years if the court respected Muslim custom by sitting for just four days a week, Friday being the Muslim Sabbath. Under Scottish Prison Service rules and Crown Office procedures, religious rights of the accused at trial had to be respected, and both defendants were Muslims. It was also thought that the judges would also prefer to sit on only four days each week, to give themselves a long weekend break.

The three Scottish High Court judges for the Lockerbie bombing trial were named on 17 November 1999 by Lord Cullen, the Lord Justice Clerk. They were Lords Sutherland, Coulsfield and MacLean, with Lord Abernethy as a substitute, meaning that he could take part in their deliberations, but not vote on admissibility of evidence or the verdicts unless one of the other three was indisposed through illness or had died. The names can have meant little to the general public, but Alistair Bonnington of Glasgow University told Reuters they were 'a team of very experienced judges. Really the top people in Scotland. Because there is no jury, the trial is likely to be very technical and full of legal points. And one common link between all the judges chosen is that they are all considered excellent lawyers.'[1]

Named president of the court, 60-year-old Lord Ranald Sutherland had been a lawyer since 1956, and was appointed Queen's Counsel in 1969. He was the second-longest serving Scottish judge. Frequently chairing appeals, he was known for expressing irritability by media portrayals of judges as out of touch and aloof. In 1997, after serving seven years on the bench, he notably proclaimed:

> I do not understand why we are so consistently represented as remote, disinterested in ordinary folk, ignorant of everyday facts and insensitive. You cannot have practised successfully and widely at the Scottish bar without learning something about the general human condition. I may never have lived in the poorest areas of our major cities, but I believe that I have some insight into what they must be like.[2]

Lord John Cameron Coulsfield had been a lawyer for thirty-nine years, was appointed Queen's Counsel in 1973 and had been a judge for twelve years. Lord MacLean had been a lawyer since 1966, was appointed Queen's Counsel in 1977 and had been a judge in Scotland since 1992. The 61-year-old Lord Alastair Cameron Abernethy had begun practising law in England in 1966, was appointed Queen's Counsel in 1979 before moving to Scotland and becoming a judge in 1992.[3] So the bench was stacked with knowledge of law and legal precedent. Since, as already mentioned, the court was to lack a jury to assess the guilt or otherwise of the accused, the judges would both determine guilt or otherwise and pass sentence if one or both defendants were found guilty.

When the trial commenced on 3 May 2000, the converted sports hall at Camp Zeist that was serving as the courtroom was packed with some 600 media representatives from all over the world, plus relatives of the victims and the families of the two accused, who were seated near them. Outside, several hundred armed Scottish Police patrolled day and night. Inside, between the public and the judges, barristers, the two accused and the witnesses was a hi-tech bullet- and bombproof glass screen. The long indictment read out included the names of all the murdered 259 passengers and crew of Pan Am Flight 103 and the eleven residents killed on the ground. The two accused denied all charges. Al-Megrahi's defence team was composed of his solicitor and three barristers, two of them QCs; Fhimah was likewise represented by a solicitor and three barristers, two of them QCs. It looked like a powerful line-up in court. They also had the support of a lawyer who was a former foreign affairs minister of the Libyan Government, but his presence turned out to be double-edged, since it was difficult on that account to object to American officials sitting in the courtroom and appearing to pass evidence to the Crown barristers and indicate to them lines of argument to follow.

Before the trial even began, defending lawyer Bill Taylor QC entered what in Scotland is called a defence of incrimination, naming the PFLP-GC, Abu Talb and his associates in Malta, Abdel and Hashem Abu Nada as responsible for downing Pan Am 103. Already by then the prosecution's case against the two Libyans on remand was weakened by MEBO's submission that the fragment of circuit board did not come from one supplied to Libya; Thurman's record of falsifying evidence debarred him from giving evidence as an expert witness; the FBI's star witness Giaka was living in a witness protection programme in the USA and had very strong motivation to say whatever would please his new masters. The judges actually said of him, 'We are unable to accept Abdul Majid as a credible and reliable witness [about the events at Luqa Airport]'.[4] Regarding identification of the customer of Mary's House who had bought the clothing wrapped around the IED, at the trial Tony Gauci appeared uncertain about the exact date he sold the clothes in question, and was visibly insecure about whether or not it was al-Megrahi to whom they were sold.

Within a week, media interest had dwindled to a handful of reporters, so that the general public was unaware of important points made by the defence. Cross-examined by Richard Keen QC, Dr Hayes was startlingly vague about chemical analysis at RARDE, or even if it had been carried out, although it was clear that neither the black plastic fragments of the Bombeat casing nor the fragment of circuit board had been swabbed for explosive residue. There were inconsistencies about dates when tests had, or had not, been carried out. Feraday also seemed to have made assumptions, of which he was now unsure, and altered notes. Cold War politics intruded, with three former Stasi officers giving questionable evidence of their dealings with MEBO for timing devices they had used in IEDs.

When Tony Gauci was called on 11 July, he chose to give evidence in Maltese through an interpreter, although his statements to police had been in English. He also contradicted in court many of the details in those statements. Asked whether the purchaser of the clothing was present, he said, facing the dock, of al-Megrahi, 'He resembles him a lot'. In passing over the darker-complexioned Fhimah, he was contradicting his repeated statements that the clothes' purchaser had been dark skinned. At the end of that day's hearing, the defence lawyers told al-Megrahi that Gauci had proven 'a very dodgy witness' and that the judges would not believe him. In this, they were wrong.[5]

Turning to security at Heathrow Airport, Advocate Depute Alan Turnbull QC, asked Sulkash Kamboj whether the X-ray scanner showed up electrical items like tape recorders or radios. The reply indicated a difficulty in distinguishing between them but Kamboj confirmed that the scanner operator could tell if there was an electrical device of some kind. Fhimah's counsel, Jack Davidson QC, also asked Kamboj questions, to which he received only vague answers. Most of the time, it was, 'I don't remember, sir'. For example, Kamboj could not recall if he was the last person to leave the interline shed on the evening of 21 December; nor apparently did he know whether it was normally locked at night. He denied having been told of the BKA's Autumn Leaves warning about looking for Toshiba radios in passengers' baggage. He also said he could not recall what he had said when interviewed by police on 28 December 1988 and 6 January 1989. Mr Davidson referred to Kamboj's statement during examination by the Advocate Depute to the effect that, if Mr Bedford said he had placed two bags into container AVE4041, he would accept this. This clearly contradicted statements given around the time of the disaster to the police and at the Fatal Accident Inquiry.

Al-Megrahi's counsel, Bill Taylor QC, raised the apparent lack of security at the interline shed which meant that *anyone* with a Heathrow Airport airside pass could have placed a bag onto the conveyor belt that carried luggage into the shed among bags from other Pan Am flights and interline bags. The routine was for the former, already scanned at the embarking airport, to be taken off the arriving aircraft by Pan Am loaders and placed straight away in a baggage container, while interline bags were scanned first, before being placed in the baggage container. Once in the baggage container, there was no further check.

Barrister David Wolchover[6] later raised on the Internet a far more likely scenario for the placing of the Samsonite case containing the bomb in baggage container AVE4041 at Heathrow Airport, which had nothing to do with the feeder flight from Frankfurt. In *Criminal Law and Justice Weekly*, Vol. 176, dated 31 March 2012, he made the point that neither Khreesat nor Dalkamoni would have had the airside access at Heathrow necessary to smuggle the Samsonite case into the shed. Khreesat, however, described Abu Elias as the Frankfurt/Neuss cell's *expert in airport security*, who disappeared at the time of the Autumn Leaves arrests, together with the missing fifth IED. So, Abu Elias would have known that many of the 38,000 genuine airside passes for Heathrow Airport, issued to outside workers employed on the construction of Terminal Three, were never handed in at the end of their jobs; that some 779 airside passes were listed as 'lost or destroyed'; and that valid passes could be bought for cash in nearby pubs.[7] To quote Wolchover's words, that hypothesis 'ticks all the right boxes'.

Pan Am loader/driver John Bedford told the court at Camp Zeist that he left the baggage area for his half-hour tea break after loading several pieces of interline baggage *upright* across the back of AVE4041. He returned *before* the arrival of PA103A at Heathrow to find that two more bags had been placed lying flat in the front of the baggage container, of which the lower one was in exactly the position later calculated as being the position of the bag containing the bomb. One of these two cases was indeed described by him as a maroon or brown Samsonite-type suitcase.

The prosecution's case relied on the testimony of the expert witnesses to connect al-Megrahi and the fragment of circuit board.

It was, however, the opinion of Professor Köchler, the official United Nations observer at the Camp Zeist trial, that Alan Feraday should not have been allowed to testify as an expert witness in the trial since three convictions of defendants in previous trials, against whom he had testified, had all been overturned on appeal. The forensic evidence given to the court on Day 15 (5 June 2000) by Dr Thomas Hayes, formerly head of the forensics explosives department at Fort Halstead, was central to the prosecution's case. At the time of the trial he was 53 years old, having retired early from his RARDE post just when the joint Scottish Police and FBI investigation was reaching its climax. A bachelor of science honours graduate in chemistry, a master of science in the faculty of forensic science, a doctor of philosophy in the faculty of forensic science, a chartered chemist, and a member of the Royal Society of Chemistry, he however seemed reluctant to tell the court exactly when he had resigned from RARDE in order to re-train and practise as a freelance chiropodist. He recalled starting work at Fort Halstead in July 1974, but was vague about the exact date of his leaving – probably, he thought, some time in 1990.

The function of expert witnesses is to be neutral, and not to try and support the prosecution case. Yet, evidence submitted in previous trials by three forensic expert witnesses at Camp Zeist cast doubt on the credibility of all three. Alan Feraday had given evidence against several defendants who had their convictions quashed, causing the Lord Chief Justice of England and Wales to rule in July 2005 that Feraday should not be allowed to present himself as an expert in the field of electronics. Dr Thomas Hayes had been a key witness in the trial of the Maguire Seven, who won their appeal after major flaws in forensic procedure were revealed. As though this was not enough, the FBI expert witness Thomas Thurman, who identified a slightly charred fragment of a circuit board as part of a sophisticated timing device used to detonate explosives, was subsequently accused of doctoring others of his purportedly scientific reports. He was 'let go' from the FBI without a trial because that would have been embarassing for the Bureau.

Al-Megrahi's legal team protested that the forensics evidence used by the prosecution was accepted by the court in the absence of any chemical testing of the circuit board fragment to check whether it had been involved in, or had even been close to, an explosion. Such an omission in the case of a trial where the defendant faced a life sentence for mass murder is inexplicable. Similarly, the eventual testimony of Tony Gauci 'identifying' al-Megrahi as the purchaser of the clothing in Mary's House that had been packed in the brown suitcase with the bomb was accepted by the court despite Gauci's contradictory statements on the nineteen occasions when he was interviewed by Scottish and Maltese police officers – particularly when he identified Abu Talb as the purchaser. In addition, some of the questions put to Gauci indicated the required answer, which would normally invalidate all that witness' evidence.

Five months into the trial there was a long hiatus when the Crown lawyers received new evidence, which had to be shared with the defence. It came from Norway, where five relatives and friends of Mobdi Goben, who had operated the PFLP-GC safe house and arms cache in Yugoslavia, had sought asylum. Shortly before dying, Goben had dictated an account of his function in the group, perhaps as an act of posthumous revenge against Jibril. In the account, he attributed an important role in the downing of Pan Am 103 to Abu Elias, the group's expert in airport security who was, Goben said, a relative of Jibril.[8]

More or less at the same time, the judges at Camp Zeist heard evidence from convicted PPSF member Mohammed Abu Talb, specially flown there from Sweden where he was serving a sentence of life imprisonment after being convicted in December 1989 for terrorist offences using explosives. Why the panel of top-rank Scottish judges thought that a convicted murderer and terrorist, designated witness 963 on the Crown list, would tell the truth about anything, is a mystery. In the *Private Eye* 'Yobs' comic strip of low-life criminals and their families, a thug in the dock is being questioned by a barrister: 'So you were caught doing 130mph in a stolen car, high on drugs and drink and your defence is …' The thug replies, 'I was trying to get

home in time to read a bedtime story to my little boy.' Mildly amus-
ing, as a joke, but were the judges at the Scottish court in Camp Zeist
surprised when Abu Talb denied that he had anything to do with the
bombing of Pan Am Flight 130? Asked by Advocate Depute Alastair
Campbell where he was on 21 December 1988, Abu Talb gave as
his unsupported alibi that he had been alone at home in Uppsala,
babysitting. According to him, a sister-in-law was having a baby in
the early hours of 22 December, so the women of the household
went to visit her in hospital while he volunteered to stay at home to
look after the younger children.

In return for testifying – and what prisoner locked away for years
would not take the chance of a brief trip by private plane with his
own bodyguards, just to get out of jail for a few days? – Abu Talb was
allegedly, according to the Crown Office, granted immunity from
prosecution by the Court. This despite the fact that, when arrested,
he was in possession of clothing made by the Maltese company that
supplied Gauci's shop. In January 2007 a spokesman for the Crown
Office corrected this inaccuracy and said that Abu Talb could still
face prosecution for the Lockerbie crash. It seems that Scottish law
gives immunity from prosecution only if a witness is called as an
accomplice to give evidence against those involved with him in the
crime. Abu Talb was not called as an accomplice of al-Megrahi and
Fhimah, but to rebut their defence of incrimination, which he did.
He returned to his Swedish jail, from which he was released with
remission in October 2009.

At the time of the trial, Swedish police gave evidence of intercept-
ing a telephone conversation in which Abu Talb's wife was recorded
after the Lockerbie crash warning another unidentified Palestinian
to 'get rid of the clothes immediately'.[9] Abu Talb had been in Malta
between 19 and 26 October 1988, and possibly also on 23 November,
travelling on different passports he was known to possess. There was
also the calendar in his apartment with the date of 21 December
1988 highlighted. Yet the judges considered there was no evidence
to indicate he and his associates had the means or the intention to
destroy a civil aircraft on that date. In the words of the late reporter

Paul Foot, who attended the Camp Zeist trial, 'No means, that is, beyond working with a bomb-maker who specialized in disguising explosive devices in cassette recorders so that they could be smuggled onto aircraft. No intention except visits to airports and the studying of aircraft schedules, including some from Pan Am.'

Syria and Iran had been cleared of any involvement in the crash of Pan Am 103 by President Bush, who said, 'A lot of people thought it was the Syrians. The Syrians took a bum rap on this.' On this side of the Atlantic, British Foreign Minister Douglas Hurd told the house of Commons that, after a four-year absence of diplomatic relations between Syria and Britain, there was now 'no evidence' linking any government but Libya's to the atrocity. To misquote the US President, 'a lot of people' thought it a strange coincidence that, within days of the redirection of the investigation, British hostage Terry Waite and American hostage Thomas Sutherland were released by their pro-Iranian captors in Beirut after spending 1,763 days and nights shackled to radiators, followed shortly afterwards by the release of other Western hostages. Even stranger, after thirteen years of icy silence between Washington and Beirut, one month later President Bush met Syrian President Hafez al-Assad to discuss some kind of Syrian military participation in the coalition force, it being considered vital by the planners of the invasion of Iraq that the presence of several Arab contingents in the coalition should show this was not another purely Western intervention in the Middle East.[10] On 24 November 1991, *The Sunday Times* reported on the hostages' release:

Our joy at their freedom should be tempered by the shame of the cost: the relatives of the victims of the Lockerbie bomb must now come to terms with the fact that most of those behind the murder of their loved ones are going to get away with it. The cause of justice is being sacrificed on the altar of diplomatic convenience. We will live to regret it.[11]

15

THE IMPOSSIBLE VERDICT

At the end of the nine-month trial in Camp Zeist, in which al-Megrahi and Fhimah refused to plead, on 31 January 2001 the judges announced their unanimous verdict in a document eighty pages long. Shortly before 11 a.m. that day, Lord Advocate Colin David Boyd led the Crown Office lawyers into the courtroom. Next came the two defendants, several observers noting how the appearance of Abdelbaset al-Megrahi had aged since he was imprisoned nearly two years before. Both men were dressed in traditional Arab robes. Equally theatrical, the four judges in their scarlet robes and wigs entered by a side door: Lord Abernathy, Lord Sutherland, Lord Coulsfield and Lord MacLean. The macer, or clerk of the court, formally asked the judges whether they had reached a verdict on the charge of murdering 270 people at Lockerbie on 21 December 1988. Under Scottish law, it was not necessary for the verdict to be unanimous: a 2:1 decision would have sufficed; and there were three valid answers to the macer's question: acquittal, conviction and 'not proven'. Lord Sutherland replied, 'We have!'

The three voting judges unanimously found al-Megrahi guilty of the murder of 259 passengers and crew of the aircraft, and of eleven people in the town of Lockerbie. They sentenced him to life imprisonment with the recommendation that he should serve at least twenty years before being eligible for parole. Members of the families of the two defendants had travelled from Libya to be present. Nobody recorded how al-Megrahi's family took the news. Also present at the reading of the verdict were a number of the victims' families. Some looked and sounded relieved, but others were visibly incredulous at the verdict. Stunned by what he had just heard, Dr Swire fainted and had to be carried out of the courtroom. The principal architect of the Camp Zeist trial, Professor Robert Black was reported as saying the prosecution case was very weak *and circumstantial*, and that he was extremely reluctant to believe that any Scottish judge would convict anyone on the basis of such evidence.

During the trial, the only evidence against Fhimah had been from the now discredited Giaka, so he was declared innocent and allowed to return to his home in Libya on 1 February 2001, leaving al-Megrahi still locked up in Camp Zeist. Fhimah may have been happy with the verdict of his innocence, but Dr Swire was far from being the only person horrified by the conviction of his co-accused because the trial had *convinced* him of al-Megrahi's innocence. At 2 p.m., Lord Sutherland clarified the sentence: life imprisonment, effectively twenty years in jail and deportation at the end of the term. Several of the American relatives present reportedly wished aloud that the trial had been held in a US court which could have imposed a death sentence.

Since it is difficult for a layman to assess the judgement of three very senior Scottish judges in the trial of al-Megrahi, it is fortunate that the Secretariat of the United Nations Organisation had appointed observers of the trial of the two Libyans by Scottish judges under pressure from the governments of the United Kingdom and the USA to convict 'the Lockerbie bomber'. Official UN observer Professor Köchler, who had attended the trial throughout, submitted a comprehensive report on its conduct to the secretary general's office.[1] This was highly critical of the proceedings and challenged the fairness and impartiality of the Scottish High Court of Justiciary. The verdict at the eight-month trial, announced on 31 January 2001, was labelled by Professor Köchler both 'inconsistent' and 'arbitrary'.

On 3 February, his twenty-point commentary on the trial was made public.[2] Point 3 raised the long detention on remand of the two accused:

> The extraordinary length of detention of the two suspects/accused from the time of their arrival in the Netherlands until the beginning of the trial in May 2000 has constituted a serious problem in regard to the basic human rights of the two Libyan nationals under general European standards, in particular those of the European Convention on Human Rights. In general, the highly political circumstances of the trial and special security considerations related to the political nature of the trial may have had a detrimental effect on the rights of the accused, in particular in regard to the duration of administrative detention.[3]

The present author, having himself been imprisoned for a far briefer period,[4] understands what lies behind that carefully worded and impersonal comment of a legal professional. To be deprived of one's liberty, freedom of movement, family contacts and personal dignity for over a year, under constant surveillance day and night and denied bail although technically still innocent, has a crippling effect on the morale of a remand prisoner like al-Megrahi or Fhimah.

Given that there had been more than a decade to prepare for the Lockerbie trial, perhaps that was not the intent of Scotland's High Court of Justiciary, but it was the effect. Perhaps, again, there were genuine reasons why the prosecution was not ready for trial, although that is difficult to believe *after eleven years of investigation*, when every trail had long since gone cold and the likelihood of finding genuine new evidence was close to zero, as demonstrated by the evidence given at the trial. Yet, it is hard for the uninvolved observer not to see this long delay as a legally permissible, although inhumane, way of breaking the spirit of the two accused men – as though they already merited punishment for a crime of which they were legally innocent until *proven* guilty. Point 4 raised an important point of courtroom procedure:

As far as the material aspects of due process and fairness of the trial are concerned, the presence of at least two representatives of a foreign government in the courtroom during the entire period of the trial was highly problematic. The two state prosecutors from the US Department of Justice were seated next to the prosecution team. They were not listed in any of the official information documents about the Court's officers produced by the Scottish Court Service, yet they were seen talking to the prosecutors while the Court was in session, checking notes and passing on documents. For an independent observer watching this from the visitors' gallery, this created the impression of 'supervisors' handling vital matters of the prosecution strategy and deciding, in certain cases, which documents (evidence) were to be released in open court or what parts of information contained in a certain document were to be withheld (deleted).

Professor Köchler's report continues:

5. This serious problem of due process became evident in the matter of the CIA cables concerning one of the Crown's key witnesses, Mr. Giaka. Those cables were initially dismissed by the prosecution as 'not relevant', but proved to be of high relevance when finally (though only partially) released after a move from the part of the defense. Apart from this specific aspect — that seriously damaged the integrity of the whole legal procedure — it has become obvious that the presence of representatives of foreign governments in a Scottish courtroom (or any courtroom, for that matter) on the side of the prosecution team jeopardizes the independence and integrity of legal procedures and is not in conformity with the general standards of due process and fairness of the trial. As has become obvious to the undersigned, this presence has negatively impacted on the Court's ability to find the truth; it has introduced a political element into the proceedings in the courtroom. This presence should never have been granted from the outset.

6. Another, though less serious, problem in regard to due process was the presence of foreign nationals on the side of the defense team in the courtroom during the whole period of the trial. Apart from the presence of an Arab interpreter (which was perfectly reasonable under aspects of fairness and efficiency of the proceedings), the presence of a Libyan lawyer who had held high posts in the Libyan government, and who represented the Libyan Jamahiriya in its case v. the United States and the United Kingdom at the International Court of Justice, gave the trial a political aspect that should have been avoided by decision of the panel of judges. Though Mr. Maghour acted officially as Libyan defense lawyer for the accused Libyan nationals and although he was not seen by the undersigned as interacting with the Scottish defense lawyers during court proceedings, he had to be perceived as a kind of liaison official in a political sense. It has to be noted that the original Libyan defense lawyer, Dr. Ibrahim Legwell (chosen by the two suspects long before their transfer to the Netherlands), resigned under protest when the Libyan government introduced Mr. Maghour as new defense lawyer for the two accused. In sum, the presence of *de facto* governmental representatives of both sides in the courtroom gave the trial a highly political aura that should have been avoided by all means, at least as far as the actual proceedings in the courtroom were concerned. Again, to [Professor Köchler]'s knowledge, the presence of foreign nationals on the side of the defense team was mentioned in no official briefing document of the Scottish Court Service.

7. It was a consistent pattern during the whole trial that − as an apparent result of political interests and considerations − efforts were undertaken to withhold substantial information from the Court. One of the most obvious cases in point was that of the former Libyan double agent, Abdul Majid Giaka, and the CIA cables related to him. Some of the cables were finally released after much insistence from the part of the defense, some were never made available. The Court was apparently content with this situ-

ation, which is hard to understand for an independent observer. It may never be fully known up to which extent relevant information was hidden from the Court. The most serious case, however, is related to the special defense launched by defense attorneys Taylor and Keen. It was officially stated by the Lord Advocate that substantial new information had been received from an unnamed foreign government relating to the defense case. The content of this information was never revealed, the requested specific documents were never provided by a foreign government. The alternative theory of the defense — leading to conclusions contradictory to those of the prosecution — was never seriously investigated. Amid shrouds of secrecy and 'national security' considerations, that avenue was never seriously pursued — although it was officially declared as being of major importance for the defense case. This is totally incomprehensible to any rational observer. By not having pursued thoroughly and carefully an alternative theory, the Court seems to have accepted that the whole legal process was seriously flawed in regard to the requirements of objectivity and due process.

8. As a result of this situation, [Professor Köchler] reached the conclusion that foreign governments or (secret) governmental agencies may have been allowed, albeit indirectly, to determine, to a considerable extent, which evidence was made available to the Court.

9. In the analysis of [Professor Köchler], the strategy of the defense team by suddenly dropping its "special defense" and cancelling the appearance of almost all defense witnesses (in spite of the defense's ambitious announcements made earlier during the trial) is totally incomprehensible; it puts into question the credibility of the defense's actions and motives. In spite of repeated requests of the undersigned, the defense lawyers were not available for comment on this particular matter.

10. A general pattern of the trial consisted in the fact that virtually all people presented by the prosecution as key witnesses were

proven to lack credibility to a very high extent, in certain cases even having openly lied to the Court. Particularly as regards Mr. Bollier and Mr. Giaka, there were so many inconsistencies in their statements and open contradictions to statements of other witnesses that the resulting confusion was much greater than any clarification that may have been obtained from parts of their statements. Their credibility as such was shaken. It seems highly arbitrary and irrational to choose only parts of their statements for the formulation of a verdict that requires certainty 'beyond any reasonable doubt.'

11. The air of international power politics is present in the whole verdict of the panel of judges. In spite of the many reservations in the Opinion of the Court explaining the verdict itself, the guilty verdict in the case of the first accused is particularly incomprehensible in view of the admission by the judges themselves that the identification of the first accused by the Maltese shop owner was 'not absolute' (formulation in Par. 89 of the Opinion) and that there was a 'mass of conflicting evidence' (ibid.). The consistency and legal credibility of the verdict is further jeopardized by the fact that the judges deleted one of the basic elements of the indictment, namely the statement about the two accused having introduced on 20 December 1988 into Malta airport the suitcase that was supposedly used to hide the bomb that exploded in the Panam jet.

12. Furthermore, the Opinion of the Court seems to be inconsistent in a basic respect: while the first accused was found "guilty," the second accused was found "not guilty." It is to be noted that the judgement, in the latter's case, was not "not proven," but "not guilty." This is totally incomprehensible for any rational observer when one considers that the indictment in its very essence was based on the joint action of the two accused in Malta.

13. The Opinion of the Court is exclusively based on circumstantial evidence and on a series of highly problematic inferences. [To Professor Köchler's] knowledge, *there is not one single piece of material*

evidence linking the two accused to the crime. In such a context, the guilty verdict in regard to the first accused appears to be arbitrary, even irrational. This impression is enforced when one considers that the actual wording of the larger part of the Opinion of the Court points more into the direction of a 'not proven' verdict. The arbitrary aspect of the verdict is becoming even more obvious when one considers that the prosecution, at a rather late stage of the trial, decided to 'split' the accusation and to change the very essence of the indictment by renouncing the identification of the second accused as a member of Libyan intelligence so as to actually disengage him from the formerly alleged collusion with the first accused in the supposed perpetration of the crime. Some light is shed on this procedure by the otherwise totally incomprehensible 'not guilty' verdict in regard to the second accused.

14. This leads ... to the suspicion that political considerations may have been overriding a strictly judicial evaluation of the case and thus may have adversely affected the outcome of the trial [and] have a profound impact on the evaluation of the professional reputation and integrity of the panel of three Scottish judges. Seen from the final outcome, a certain coordination of the strategies of the prosecution, of the defense, and of the judges' considerations during the later period of the trial is not totally unlikely. This, however, [if] actually proven, would have a devastating effect on the whole legal process of the Scottish Court in the Netherlands and on the legal quality of its findings.

15. In the above context, [Professor Köchler] has reached the general conclusion that the outcome of the trial may well have been determined *by political considerations* and may to a considerable extent have been the result of more or less openly exercised influence from the part of actors outside the judicial framework — facts which are not compatible with the basic principle of the division of powers and with the independence of the judiciary, and which put in jeopardy the very rule of law and the confidence citizens

must have in the legitimacy of state power and the functioning of the state's organs — whether on the traditional national level or in the framework of international justice as it is gradually being established through the United Nations Organization.

16. On the basis of the above observations and evaluation, [Professor Köchler] has — to his great dismay — reached the conclusion that the trial, seen in its entirety, was not fair and was not conducted in an objective manner. Indeed, there are many more questions and doubts at the end of the trial than there were at its beginning. The trial has effectively created more confusion than clarity and no rational observer can make any statement on the complex subject matter "beyond any reasonable doubt." Irrespective of this regrettable outcome, the search for the truth must continue. This is the requirement of the rule of law and the right of the victims' families and of the international public.

17. The international observer may draw one general conclusion from the conduct of the trial, which allows to formulate a general maxim applicable to judicial procedures in general: proper judicial procedure is simply impossible if political interests and intelligence services — from whichever side — succeed in interfering in the actual conduct of a court. The purpose of intelligence services — from whichever side — lies in secret action and deception, not in the search for truth. Justice and the rule of law can never be achieved without transparency.

In signing off the report, Professor Köchler expressed the hope that an appeal, if granted, would correct the deficiencies of the trial as exposed in his report. He added

Truth in a matter of criminal justice has to be found through a transparent inquiry that would only be possible if all considerations of power politics were put aside.[5]

Interviewed by *The Scotsman* on 1 November 2005, Professor Robert Black labelled al-Megrahi's conviction 'the most disgraceful miscarriage of justice in Scotland for 100 years'. According to the interview, every lawyer who had read the judgement said it was nonsense. Black's reason for speaking out was twofold. He had practised law as well as being an academic, and strongly believed that no Scottish jury of fifteen members, if given the standard instructions about dealing with reasonable doubt, would have convicted al-Megrahi on the evidence produced at the trial. Also he felt a personal responsibility for al-Megrahi's situation, having proposed the solution of the trial being held in Holland and encouraged the Libyan authorities to accept this solution to a knotty problem. In his professional opinion, al-Megrahi stood a better than fifty–fifty chance of being acquitted on appeal. Yet, al-Megrahi's appeal against his conviction was turned down on 14 March 2002 by a panel of five Scottish judges at Camp Zeist. On the same day, Professor Köchler described the dismissal of the appeal as 'a spectacular miscarriage of justice'.

Early in 2003, South African President Nelson Mandela – who knew from personal experience the effects of long-term incarceration on a prisoner – asked the Western Christian churches to intervene in what he described as 'a clear miscarriage of justice'. Mandela had earlier offered South Africa to host the trial, but this suggestion was turned down due to just one of the many murky possible explanations for the destruction of Pan Am 103 revealed by the investigation. On 22 December 1988, the day after the Lockerbie disaster, the then apartheid-supporting government of South Africa had been due to end its illegal occupation of Namibia,[6] during which the De Beers–Anglo American mining conglomerate had removed from the territory diamonds, uranium and other minerals to the value of £11 billion. Bernt Wilmar Carlsson, Assistant Secretary General of the United Nations Organisation and UN Commissioner for Namibia, was travelling to New York on Pan Am 103 for the signing of the Namibian independence accord, and had died with all the other victims on Pan Am 103.

The theory alleged that he was the intended target for which the aircraft had been blown up. The reason? He 'knew too much' about the purchase by Britain, among other countries, of one-third of its annual requirements of yellowcake – a form of processed uranium ore – from the Rössing uranium mine in Namibia[7] between 1976 and 1989 allegedly through the British-registered Rio Tinto Zinc Corporation. That traffic was in blatant contravention of Decree No. 1 of the UN Council for Namibia – a decree observed only by Mr Carlsson's native Sweden – as was the processing of the ore by URENCO, a multinational company with a refinement facility in Capenhurst, Cheshire, of which the British Government was one-third owner. The theory that Carlsson's presence on the flight caused the bombing of Pan Am 103 was, of course, a re-run of the murder of UN Secretary General Dag Hammarskjöld in 1961 in the shoot-down of his Swedish-owned aircraft over Zambia by mercenary forces employed by mining companies working in the Katanga province of the former Belgian Congo.

Mandela's new intervention in the Lockerbie appeal negotiations led to the production of a highly critical report of the scientific and forensic evidence presented at the original trial by the Church of Scotland's leading scientist Dr John Urquhart Cameron. Based on this, in July 2003 Dr Iain Torrance, Moderator of the General Assembly of the Church of Scotland petitioned British Prime Minister Tony Blair to release al-Megrahi.

PART 4

16

THE MOST HATED MAN IN EUROPE

It is no exaggeration to say that, after the verdict was announced, al-Megrahi was the most hated man in Europe. A number of the American victims' relatives had wanted punishment going as far as death – a penalty still available in thirty-one of the USA and within the power of the federal government. The predominant feeling in Britain was of relief that 'the truth had been found' and a legitimate legal process had handed down the most severe penalty available under Scottish law for the murder of 270 people on that night in December 1988. Yet a small number of people who had concerned themselves with the details of the trial – including relatives of the victims – considered that the verdict was unsound and the sentence *ipso facto* unjust. Why was the Justice for Megrahi campaign supported by people like Dr Jim Swire and Rev. John Mosey, each of whom lost a daughter in the bombing, by Archbishop Desmond Tutu, by the head of the Catholic Church in Scotland, Cardinal Keith O'Brien, and by Scottish QC Ian Hamilton, who went on record as saying on the Internet, 'I don't think there's a lawyer in Scotland who now believes Mr Megrahi was justly convicted'.

What sort of man was Abdelbaset Ali Mohmed al-Megrahi, dubbed in the media 'the Lockerbie Bomber'? He was born on 1 April 1952 as one of eight siblings in a poor family that shared a house with two other families in the Libyan capital Tripoli. Having what was called 'a weak chest', he was often ill in childhood, which makes for a miserable start to life. The boy's father being a lowly customs officer, his mother had to earn occasional extra money for food by taking in neighbours' sewing. Their living standards improved with Gaddafi's coup and introduction of 'Islamic socialism' in 1969 after the declaration of the Libyan Arab Jamahirija. After finishing secondary school the following year, Abdelbaset spent nine months studying at Rumney Technical College in Cardiff, hoping to become a merchant navy ship's captain. His poor eyesight making this ambition unrealistic, he left Rumney and returned to Tripoli, receiving training as a flight operations officer[1] for the national carrier, Libyan Arab Airlines. The work consists of planning suitable flight paths with pilots, bearing in mind the performance of the aircraft, their fuel loads and passenger/cargo loading as well as metereological conditions en route, airport conditions and airspace restrictions. Responsibility is high: in the US and Canada, the operations officer shares legal responsibility for flight safety with the pilots on a fifty–fifty basis. He can delay, cancel or divert a flight and is responsible, after take-off, for advising pilots of any change in conditions.

The training curriculum is laid down by the ICAO. Although some airlines and countries do not require the full course stipulated by the organisation, Megrahi obtained his licence in the USA, which required a wide knowledge of meterology and aviation matters generally to the same level as a certificated airline pilot. It is certainly no easy job. Overseeing as many as twenty flights and planning new ones while monitoring those already in the air produces a high level of stress with which not everyone can cope by any means. So we know he was a calm and serious man, able to handle stress, with a professional appreciation of aviation safety. He was also a good manager, earning promotion to Head of Operations at Tripoli Airport. Taking a course in geography at the University of Benghazi, he was the top student in his year, and intended taking a year out to study for a master's degree in climatology at an American university.

Megrahi married in 1982, when he was 30. The marriage produced five children: four boys and a girl. His life moving in a less academic direction, at the age of 34 al-Megrahi became a business partner in a small company whose clandestine function was obtaining spare parts for LAA aircraft despite US sanctions against this. To conceal his aviation background, he was issued with a 'coded' passport in the name of Ahmed Khalifa Abdusamad. From whatever snooping operation, this was picked up by NSA,[2] which enabled the prosecution at Camp Zeist to allege that al-Megrahi was an active officer in Libyan intelligence, Mukhabarat el-Jamahiriya.[3] It is quite probable that he did effect missions for the Mukhabarat, in the same way as many British and other business travellers do so from time to time for the intelligence services of their countries. But that does not mean that he was an Arab James Bond, shooting his way around the world. On his travels, he visited the USA and the UK many times, also becoming head of security for Libyan Arab Airlines and a consultant to the Libyan Centre for Strategic Studies.

Inside Glasgow's Barlinnie Prison after the verdict, al-Megrahi's dignified bearing and good manners impressed all the staff. He put aside any natural bitterness and joined in impromptu football matches with them. John Ashton, writer of al-Megrahi's account *You are my Jury*,[4] recalls him as beng immensely cheered by many hundreds of letters of support and the visits of well-known people including Nelson Mandela, who knew what he was going through, having himself spent twenty-seven years in prison. Neither the other prisoners nor the prison officers shunned him as a terrorist, one of the latter telling Ashton off the record, 'We all know he didn't do it'.[5] It was a significant remark, inasmuch as experienced prison officers get pretty good at knowing which of their charges are innocent and which are guilty.

Ashton visited al-Megrahi in the prison many times. Lest that be thought likely to suspend his critical faculty, the reverse is more probable: in a collaboration lasting years like this one did, al-Megrahi would almost certainly have betrayed his guilt at some moment. Instead, Ashton wrote of visiting him in one of the tiny rooms at the prison set aside for legal visits, where al-Megrahi always arrived with a bundle of papers in order to discuss fine points of evidential detail. Ashton described him as demanding, but friendly and humorous – a man sustained by the support of his family and by regular prayer, who was in tears at the news of the 9/11 attacks. His initial optimism that the second appeal would succeed gradually gave way to pessimism with all the delays in the judicial process.

After lingering in Barlinnie Prison until February 2005, al-Megrahi was then transferred to the open wing at Gateside Prison in Greenock. At first nervous of the reaction of the other long-term prisoners there – many of them Scottish – to his reputation as a terrorist guilty of the mass murder of so many men, women and children above and on Scottish soil, he was reassured by the governor that none of them would want to lose their approaching chance of liberty by attacking him.

At a preliminary hearing in Camp Zeist during October 2001 – just a few weeks after the destruction of the Twin Towers on 11 September – Marina Larracoechea told the five Scottish judges nominated to hear the appeal that, in her opinion, the human rights of the two accused Libyans had been violated. Additionally, she held that key points had been ignored in the Fatal Accident Inquiry for fear of prejudicing later criminal proceedings, yet had not been treated at the trial either, leaving her and many others unconvinced of al-Megrahi's guilt. It was necessary, she argued, for a completely new investigation, overseen by two delegated states other than Britain and the USA,[6] to take place with none of the political manipulation that had bedevilled both the investigation and the trial. The investigation should have the widest possible remit and examine, for example, the responsibility of intelligence and security organisations, which had knowledge of the Helsinki warning and used this to save the lives of diplomats but allowed the crew and passengers on board Pan Am 103 to be 'massacred' – as she graphically expressed it. Present in court were Dr Swire and the Reverend John Mosey, representing other relatives of victims who had voiced similar desires for an independent review. Her request was rejected by Lord Cullen, the presiding judge, who considered it 'not competent'. He ruled that the role of himself and the other four judges was simply to hear al-Megrahi's appeal against sentence, as presented by his lawyers.[7]

In late January 2002 a self-styled 'retired CIA Middle East specialist' named Robert Baer, who had been involved in the Lockerbie investigation from December 1988 to August 1991, published a book,[8] which stated that Dalkamoni and other PFLP-GC members met with the Iranian Pasadarn intelligence service a few days after the shoot-down of IR655 to discuss execution of the *qisas*. That made sense, but other details in the book did not. It was as though the enormous body of true and fabricated 'evidence' could be used to justify just about anyone's theory about Lockerbie.

Al-Megrahi had to wait a year for his appeal to be heard. This is not an inordinately long time in legal matters. In their written judgement, the Scottish judges at the appeal in Camp Zeist had to set aside 'the absence of any explanation of the method by which the primary suitcase might have been placed on board KM180, [which is] a major difficulty for the Crown case'.[9] As Lord Osborne QC remarked at the appeal, 'There is considerable and quite convincing evidence that [the smuggling of an unaccompanied suitcase on board KM180] could not have happened. Now, it's quite difficult rationally to follow how the Court can take the step of saying, "Well, we don't know how it got on the flight. We can't say that. But it must have been there." On the face of it, it may not be a rational conclusion.'

Indeed, it is not. Lord Osborne also asked in court why an experienced terrorist would send the bomb on such a long journey involving three take-offs and two landings, with the risk the bomb could go off at the wrong time or in the wrong place, or have been detected during the baggage transfers in Frankfurt and London. 'He would,' said Lord Osborne, 'be taking a lot of chances of failure by having the bomb ingested [into the baggage system] in Malta and not in Heathrow. All sorts of things could have gone wrong with the sequence of flights.'[10]

Once again, Professor Köchler was present at Camp Zeist throughout: from 23 January 2002 until the last session on 14 February 2002 and also on 14 March 2002 for the announcement of the decision of the five Scottish judges charged with hearing the appeal: Lord Cullen, Lord Kirkwood, Lord Macfayden, Lord Nimmo-Smith, and Lord Osborne. His Report to the UN Secretary General's office was datelined Vienna, 26 March 2002.

Points 1 to 3 of this report covered formalities, with Point 4 noting that the Crown Office had avoided answering Professor Köchler's questions about the withholding of evidence by the police authorities. Point 5 raised what he described as 'the total lack of transparency in regard to the Defense's actions'. Points 6 and 7 again criticised the presence in court of representatives of the US Department of Justice and of the Libyan state which 'introduced into the appeal proceedings a political element that should have been avoided'. Point 8 raised the overshadowing of the appeal proceedings by 'at least two meetings between Libyan, U.S. and U.K. intelligence-cum-political officials in the United Kingdom' which apparently dealt with 'the issue of Libya's acceptance of responsibility for the Lockerbie bombing and with her obligation for compensation – at a time when the matter was still *sub judice* in an independent court – which might have been prejudicial to the outcome of the appeal'. This is a reference to Gaddafi agreeing to pay damages for the Lockerbie bombing in order to free his country from the international trade sanctions that had been crippling the Libyan economy. To the general public, that may have looked like an admission of guilt, although it should not have carried any weight in the minds of the learned Lords, supposedly concentrating exclusively on whether the evidence at the trial was such as to justify *without any doubt* the verdict that al-Megrahi was guilty of a crime with which there was no material evidence connecting him, and that he merited a life sentence.

Point 9 dealt with the opinion of Professor Köchler that al-Megrahi's defence team had been so inadequate that 'the requirements of Art. 6 ("Right to a fair trial") of the European *Convention for the Protection of Human Rights and Fundamental Freedoms* were not met'. Point 10 held that there 'was insufficient evidence in law to convict the appellant' and that Section 106 (3) of the Criminal Procedure

(Scotland) Act 1995 stated that an appellant might bring under review 'any miscarriage of justice, which may include such miscarriage based on "the jury's having returned a verdict which no reasonable jury, properly directed, could have returned"'. Point 10 included the following passage:

> The Defense [*sic*] did not did not raise any of the technical issues, particularly in regard to the timer used in the explosive device, on which new information had become available since the Verdict on 31 January 2001. [Nor did it] raise the issue of Mr. Anthony Gauci, key witness of the Prosecution, having been invited repeatedly for holiday trips to Scotland by the Scottish police. This information was available before the beginning of the appeal hearings; it calls into question the trustworthiness and reliability of the prosecution witness on whose testimony the verdict substantially depended. [Nor did it] raise the issue of *why* important evidence about the breaking of a lock at the luggage storage area at Heathrow airport had disappeared from the police records and why it was not made available to the trial court.

In the same point, Professor Köchler commented that a defence counsel stated at the beginning of the appeal hearings that there was no fault on the part of the Prosecution in regard to the unavailability of this important evidence. He rightly pointed out that it was 'hard to understand why, in an adversarial system, the Defense should come to the defense of the Prosecution on such a crucial matter which could cast doubt over the entire strategy of the prosecution'.

Points 11 and 12 dealt with the withholding of evidence, since it was a principle of Scottish and English law that, even in an adversarial system of criminal law – unlike in the Continental system, where the judge may also be the investigator and prosecutor – the trial judges had the obligation to scrutinise any information witheld by the prosecution because failure to do so would result in the unfairness of the trial since the prosecution authorities should disclose to the defence all material evidence in their possession to be used against the accused. The defence in the present appeal, he said, had completely failed to raise this basic issue and thus gave up one of the main legal instruments at its disposal, which also may seriously have compromised al-Megrahi's ability to eventually claim his rights at the Privy Council and/or at the European Court of Human Rights. Because of their actions, or lack of action, during the trial the defence lawyers could be seen as complicit in the lack of fairness of the proceedings.

Point 13 seemed to infer that the security guard Mr Manly had been under considerable pressure – from whom was not said – to withdraw his evidence about the break-in at Heathrow on the night of 20–21 December 1988. The report continued:

> While being adamant about the technical details about how the padlock at Heathrow airport was broken ('cut like butter'), [Mr Manly] was highly confused and proven totally wrong in regard to the exact location of the door and the way in which the padlock was attached to the door. At the beginning of his testimony he told the court that, because of an accident, he was under medication and that he was afraid he might have to vomit in the course of his testimony. He looked very frail and behaved in a highly emotional, at times even aggressive manner. It was impossible [for Professor Köchler] to obtain any specific information about the factors which led to this deplorable state of health. In spite of the efforts promised by the Scottish Court Service, it was not possible to obtain any information on the kind of medication under the influence of which Mr. Manly may have acted in the way he did, or on the time and nature of the accident that made this medication necessary. In fact, Mr. Manly's testimony – seen in its entirety – may even have been counterproductive in regard to the defense strategy. The question remains why the Defense introduced Mr. Manly as an additional witness under these particular circumstances.

Point 14 commented on the judges being 'satisfied to analyze [*sic*] the verdict of the trial court in a merely formal manner, not dealing with the substance of the argument nor with its plausibility and logical consistency':

> In the Opinion of the Appeal Court they repeatedly expressed the view stated in Par. 25 that 'once evidence has been accepted by the trial court, it is for that court to determine what inference or inferences should be drawn from that evidence.'

Professor Köchler made the point that, if this is the attitude of an appeal court in the Scottish system of criminal law, then the question arises how a meaningful role of an appeal court can be defined at all. He particularly criticised in Points 15 and 16 the court's passing over the meteorological evidence that the most probable date of the purchase of the clothes was 23 November 1988, rather than 7 December 1988, when al-Megrahi was in Malta. Point 16 reads:

> Because *in this entirely circumstantial case*, in the absence of any material evidence, everything finally depends on whether the appellant bought the clothes or not, the entire verdict collapses if this fact cannot be proven 'beyond a reasonable doubt'. If the evidence presented during the trial and the additional evidence made available during the appeal is analyzed in its entirety, it becomes clear to any rational observer that the theory of ingestion of the luggage containing the explosive device in Malta needs considerably more assumptions and is based on much lower probability than the theory of ingestion at Heathrow. *In an entirely circumstantial case like the present one*, this means that a determination 'beyond a reasonable doubt' cannot honestly be made if one bases one's argumentation and inferences upon reason and common sense. The trial verdict, confirmed by the appeal judges, would not stand a plausibility test in a scientific context defined by the rules of logic and reason [author's italics].

Point 17 quoted the observation of Lord Osborne on Day 96 of the trial regarding the theory, unsupported by any material evidence, that the bomb suitcase had travelled from Malta to Frankfurt to Heathrow on 21 December. For the Court to accept this theory as fact, Lord Osborne had said, was 'not a rational conclusion'. In Point 18 Professor Köchler described the unanimous rejection by the five appeal judges of all grounds for an appeal in mid March 2002 as 'this rather drastic *sacrificium intellectus*'. His report totalled over 7,000 words that could be summed up by one sentence in its final paragraph:

> Regrettably, the decision of the Appeal Court in the case of Abdelbaset Ali Mohamed Al-Megrahi v. H. M. Advocate was not a victory for justice, but for power politics.[11]

It was, he said, 'a spectacular miscarriage of justice' – a statement with which Dr Swire and Sra Larracoechea and other relatives of Lockerbie victims who had attended hearings at Camp Zeist, agreed. Statements collectively signed by lawyers, legally trained academics, politicians, other public figures and relatives of the victims all concurred.

THE SECOND APPEAL

After the rejection of al-Megrahi's appeal, the due process of law ground slowly on until on 15 August 2003, Libya's Ambassador to the United Nations submitted a letter to the Security Council formally accepting responsibility for the Lockerbie bombing. Compensation was paid into a fund for each bereaved family to receive $8 million, less $2.5 million deducted for legal fees.[1] In return, the UN cancelled the sanctions that had been suspended four years earlier, and the US lifted its trade sanctions. Each family would have received $2 million more if the State Department had removed Libya from the List of States Supporting Terrorism, but this did not happen before the deadline set by Libya. The US did however resume full diplomatic relations with Libya after deciding to remove it from the list in May 2016.

When relatives were informed that Libya had made available the fund to provide payment for each of the victims' families, reaction varied, from those who numbly accepted the compensation for their grievous loss fifteen years earlier to a bitter accusation by the parents of Theodora Cohen that this was a bribe to induce the families to cease making politicians' lives difficult. It seems that most American families still wanted revenge; in the words of their representative George Williams, 'to have Gaddafi's head on a plate'.[2] In Sra

Larracoechea's words, 'We have never been further from the truth.' She analysed exactly Gaddafi's motives in paying out as being the only way to free his country from the sanctions and get back to selling the country's oil, but nothing to do with the guilt or otherwise of al-Megrahi, whom she and other relatives considered a deeply unfortunate scapegoat.

Also in 2003 Professor Köchler authored a book entitled *Global Justice or Global Revenge?*[3] Not a man to let his sword sleep in his hand, five years later, during a visit to Scotland, he gave a speech sponsored by the Scottish lawyers' magazine *The Firm* at the Glasgow Hilton, in which he referred to a public interest immunity certificate issued by the British Government:

> Whether those in public office like it or not, the Lockerbie trial has become a test case for the criminal justice system of Scotland. Its handling will demonstrate whether a domestic system of criminal justice can resist the dictates of international power politics or simply becomes dysfunctional as soon as 'supreme state interests' interfere with the imperatives of justice. If the rule of law is to be upheld, the requirements of the administration of justice may have to take precedence over public interests of a secondary order – such as a state's [current] foreign policy considerations or commercial and trade interests. The internal stability and international legitimacy of a polity in the long term depend on whether it is able to ensure the supremacy of the law over considerations of power and convenience.[4]

On 23 September 2003 lawyers acting for al-Megrahi applied to the Scottish Criminal Cases Review Commission (SCCRC) for a review of the case (both sentence and conviction), arguing that there had been a miscarriage of justice. Yet another Kafkaesque nightmare lay ahead for al-Megrahi: on 24 November he was taken to the High Court in Glasgow to appear before the three judges who had sentenced him at Camp Zeist. They informed him that he was facing, not twenty, but *at least* twenty-seven years, in jail, counting from April

1999 when he was placed on remand, before he could be offered parole.[5] On 31 May 2004 he was granted leave to make a second appeal, to be heard in Edinburgh by a panel of five judges on 11 July 2006.

On 16 November 2005 Dr Swire met al-Megrahi in prison, to urge him not to give up his fight. As the founder and spokesman of UKFF103, Dr Swire was adamant that the search for truth and justice required a full and independent review of the whole process from 21 December 1988 onwards, and was not deterred by hate mail received after his prison visit. The attitude of the Scottish legal system was made plain when Lord Fraser of Carmyllie, formerly the Lord Advocate, said in December 2008 that Dr Swire's insistence on al-Megrahi's innocence was 'comparable to the Stockholm syndrome' by which hostages come to identify with and protect their captors.[6] Dr Swire's positive reaction to Lord Fraser's dismissal was to found the Justice for Megrahi campaign, which, among other aims, held that al-Megrahi should be allowed to return to his family in Libya pending his second appeal. It was a point of view not shared by members of the US group VPF103 like Susan and Daniel Cohen, whose daughter Theodora had been killed. Having initially admired Dr Swire's stand, they put in writing that his several trips to Libya reminded them 'of Colonel Nicholson in the film *Bridge on the River Kwai* – a brave and decent man whose obsession led him unwittingly to serve the enemy cause'.[7]

The gulf between VPF103 and UKFF103 yawned wider still. After a television showing of the film *The Maltese Double Cross* on 11 May 1995, Dr Swire had asked the FBI Assistant Deputy Director Oliver 'Buck' Revell via a satellite link why his son cancelled his booking on Pan Am 103 'instead of getting murdered like my daughter'. Revell Senior's answer had been that Revell Junior had received an unexpected last-minute change of leave dates from the US Army, in which he was serving at the time. Against that, an unidentified Pan Am security man at Heathrow alleged that Revell had personally intervened at Heathrow at the last moment to stop his son and daughter-in-law boarding the aircraft. Less dramatically, other sources had it that

Oliver Revell Jr and his wife changed their bookings two weeks before 21 December – which could be completely innocent. There were also twenty-nine other no-shows – passengers booked onto Pan Am 103 who failed to check in for whatever reason.

Much later, in November 2013, the VPAF103 president Frank Duggan accused Dr Swire and other UK relatives of being liars. Dr Swire's reaction was measured, as always:

> I do not normally reply to statements in the media from Mr Frank Duggan. However, he had recently very publicly accused me of lying, concerning an event which happened in the United States Embassy [in London], where Mr Duggan was present. I was also present.

The disagreement concerned a remark by a member of the President's Commission on Aviation Security and Terrorism made off the record at the embassy in February 1990 to Martin Cadman, who had lost his son on board Pan Am 103: 'Your government and ours know exactly what happened, but they're never going to tell.'[8] Mr Duggan had not been in a position to overhear this remark, but Dr Swire believed Cadman's account.

Back to 2007, in May of which year 49-year-old Kenny MacAskill was appointed Justice Secretary of the Scottish National Party Government and, as such, became responsible for oversight of the Scottish Prisons Service. This government was sworn in on 16 May, soon after which the UK Government in London started negotiations for a prisoner transfer agreement (PTA) with Libya. As MacAskill diplomatically put it, 'Given that there was only one Libyan prisoner in Scotland and few elswhere in the UK, the implications were clear'.[9] Although the UK Government stressed that al-Megrahi would be specifically excluded from the PTA, the Libyans did not agree so that, when the agreeement was concluded, no mention was made of any exclusion.

MacAskill's position made him responsible for prisoner transfers and all questions of compassionate release. He also wrote, 'At that early stage in the SNP administration [any question of releasing al-Megrahi] would for good or ill be dealt with by me alone.'[10] It was a peculiar situation in that the Foreign and Commonwealth Office in London was supposed to represent the entire United Kingdom, including the devolved Scottish administration, in foreign affairs yet the British Government in London left the new Scottish Government holding what was a political hot potato.

In June 2007, after a number of technical issues had been resolved, the SCCRC finally approved a second appeal for al-Megrahi. One problem was that Scotland did not have a wide choice of senior judges to hear it, and it took some time to choose five suitable names. Al-Megrahi's initially high hopes of thus clearing his name eventually dwindled as other delays were introduced. After twelve months, in the June 2008 edition of the Scottish legal periodical *The Firm*, the UN Observer at Camp Zeist, Professor Köchler, accused the British Government of deliberately delaying al-Megrahi's second appeal.

An article in *The Guardian* of 17 June 2007[11] summarised the situation. Al-Megrahi's legal team had submitted evidence to the SCCRC contending there were major flaws in his prosecution and conviction at Camp Zeist, as a result of which he had spent ten years in Scottish prisons. The two journalists who wrote this believed that the SCCRC would announce its ruling about a second appeal in the following week.

The *pièce de conviction* said to link al-Megrahi to the destruction of Pan Am Flight 103 was that small fragment of circuit board, which *could* have been part of the IED's countdown timer, and had allegedly been found in woodland 25 miles from Lockerbie months after the crash. The prosecution's case was that expert witnesses had established a link between al-Megrahi and the fragment. *Yet, there was no evidence of this* and the three key forensic witnesses involved – Feraday, Hayes and Thurman – had been demonstrated to lack credibility and should not have been accepted as experts by the court. To recapitulate:

- Alan Feraday, head of the Forensic Explosives Laboratory at RARDE had given evidence against other defendants who later had their convictions quashed, as a result of which in July 2005 the Lord Chief Justice ruled that Feraday should not be allowed to present himself as an expert in the field of electronics.

- Dr Thomas Hayes, Senior Scientific Officer at RARDE had given misleading evidence that led to the Maguire Seven being imprisoned in 1976 for handling explosives in connection with the IRA bombings in Guildford. Their sentences were later quashed.
- At the FBI, Thomas Thurman held a degree in politics and had some training as a bomb disposal technician at the USN Explosive Ordnance Disposal School, but had been accused in another trial of testifying to matters outside his area of expertise and fabricating evidence. He was quietly sacked from the Bureau.

In June 2007 al-Megrahi's new defence team was making the legal point that the forensics case provided by the prosecution was taken at face value by the trial and first appeal judges although there had never been a chemical analysis or swabbing for the gaseous reaction that would indicate whether or not the fragment had survived an explosion. Evidence given had been based exclusively on the slightly charred appearance of the fragment. Al-Megrahi's new lawyers were intending to call 'a legal source close to the investigation', who would say that such a process of forensic analysis was unheard of in criminal trials.

Apart from the untested circuit board fragment, the prosecution of al-Megrahi had only two other pillars on which to rest:

- Giaka's testimony of seeing al-Megrahi arrive in Luqa Airport with the Samsonite suitcase on 20 December 1988 and seeing Fhimah place it on KM180 the following morning. Yet Giaka was a witness with a very doubtful previous record, to put it mildly. And Fhimah had been found not guilty at the trial …
- Tony Gauci's uncertain identification of al-Megrahi as the man who bought the clothing wrapped around the bomb. Yet this conflicted with his nineteen previous statements to investigators, which alone should have invalidated Gauci's evidence.

The two *Guardian* writers reporting all this added,

> A key witness who could be proven to be so unreliable is more
> than sufficient to collapse any trial. Plus there was evidence of lead-
> ing questions put to Gauci, a practice known to distort evidence.[12]

Apparently unaware that Tony Gauci was motivated to testify by his
interest in a substantial reward for information leading to the arrest
of 'the Lockerbie bomber', the judges at Camp Zeist had decided he
was an honest and reliable witness, whose hesitant testimony of al-
Megrahi as *resembling* the clothes purchaser they considered as proof
beyond reasonable doubt that he had indeed purchased the clothes
in the Samsonite suitcase and was therefore the Lockerbie bomber.[13]

Among the many items of evidence of which the defence lawyers
were not informed was an early statement to police of a frequent
British visitor to Malta named David Wright. He told Dumfries and
Galloway officers on 3 November 1989 that he had recently seen two
other Libyan men at Mary's House buying clothing similar to the
contents of the Samsonite suitcase.[14] This is not surprising, since the
shop was a narrow-fronted establishment in a side street that could
not have carried a massive stock to give a wide variety of choice for
its customers. On 18 December 1989 DS Armstrong and DC Kirk
took a statement to this effect from Mr Wright.[15] Had this public-
spirited visitor to Malta been called as a witness, his testimony might
have completely demolished the only reason the judges had to connect al-Megrahi with the crash.

As to the reward, in discussions with Scottish Police, the Gauci
brothers had made no secret that the family had financial problems,
which made them very keen to receive the reward being offered by
the US Department of Justice under its programme 'Rewards for
Justice', of which they had been told by a CIA officer. Scottish Police
did not inform the defence lawyers of the Gaucis' expectation of this
reward, which was known to them when interviewing the brothers.[16]
A memo from DI Dalgleish to ACC Graham refers to this. One of

the pieces of undisclosed evidence to be considered in the second appeal was that Tony Gauci did receive 'in excess of US $2 million' and Paul 'in excess of $1 million' – in his case for 'sustaining Tony's resolve'. What does that mean? Well, the Scottish Lord Advocate Lord Fraser of Carmyllie described Tony Gauci, whose testimony was crucial in identifying al-Megrahi, as 'an apple short of a picnic', and said that even his family 'would say he was not the full shilling'.[17]

Through the CIA the Gauci brothers were also offered places in a witness protection programme in the USA if things got too hot for them in Malta[18] – which was a distinct possibility in the Mediterranean island republic with its own Mafia, where the sixth car bomb in eighteen months killed the courageous investigative journalist Daphne Caruana Galizia on 16 October 2017 during the writing of this book.

A former Chief Assistant District Attorney – the highest non-elected law officer in the district of Manhattan – Jessica de Grazia was hired by al-Megrahi's defence team to go to Malta after the failed first appeal. Her brief was to check out a story in a Maltese newspaper of October 1988 about a meeting there between Abu Talb and members of PFLP-GC's Malta cell. They had had a previous meeting there in March of the same year. On the island, de Grazia interviewed a witness who claimed to have been present at the October meeting 'in a room behind a baker's shop between Abu Talb and Dalkamoni discussing the best way to get a bomb on an airliner'.[19] Had all those visits to Malta by British, German and American police and intelligence operatives failed to uncover that lead, or had it just been discarded as inconvenient?

18

'MR MEGRAHI, YOU MAY GO HOME!'

Each day of the four years al-Megrahi was kept waiting for the SCCRC to announce that he could have a second appeal was cruelly long. After it undertook to rule about a second appeal by the end of June 2007, it was literally at the last possible moment, on 28 June, that the SCCRC concluded its review of the case and, accepting that a miscarriage of justice *could* have occurred, granted al-Megrahi leave to appeal again.

Why did it take four years for this review body to examine the transcripts of the trial and first appeal? Was it because al-Megrahi was increasingly unwell and the Scottish legal system hoped he would die in the meantime? Professor Köchler expressed surprise that the review was blatantly biased in favour of the judicial establishment in Scotland:

> In giving exoneration to the police, prosecutors and forensic staff,
> I think [the Scottish Law Lords] show their lack of independence.
> No officials to be blamed: simply a Maltese shopkeeper.[1]

In letters to Scotland's First Minister Alex Salmond, the British Foreign Secretary David Miliband, the Home Secretary Jacqui Smith and others, Professor Köchler called for the full report of the SCCRC to be published and for a *full and independent* public inquiry into the Lockerbie bombing to be held in the presence of UN-appointed legal experts from uninvolved countries. He went into print in the Scottish lawyers' magazine *The Firm* with the accusation that the totalitarian nature of the second Lockerbie appeal process 'bore the hallmarks of an intelligence operation'.[2]

What did he mean by that? Foreign Secretary Miliband had issued a public interest immunity certificate (PIIC), the effect of which was to exempt the prosecution from revealing to al-Megrahi's defence team *anything* it chose to hide. This was said to be necessary in order not to embarrass a foreign government which had supplied information acquired by its intelligence service. The important principle of law that the courtroom is a level playing field, obliging the prosecution to reveal to the defence in advance all the evidence it will use, was therefore annulled by this PIIC, to the disadvantage of the defence. The original function of a PIIC was to conceal, for example, the identity of 'supergrasses',[3] e.g. paramilitaries in Northern Ireland who would have been murdered if their identity had been made public after they turned Queen's evidence and informed on their former comrades in return for their own immunity from prosecution. Sources of intelligence in a hostile country – such as a CIA or SIS 'asset' in the KGB during the Cold War – also needed this kind of anonymity. The reason for this particular PIIC was reportedly a letter sent by King Hussein of Jordan to Prime Minister John Major shortly after the destruction of Pan Am 103 identifying the Palestinian terrorists who had made and placed the bomb on *Maid of the Seas*. The Cabinet Office was still blocking the publication of that letter two decades later on the grounds that it could destabilise the government of Jordan.[4]

Placing 'the public interest' or interests of the state, as decided by a civil servant, intelligence officer or politician, above the principle of a fair trial in the case of the Lockerbie court at Camp Zeist may have been done for solid reasons, but, whatever the ostensible 'justification', the effect was to exempt the prosecution from revealing to al-Megrahi's defence team important evidence, *so that he could not have a fair trial.*

On 11 October 2007 the Judicial Appeal Court in Edinburgh examined new information that cast doubts on al-Megrahi's conviction. His lawyers were claiming that vital CIA documents relating to the MEBO timer which allegedly detonated the Lockerbie bomb, were withheld from the defence at the trial. There was also never any proof to connect al-Megrahi and the fragment, nor was any proof advanced in court that the fragment had been in contact with the intense heat of a Semtex explosion.

On 14 September 2008, the Arab League Ministerial Council passed a resolution calling for al-Megrahi, described as a political hostage, to be released from prison in Scotland. It also demanded that the Scottish Government hand to the defence lawyers documents which the SCCRC had identified, and which had previously been witheld. As Professor Robert Black commented, there was an obligation on the Crown Office 'to disclose evidence, but it need only disclose as much evidence as it decides is relevant to the defence case which leaves the anomaly that the prosecution has to second-guess what the defence would want and need to know'.[5]

Also in September 2008, following a meeting organised by Justice for Megrahi – or Lockerbie Justice Group, as it was now known – on the Isle of Skye, Professor Köchler and Professor Robert Black jointly called for a new public inquiry into the Lockerbie bombing. Leaving aside all legal niceties, Professor Köchler expressed his thinking with crystal clarity:

> Irrespective of the outcome of the current appeal, there should be a reinvestigation of the [Lockerbie bombing] by the Scottish authorities. It is extremely frustrating that with regard to such an incident just one person has been presented as the culprit and no further questions asked. Only a child would believe such a story.[6]

Indeed. Where was the motive for al-Megrahi, whose work had been largely in aviation *security*, to blow up an aircraft in mid-air with hundreds of people on board? Where were the accomplices he would have needed? The only other person mentioned in the indictment was Lamin Fhimah and he had been declared innocent of any involvement by the judges at Camp Zeist. Giaka had told the CIA, but did not repeat in the court, when testifying as witness No. 684 at Camp Zeist, screened from the public and protected outside the courtroom by a posse of thirty US marshals, that it was Fhimah who put the Samsonite suitcase on flight KM 180 in the morning of 21 December. Surely the judges' exoneration of Fhimah invalidated all Giaka's other evidence? As Lord Osborne had pointed out, the unlikely scenario of al-Megrahi and/or Fhimah placing the bomb on a flight from Malta to Frankfurt, there to be unloaded and placed on the feeder flight to Heathrow, and there to be unloaded again and placed on Pan Am 103 depended *entirely* on the evidence of this one unreliable witness. Most importantly, since numerous IRA and other IED-makers had killed themselves while trying to assemble their devices, where was the infrastructure that al-Megrahi would have needed to make one without blowing himself up in the process? The official Camp Zeist version of the destruction of Pan Am 103 was indeed a story that only a *very young* child would have believed, yet the three trial judges and five appeal judges apparently had believed it.

And where was the sizeable reward al-Megrahi would have received from whatever person or entity might have commissioned such a mass murder, since he had no conceivable personal reason to kill all those people? A *Sunday Times* report that, at the time he was convicted, al-Megrahi had $1.8 million in a Swiss bank account seems to have been pure speculation. According to John Ashton, the account, which had been used for al-Megrahi's various international business deals, had been dormant since 1993, when it had a balance of $23,000.

During the summer of 2008, al-Megrahi felt increasingly unwell and noticed blood in his stools A prostate specific antigen (PSA) test of a healthy man shows a reading between zero and 6.5. Al-Megrahi's PSA reading was 363.[7] An MRI scan on 23 September 2008 at

Inverclyde Royal Hospital revealed a highly aggressive tumour on his prostate gland with incurable metastasised invasion elsewhere in the body, including his bones. It was a death sentence. The diagnosis calls into question what level of routine health check-ups had previously been available to the prisoner, seeing that the disease was so advanced. It was then estimated that someone in his condition was likely to live for between eighteen months to two years, possibly longer, but less under stress – which was certainly the case here. On 26 October 2008 Professor Robert Black wrote on his blog:

> More than thirteen months have passed since the first procedural hearing in the new appeal was held. More than ten months have passed since the appellant's full written grounds for appeal were lodged with the court. Why has no date yet been fixed for the hearing of the appeal? Why does it now seem impossible that the appeal can be heard and a judgement delivered by the twentieth anniversary of the disaster of 21 December 1988? The answer is simple: because the Crown, in the person of the Lord Advocate, and the United Kingdom government, in the person of the Advocate General for Scotland, have been resorting to every delaying tactic in the book (and where a particular obstructionist wheeze is not in the book, have been asking the court to insert it).[8]

On 6 November 2008, three Scottish Criminal Appeal Court judges reserved judgement on an application by al-Megrahi's new defence counsel Maggie Scott QC for him to be released on bail pending his second appeal against conviction which was expected to be heard in 2009. If out on bail, he would live with his family in a rented house in Glasgow, and was regarded as a 'low flight risk'. The bail application was refused on 14 November, with the judges commenting:

> While the disease from which the appelant suffers is incurable and may cause his death, he is not at present suffering material pain or disability. The full services of the National Health Service are available to him, notwithstanding he is in custody.[9]

On 21 December 2008 – the twentieth anniversary of the Lockerbie crash – the *Independent* published this passage:

> Since the Crown never had much of a case against Megrahi, it was no surprise when the Scottish Criminal Cases Review Commission (SCCRC) found prima facie evidence in June 2007 that Megrahi had suffered a miscarriage of justice and recommended that he be granted a second appeal. If Megrahi didn't do it, who did? Some time ago suspicion fell on a gang headed by a convicted Palestinian terrorist named Abu Talb and a Jordanian triple agent named Marwan Abdel Razzaq Khreesat. Both were Iranian agents; Khreesat was also on the CIA payroll. Abu Talb was given lifelong immunity from prosecution in exchange for his evidence at the Lockerbie trial; Marwan Khreesat was released for lack of evidence by German police even though a barometric timer of the type used to detonate the bomb on Pan Am Flight 103 was found in his car when he was arrested [in Neuss].

Libya accepted responsibility for the bombing, although it never admitted guilt. Gaddafi paid $2.7 billion (£1.8 billion) in compensation to the victims' families – $10 million for every victim. The final payment was made this year. US lawyers took approximately a third of the final amount. But the economic and humanitarian price for Libya was far higher: UN sanctions over an eleven-year period inflicted billions of dollars' worth of economic damage on Libya and prevented thousands of Libyan citizens from travelling abroad.[10] The Arab League supported Libya's right to compensation for the considerable damage done to its economy by UN sanctions between 1991 and 1999.

No less than thirteen procedural hearings took place at the High Court of Appeal in Edinburgh. It was finally announced in January 2009 that the second appeal was scheduled to start three months later at the end of April and that the hearing could last as long as twelve months because of the complexity of the case and volume of material to be examined. Given Professor Köchler's misgivings about the performance of the defence lawyers at the trial and first appeal, it is understandable that al-Megrahi had engaged a new team for the second appeal. At a preliminary High Court hearing in Edinburgh on 20 February 2009, his counsel Maggie Scott QC was informed that a delegation from the Crown Office was due to travel to Malta to seek consent for disclosure of sensitive documents that could be crucial – whatever that might mean.

The judges appointed to hear the second appeal had little liking for a job which required them either to justify a grossly wrong verdict, under which an innocent man had spent the last decade in prison, or to condemn three of their fellow High Court judges for handing down that grossly wrong verdict and five others for refusing the first appeal against it. Given the age of senior judges appointed to hear the second appeal, illness not surprisingly gave one of them an escape route: Lord Wheatley had to undergo heart surgery and was said not to be fit to hear the case until the following autumn. The hearing was postponed until then, posing the question: was there no possible substitute for him?

At the end of April 2009 the United Kingdom Government ratified the PTA with Libya. Since he had not been excluded from its provisions, this provided what Scottish Justice Secretary MacAskill described as a 'legal route ... to have Megrahi [sic] repatriated'. On 5 May a Libyan delegation in Glasgow made a formal application for the transfer of al-Megrahi. However, a possible hitch lay in the provisions of Article 3 of the PTA, which required that 'no other criminal proceedings related to the offence ... are pending'. Was the application for the second appeal such a proceeding?

On 26 June, MacAskill received a telephone call from US Attorney General Eric Holder, who made it clear he was unhappy with any talk of transferring al-Megrahi to Libya. There was an implication that, if he was sent anywhere, it should be to the USA, to serve the rest of his sentence. As officials of the Scottish Justice Department advised MacAskill, very few convicted US citizens in British custody ever opted to be repatriated because conditions were inevitably more severe in US prisons, so they preferred to remain locked up in Britain.

In al-Megrahi's case there was even the possibility that he would be re-tried and executed for the crime of mass murder, if shipped across the Atlantic.[11]

In an attempt to bridge the ocean, on 9 July MacAskill in Edinburgh listened to representations of some of the American families concerned by video conference from New York and Washington. Some relatives sat facing the camera, holding up photographs of their lost loved ones. He wrote afterwards:

> The grief of all was evident and the simmering rage of some was palpable. Frank Duggan expressed his thanks for the opportunity to present their views. Others related their personal testimonies of pain and sorrow. One lady spoke of the loss of her husband, aged just forty, who had been the father of three children, aged just ten, seven and two years old at the time. Another woman said she had been just two years old when her father had died on the flight. A further widow told how her husband had been working in Austria in the pursuit of Nazi war criminals and that he had left two children who were aged just seven and a half and four at the time. An older couple spoke of losing their twin sons aged just twenty on Pan Am 103. The bereaved mother added that President Clinton, speaking on the tenth anniversary of the tragedy, had confirmed that sentences would be served in Scotland. And so it continued, with spouses and parents all narrating their self-evident sorrow and often continuing anger. [They] were almost uniformly opposed to transfer or release on any grounds.[12]

It was, MacAskill declared, 'the hardest meeting', but he did not allow it to deflect him from his chosen course, accepting an application for compassionate release on 24 July. On 4 August the US Consul General expressed in person his government's opposition to either prisoner transfer or compassionate release. This was followed by calls from Secretary of State Hilary Clinton, personally telephoning MacAskill several times from various African countries while he was travelling in Orkney and the Shetland Islands, to tell him how to do his job. Assistant to the President for Homeland Security John Brennan also called, to relay President Obama's views on what should be done with al-Megrahi, but more politely. There was also in existence an appeal by the Crown Office on the grounds that the trial sentence was too lenient! To understand the pressure on MacAskill, one has to reflect that he was not only the head of the Scottish justice system, but also a politician, whose decision on whether or not to release al-Megrahi would reflect on the Scottish National Party's administration.

On 5 August 2009 Professor Köchler gave an interview to reporter Glenn Campbell for the BBC *Newsnight* programme, reiterating his support for the compassionate release of al-Megrahi. Unlike a transfer to serve jail time in one's own country under the Prisoner Transfer Agreement, a compassionate release should have allowed al-Megrahi's second appeal to continue. Professor Köchler considered that this was important not only for the prisoner, but also for all the families of the victims, who wanted to know who was responsible for the mid-air explosion of Pan Am 103 over Lockerbie. Professor Köchler made it clear that a compassionate release should only be approved by Scottish Justice Minister Kenny MacAlister if he considered al-Megrahi was the victim of a miscarriage of justice, and therefore not 'guilty as charged'. The professor referred in the interview to his previous statements that the opinions given by the judges on the trial and the first appeal in 2001 and 2002 were based on dubious circumstantial evidence and the testimony of unreliable witnesses.

He also criticised the delays imposed on the two reviews by the Scottish legal system: more than five years elapsed with al-Megrahi in jail between the end of the first appeal and the decision of the SCCRC to refer the case back to the appeal court in June 2007. In addition, more than two years later, the second appeal was still in its earliest stage. Deliberate delaying tactics included the scheduling of procedural hearings with intervals of several months between and the appeal judges' decision not to replace a colleague who had fallen ill, but to delay the hearing until his projected recovery some time in September.[13]

On 6 August 2009, MacAskill visited Greenock Prison to hear al-Megrahi's request for a prisoner transfer to Libya under the PTA ratified on 29 April. Before meeting the prisoner, MacAskill had a discussion with the prison governor, who confirmed that al-Megrahi was a model prisoner, who had no issues with the other prisoners or the staff. His health, however, was a general concern, since there were no specialist oncological facilities or treatment within the Scottish Prison Service and transporting outside for specialist treatment the prisoner regarded by many as 'the Lockerbie bomber' was a major security headache. After the meeting with al-Megrahi, who had had a relapse that week, MacAskill wrote,

> what confronted me seemed a tired old man; fifty-six years old, but looking a decade more than that. He had a persistent cough and looked like someone suffering from the flu. His English was very good and he was polite, though direct in his remarks. There was no obvious remorse, but he was neither threatening nor frightening. He did acknowledge the suffering of the victims' families, and accepted that many viewed him with hatred; feelings he stressed that he did not reciprocate. Chemotherapy would need to commence soon and he felt he needed his family around him for that.[14]

As anyone who has lived with a cancer patient undergoing intense chemotherapy knows all too well, the side-effects can be exceedingly unpleasant. To suffer them in the company of loving relatives is bad enough; to undergo the therapy in a prison cell in a hostile country amounts to torture.

In the week following MacAskill's prison visit it was reported in the media – and denied by the Scottish Government – that al-Megrahi was likely to be released within a few days on compassionate grounds due to the terminal cancer from which he was suffering. Official and unofficial American opinion was that he should stay in a Scottish prison, no matter what was his state of health, and eventually die there. On 10 August MacAskill told Libyan officials off the record that it would be easier for him to grant a compassionate release if the second appeal was abandoned, although this might not technically be necessary for a prisoner transfer. From all these high-level international negotiations the people of Lockerbie felt excluded, as though the deaths of *only* eleven innocent people on the ground, plus others injured, many more traumatised and the considerable damage to property in the dreadful events of 21 December, were not important by comparison with the deaths of those in the aircraft.

On 14 August, lawyers representing al-Megrahi announced that he had applied to the High Court in Edinburgh two days previously to withdraw his second appeal and MSP Christine Grahame announced that she was clear 'vested interests' wanted the second appeal abandoned because, if it went ahead, al-Megrahi's lawyers were going to expose the truth about Lockerbie, the miscarriage of justice and the suppression of evidence. Former Scottish Westminster MP Tam Dalyell, who had been involved since the early days of the investigation, when a police officer told him in confidence that search results were being manipulated, now stated publicly that al-Megrahi was merely a scapegoat.

The Director of Health and Care at the SPS wrote a helpful assessment of the medical condition of this high-profile prisoner, which included a critical sentence: 'The clinical assessment, therefore, is that a three-month prognosis is now a reasonable estimate for this patient.'

On 20 August 2009 MacAskill announced the release on the compassionate grounds that al-Megrahi was in the final stages of terminal prostate cancer. After being locked away from the world for ten years, four months and fifteen days, he was given a few minutes to collect his belongings, and dressed in a white tracksuit and bulletproof vest, to be escorted in a convoy by Strathclyde Police and SPS officers, also wearing bulletproof vests, to Glasgow Airport. There, he boarded an Airbus A340-200 of Afriqiyah Airlines – the smaller Libyan carrier – registration 5A-1AY, which was used as President Gaddafi's personal aircraft. Waiting on board were Gaddafi's son Saif al-Islam, who had played a part in the diplomatic negotiations, and al-Megrahi's son Khaled, who wept for joy on seeing his father a free man at last.

At exactly the same time, MacAskill was delivering live to television cameras a detailed statement of the reasons for his release.

On 3 September 2009 the respected investigative journalist John Pilger posted this succinct commentary on his website:

> No one in authority has had the guts to state the truth about the bombing of Pan Am Flight 103 above the Scottish village of Lockerbie on 21 December 1988, in which 270 people were killed. The governments in England and Scotland in effect blackmailed Megrahi [*sic*] into dropping his appeal as a condition of his immediate release. Of course there were oil and arms deals under way with Libya, but had Megrahi proceeded with his appeal, some 600 pages of new and deliberately suppressed evidence would have set the seal on his innocence and given us more than a glimpse of how and why he was stitched up for the benefit of 'strategic interests'.

19

LATE NEWS

The Airbus arrived back in Libya during celebrations of the fortieth anniverary of Gaddafi's *coup d'état*, but not, as portrayed by British and American media outlets, in the midst of a vast rally to welcome the returning hero – or villain, as the Scottish judges might have said. Quite the reverse: the Libyan Government diverted the aircraft away from Tripoli's International Airport to a smaller one and did not allow the international media and a vast crowd of well-wishers access. After a long wait on board while the airport was cleared of spectators, al-Megrahi was welcomed on the steps of the aircraft by his old friend and colleague Lamin Fhimah before being driven away to meet his 86-year-old mother, who had not been told of his terminal cancer condition in case the shock would be too much for her.

Al-Megrahi was transported to Tripoli Medical Centre, the country's most modern public hospital, for treatment. There, on 2 September 2009, it was reported that his metastasised cancer had worsened, and that he had been transferred to the intensive care unit. Libyan Foreign Ministry spokesman Mohammed Seyala announced that al-Megrahi had been moved to a special VIP wing of the hospital, was receiving full treatment from a team of doctors and was able to telephone his mother. He was released on 2 November after beginning chemotherapy, to live with his family in West Tripoli, in a villa paid for by the Libyan Government, while continuing to make regular visits to the hospital for treatment.

Alastair Darling, Britain's finance minister at the time, denied that fear of revocation of British Petroleum energy contracts with the Libyan Government had anything to do with the release. Toeing the same line, on 28 August 2009 in an interview reported in the Scottish newspaper *The Herald*, Saif al-Islam also stated that al-Megrahi's release was not connected to any oil deals but was an entirely separate issue. He said people should not get angry because the UK and Libya were talking about commerce or oil. An oil deal was signed at the same time as the release, but they were 'completely different animals', according to him.[1]

Two days later the London *Sunday Times* reported that ministers at Westminster had agreed in 2007 not to exclude al-Megrahi from the Prisoner Transfer Agreement with Libya because of what it called 'overwhelming national interests'. Like an oil deal? In December 2007 Secretary of State for Justice Jack Straw had written to his opposite number in Scotland, Kenny MacAskill:

> I had previously accepted the importance of the al-Megrahi issue to Scotland and said I would try to get an exclusion for him on the face of the agreement. I have not been able to secure an explicit exclusion. The wider negotiations with the Libyans are reaching a critical stage and, *in view of the overwhelming interests for the UK*, I have agreed that in this instance the [PTA] should be in the stand-ard form and not [exclude] any individual.[2]

In this tangle of party political and international wheeler-dealing, Scottish First Minister Alex Salmond reiterated that al-Megrahi's release had been granted on compassionate grounds and not as part of any deal struck by the British Government. In July 2010 four sena-tors in Washington made public their belief that British Petroleum had persuaded the British Government to grease the wheels of the oil deal by releasing al-Megrahi. BP confined itself to saying it had pressed for the Prisoner Transfer Agreement because a delay might have had negative consequences for UK commercial interests, yet did not admit to being involved in any discussions regarding al-Megrahi's release. The Scottish Government insisted that it had had no contact with BP in relation to al-Megrahi's release. Yet any sober examination of these exchanges makes it impossible not to suspect that al-Megrahi was being used as a bargaining chip. As the fur flew in all political directions, MacAskill and his staff had to withstand personal attacks, some of an obscene and threatening nature.

Bearing in mind that the bombing of Pan Am Flight 103 over Lockerbie on 21 December 1988 was to any informed observer a revenge in accordance with the *qisas* ordained under sharia law after the unjustified USS *Vincennes* shoot-down of the Iranian Airbus over the Strait of Hormuz on 3 July 1988, it is interesting that the American desire to revenge the destruction of Clipper *Maid of the Seas*, as though it was completely unprovoked, should continue unabated. There was even the horrible refinement of the timing of the Lockerbie crash – just a few days before Christmas, echoing exactly the shooting down of IR161 a few days prior to the feast of Eid al-Fitr that ends the fasting month of Ramadan. Professor Köchler was far from being the only member of the legal profession who was clear that al-Megrahi was in jail due to not one, but two gross miscarriages of justice: the trial and the first appeal.

That sober journal *The Scotsman* quoted on 27 August 2009 comments of four unnamed medical 'specialists' that MacAskill ignored their advice when they refused to give an expert opinion as to how long al-Megrahi would live. The only medical professional who supported the release on medical grounds was the Scottish Prison Service doctor who had been treating al-Megrahi's case of metastatatic cancer in conjunction with an experienced NHS oncologist. However, Scotland's Justice Committee, although quite definite that Scottish Prison Service medical guidelines were not followed in the decision to release al-Megrahi, also acknowledged that the decision to release a prisoner on compassionate grounds was the responsibility of the Minister of Justice and not of the Committee.

On 18 September 2009 al-Megrahi's representatives released a 300-page document challenging the prosecution case at Camp Zeist, but Lord Advocate Elish Angiolini ruled that the second appeal had been abandoned by al-Megrahi as a condition of his compassionate release. In early April 2010 it was reported that his cancer was not responding to treatment. Oncologist Karol Sikora, who had originally supported the three months prognosis (although his evidence was not allowed to contribute to the release decision as his fee had been paid by the Libyan authorities), reported that al-Megrahi was bedridden and had probably no more than four weeks to live, with his earlier apparent remission probably due to the positive emotional effect of being back with his family. The Libyan Consul General in Glasgow also reported that his condition had rapidly deteriorated. Nothing was straightforward. Scottish First Minister Alex Salmond compared al-Megrahi's experience with that of Great Train Robber Ronald Biggs, who had also been accorded compassionate release on health grounds and was still alive.

In October 2009 the satellite tv channel Sky News, in its eagerness to be 'first with the news', reported that al-Megrahi had died. Coincidentally, his biographer John Ashton was interviewing him on that day, when their conversation was constantly interrupted by telephone calls offering condolence to his family. The previous meeting Ashton had had with al-Megrahi was in a hotel in Tripoli. Of this, Ashton wrote:

> It was the only time I saw him among ordinary Libyans. Again we were repeatedly interrupted, this time by strangers thanking him, not for an act of terrorism, but for sacrificing his liberty for the good of the nation. His decision to stand trial [and not defend himself] helped free the country from UN sanctions that imposed twelve years of collective punishment [on the Libyan population] on the assumption of his guilt.[3]

On 26 July 2011, during the Libyan Civil War, al-Megrahi was seen on Libyan state television, attending a pro-Gaddafi political rally in a wheelchair, looking weak and ill. On 30 August 2011 Scottish First Minister Alex Salmond said that, with al-Megrahi dying and dependent on oxygen and an intravenous drip, what American lawyers and politicians had to say on the matter was 'neither here nor there'.

Gaddafi was brutally assassinated on 20 October 2011, prompting US Secretary of State Hilary Clinton to demand that al-Megrahi be returned to prison in Scotland. She turned the facts on their heads by subsequently insisting that his release was a miscarriage of justice and pressing for his extradition to the USA. By then it would anyway have been grotesque to remove this suffering man from his family and transport him back to a prison cell in a hostile country. Nevertheless, in early November, the State Department announced that it was preparing a formal demand for extradition to the USA. The Scottish Government rightly said that only it, as the authority which had repatriated al-Megrahi, could make such a request to the NTC; this, it would not do because al-Megrahi had abided by the conditions of his release.

With frequent hospital visits for treatment, al-Megrahi managed to live at home with his family until 13 April the following year, when he re-entered hospital, emerging to die at home with his family on 20 May 2012, aged 60. Following Muslim custom, his funeral took place the following day. In Britain many families of the Lockerbie victims called for al-Megrahi's second appeal to be heard for posthumous rehabilitation. Prime Minister David Cameron refused, apparently believing that the Camp Zeist trial and the first appeal had been correctly conducted. In theory, the al-Megrahi family could have applied to the SCCRC for the second appeal to be heard, but with all the political and military unrest in Libya and the enormous burden under which the family had lived, that was unlikely to happen until Scottish criminal lawyer Aamer Anwar, supported by a group of relatives of the Lockerbie victims, commenced acting for the family in June 2014, with the aim of presenting the verdict of the first appeal at Camp Zeist as a miscarriage of justice. The battle lines still clearly drawn, in December of that year the Lord Advocate Frank Mulholland declared that, on the contrary, al-Megrahi was indeed the Lockerbie bomber. Although he was by then dead, Mullholland was still talking of tracing his accomplices, twenty-six years after the downing of Pan Am 103!

So, where does that leave us? It is true that Abdelbaset al-Megrahi was for some years occasionally employed by a Libyan intelligence organisation, and that, from time to time, he circumvented international sanctions for the benefit of his country, but that alone does not make him a terrorist, any more than we suspect every officer of MI5 and MI6, or even the CIA, of carrying out James Bond-style assassinations. Despite the modern credo of *Need to know*, it is possible that he may have had some knowledge of the PFLP-GC plan to sabotage an aircraft, without knowing all the details, because intelligence officers often hear things on the professional grapevine. He would not have been alone in that. But no evidence was ever presented in court connecting him with the making of the IED or its placing on the Pan Am Clipper *Maid of the Seas.* Yet a man, never proven in the eyes of many lawyers, politicians and investigative reporters to be guilty of the crime for which he was prosecuted, spent over ten years in prison in a country where millions of people believed they had good reason to hate him. In addition, an investigation by thousands of detectives and other investigators, spread over several countries, lasting a considerable time and costing millions of pounds, was simply wiped out for geopolitical motives. The father of victim Theodora Cohen summed up the whole scandal:

> We've heard all [the excuses]. We can't do anything now because of the hostage crisis. We can't do anything now because of Desert Storm. There are always bigger fish to fry. It's amazing how many people have told me, 'Why are you doing this? You can't bring her back to life. Well, they're dead. You can't bring them back, so let's not bother with this.' The murderers are too powerful; the murderers are too useful.[4]

Shortly after Bill Clinton became US President in January 1993, Daniel and Susan Cohen received a letter from the White House, in which Clinton wrote:

I will assure you that all questions regarding Syrian and Iranian involvement in the Pan Am 103 tragedy are addressed and fully answered. The US owes it to the victims' families to see that these charges are throroughly investigated.[5]

Hence, perhaps, Hilary Clinton's obsession with her form of justice. Much later, in Britain, Mr Brian Pluthero contacted Dr Swire in January 2015 by e-mail, claiming that he had been the Pan Am ground security coordinator on duty at Heathrow on the evening of 21 December 1988. At the time, he wrote, his 'views had been silenced by Pan Am management'. He now wanted to speak to Dr Swire. It seems that he was never able to do that, for reasons unknown. If they did talk, the conversation was never made public.

At the time of writing this book, no one other than al-Megrahi has been indicted, arrested or tried for the murder of those 270 people on 21 December 1988.

Following the careers of terrorists is not easy, but Ahmed Jibril was reported to have died at the age of 76 on 26 August 2014 when his car was blown up by a roadside IED placed by the al-Qaeda-linked Jabhat al-Nusra terror group. His followers, however, protested that he died of a stroke. His son Mohammed Jihad Ahmed Jibril, the head of PFLP-GC's military wing and presumed eventual successor to the group's leadership, was killed by a car bomb containing 2kg of TNT in Beirut's Mar Elias district on 20 May 2002.

Marwan Khreesat reportedly died in October 2016 after complaining that all his troubles were because of Lockerbie. There is, unbelievably, a Facebook page purporting to be of him as a cuddly grandfather.

Abu Talb's wife Jamila Mograbi is one of nine siblings, several of whom have been involved in terrorism. She was herself an active member of the PLO and later a combat nurse for PPSF. So when she telephoned the other Palestinian resident in Sweden after Lockerbie and told her to 'get rid of the clothes', it was an order, not a suggestion. Jamila met Abu Talb in 1977 and married him in the following year. Her sister Dalal was one of thirteen Fatah terrorists who landed from an Egyptian ship on a deserted stretch of the coast of Israel on 11

March 1978. Completely lost, they found Gail Rubin, an American woman photographer, taking nature shots on the beach. After she told them where they were, Dalal Mograbi killed her. The thirteen terrorists then walked inland a mile to a highway, where they fired on traffic indiscriminately and hijacked a taxi and later a bus. Filled with hostages, it careered south along the Coastal Highway towards Tel Aviv with the Fatah group firing at, and throwing grenades at, other vehicles, killing and wounding travellers randomly. They hijacked a Tel Aviv–Haifa service bus, forced their hostages onto it and crashed in a hail of bullets through improvised roadblocks until brought to a halt at a more formidable roadblock near Herzliya by calthrop strips puncturing the tyres of the bus.

Some of the hostages were killed on the way and others were gunned down when they tried to escape from the immobilised vehicle. The head of the police anti-terrorism unit arrived in advance of his men and stormed the bus, single-handedly killing two terrorists and sustaining a shoulder wound himself. The bus exploded and burned out, probably as the result of a hot grenade fragment piercing the fuel tank. In this appalling carnage, thirty-eight civilians were killed, including thirteen children, and seventy-one others injured, some seriously. Dalal Mograbi was among the eleven terrorists who died. The two survivors spent seven years in prison until released in a prisoner exchange in 1985. In reward for Dalal's 'act of martydom', the President of Algeria gave all her siblings Algerian passports.

Jamila used her genuine Algerian passport when arriving in Sweden in November 1983, with Abu Talb using a forged Moroccan passport. Claiming asylum as refugees, under the liberal Swedish immigration policy they were swiftly given residence permits, settling in the cosmopolitan city of Uppsala, where two of Jamila's brothers, Mahmoud and Mustafa Mograbi, joined Abu Talb and his friend Marten Imandi planning a terror campaign across Europe.

Imandi, from a poor Damascene family with nine children, joined the PLO at the age of 15 and was trained as a terrorist. In 1972, he moved to Lebanon and fought there in militia operations for two years. While working apparently as an apprentice welder in Malta, he married a Swedish woman in September 1977, moving to Sweden, where he was able to gain citizenship in 1980, earning a living running a Middle Eastern grocery store. It is a mystery how the other men of the group ever earned any money. In 1985 and 1986 the two Mograbi brothers, Abu Talb and Imandi set out to bomb premises in Copenhagen, Amsterdam and Stockholm. None of them was convicted for the bomb in Stockholm because of a technical error in the prosecution's case. Abu Talb and Imandi got life sentences. Mahmoud Mograbi got a six-year sentence for his part in the affair. His brother Moustafa was so scared, walking around Copenhagen with an IED in his rucksack, that he ran out of the El Al office there on being confronted by a member of staff and threw the rucksack into a waterway, from where it was later recovered by police. Back in police custody in Stockholm, he confessed his actions to his lawyer, who advised him to repeat it in Stockholm District Court, where he was given a very lenient six-month sentence.

Imandi managed to escape from the allegedly secure prison at Kumla by climbing over the wall with another man, and was on the run for five days. Since his release in 2009, he continues to live in Sweden under the name of Caanan Marten Deimamdi. Apart from one sentence for assault, he seems to have kept his hands clean since then, so to speak.

Another of Jamila's sisters named Khalid or Rashidi made her debut in the headlines when she was arrested in London during 1978 after throwing a hand grenade under the car of the Iraqi Ambassador to the Court of St James, His Excellency Taha Ahmed Daud. Probably the car was armoured, because the ambassador sustained no serious injury.

Mohammed Abu Talb was released from prison at Hall, 50 kilometres south of Stockholm, in early 2010, having served twenty years. Although his sentence on 21 December 1989 stipulated that he was to be deported on release, it is not surprising that no country will accept him. His country of birth, Egypt, specifically refused to have him back, as have Lebanon, Jordan and Syria. The Swedes seem unable to decide what to do with him, so he remains a free man there, needing only to renew his residence permit annually. He has changed his name to Mohamed Adam Mograbi, taking the family name of his wife. Although he had divorced her, the couple has remarried. They have four sons: Sami Abu Talb, aged 17 and presumably conceived during a conjugal visit in prison; Samar Abu Talb, aged 27; Samer Abu Talb, aged 34; and Samir Abu Talb, aged 38. The similarity of names is confusing, and makes more difficult any investigation of a crime committed by any one of them. Nevertheless, Samir Abu Talb has served a twenty-month prison term for what were called 'economic crimes'.

Where is Abu Elias, aka Khaisar Haddad, the blond, blue-eyed Lebanese Christian nephew of Ahmed Jibril and expert in airport security who was thought the person most likely to have placed the Samsonite suitcase on board *Maid of the Seas*? MSP Christine Grahame and others believe that he lives in Washington DC, not far from Dulles International Airport under some kind of witness protection pro-gramme, employed by the local education authority under the name of Basel Bushnaq. He may be the man who did the dirty work of placing the bomb aboard *Maid of the Seas*, but the conspiracy theorists who think Elias/Haddad/Bushnaq was working for a US intelligence agency overlook one thing. If the downing of Pan Am 103 was the work of such an agency, it is extremely unlikely that he would still be alive. One thinks back to the statistically improbable chain of sudden deaths after the Kennedy assassination.

Searching for Abu Elias by name leads only to a Lebanese restau-rant, butcher's shop and Middle Eastern take-out in Montreal, which sells such delicacies as calf's brain sandwiches, tabouleh and kebabs. So, it seems we shall never know *officially* who killed all those people above and in Lockerbie on 21 December 1988.

ANNEXE

LIST OF FATALITIES AT LOCKERBIE

Note: Strangely, after so many years, there are differences between the published lists of victims of the crash of Pan Am 103. The Crown Copyright list below is extracted from the Scottish Fatal Accident Report. Para (4) is included as the most succinct description of the worst aviation accident in British history.

The Sheriff Principal Determines:

(1) That
ELISABETH NICOLE MARIE AVOYNE, born on 5 May 1944, and residing at 2 Avenue Francois Patrocle, 78290 Croissy Sur Seine, France
JERRY DON AVRITT, born on 30 July 1942, and residing at 14031 Bexley Street, Westminster, California 92683, USA
NOELLE LYDIE BERTI, born on 24 December 1947, and residing at 1 Rue D'Armenomville, Paris, France 754017
SIV ULLA ENGSTROM, born on 21 September 1937, and residing at 6 Rays Avenue, Windsor, Berkshire
STACIE DENISE FRANKLIN, born on 16 February 1968 and residing at 1366 Thomas Avenue, San Diego, California 92109, USA
PAUL ISAAC GARRETT, born on 16 November 1947, and residing at 482 Cross Street, Napa, California 94559, USA
ELKE ETHA KUHNE, born on 17 March 1945, and residing at Langensalza Strasse 20, 3 Hanover, West Germany
MARIA NIEVES LARRACOECHEA, born on 3 March 1949, and residing at Castello 83, Madrid 28006, Spain

JAMES BRUCE MacQUARRIE, born on 30 September 1933, and residing at
32 North Road, Kensington, New Hampshire, 03833, USA

LILIBETH TOBILA MACALOLOOY, born on 2 November 1961 and residing at
Morfelder Strasse 97, 6092 Kelsterbach, West Germany

MARY GERALDINE MURPHY, born on 14 May 1937, and residing at
1 Cranebrook Manor Road, Twickenham, Middlesex

JOCELYN REINA, born on 26 May 1962, and residing at 732 Great Western
Road, Isleworth, Middlesex

MYRA JOSEPHINE ROYAL, born on 20 December 1958 and residing at
30 Clitherow Avenue, Hanwell, London

IRJA SYHNOVE SKABO, born on 3 July 1950 and residing at Ankerveien
17-0390, Oslo, Norway

MILUTIN VELIMIROVICH, born on 14 October 1953, and residing at 33 Dorset
Way, Heston, Hounslow, Middlesex

RAYMOND RONALD WAGNER, born on 18 January 1936, and residing at
165 Pennington-Harbourton Road, Pennington, New Jersey 08534, USA.

died from multiple injuries at about 1905 hours on Wednesday 21 December 1988
at or near Lockerbie, Dumfriesshire in the course of their employment with Pan
American World Airways as members of the flight crew of Pan American World
Airways Flight 103 on Boeing 747-121 Registration N739PA en route from
London Heathrow Airport to John F Kennedy Airport, New York.

(2) That

JOHN MICHAEL GERARD AHERN, born on 16 April 1962, and residing at
127 Sherman Avenue, Rockville Centre, New York 11570, USA

SARAH MARGARET AICHER, born on 9 February 1959, and residing at
30E Stanhope Gardens, London

JOHN DAVID AKERSTROM, born on 20 May 1954, and residing at 6822 Ryan
Road, Medina, Ohio 44256, USA

RONALD ELY ALEXANDER, born on 15 July 1942, and residing at 425 East
58th Street, New York, New York 10022, USA

THOMAS JOSEPH AMMERMAN, born on 6 August 1952, and residing at
2 Forrest Avenue, Old Tappan, New Jersey 07676, USA

MARTIN LEWIS APFELBAUM, born on 16 August 1929, and residing at
2505 18th Street, Philadelphia, Pennsylvania 19103, USA

RACHEL MARIE ASRELSKY, born on 26 November 1967, and residing at
605 Water Street, New York, New York 10002, USA

JUDITH ELLEN BERNSTEIN or ATKINSON, born on 18 January 1951, and
residing at Flat 3, 32 Cranley Gardens, South Kensington, London

WILLIAM GARRETSON ATKINSON III, born on 18 August 1955, and residing at Flat 3, 32 Cranley Gardens, South Kensington, London

CLARE LOUISE BACCIOCHI, born on 15 March 1969, and residing at
21 Hillside, Kingsbury, Tamworth, Warwickshire

HARRY MICHAEL BAINBRIDGE, born on 16 November 1954 and residing at
9 Marisa Court, Montrose, New York 10548, USA

STUART MURRAY BARCLAY, born on 28 November 1959, and residing at
Honey Hill Farm, Barnard, Vermont 05031, USA

JEAN MARY CRISPIN or BELL, born on 16 March 1944, and residing at
The Silver Suite, Mellor House, Charles Street, Windsor, Berkshire

JULIAN MacBAIN BENELLO, born on 28 December 1962, and residing at
143 Longwood Avenue, Apartment 4, Brookline, Massachusetts 02146, USA

LAWRENCE RAY BENNETT, born on 5 November 1947 and residing at
2828 McKinley Street, Chelsea, Michigan 48118, USA

PHILIP VERNON BERGSTROM, born on 21 December 1966, and residing at 400 South Lake Street, Apartment 9, CMA Forest Lake, Minnesota
55025, USA

ALISTAIR DAVID BERKLEY, born on 11 April 1959, and residing at 30 Sutton
Square, London

MICHAEL STUART BERNSTEIN, born on 3 July 1952, and residing at
6012 Cairn Terrace, Bethesda, Maryland 20817, USA

STEVEN RUSSELL BERRELL, born on 19 June 1968, and residing at 1216 South
Ninth Street, Fargo, North Dakota 58103, USA

SURINDER MOHAN BHATIA, born on 21 May 1937, and residing at 810
Camino Real Road, 202 Redondo Beach, Los Angeles, California 90277, USA

KENNETH JOHN BISSETT, born on 19 December 1967, and residing at
120 East Hartsdale Avenue, Apartment 1K, Hartsdale, New York 10530, USA

DIANE ANN BOATMAN-FULLER, born on 8 January 1953, and residing at
58 Swinburn Court, Blanchedowne Road, Denmark Hill, London

STEPHEN JOHN BOLAND, born on 28 September 1968, and residing at
4 Century Road, Nashua, New Hampshire 03060, USA

GLENN JOHN BOUCKLEY, born on 24 February 1961, and residing at
7300 Cedarpost Road, Apartment Cl, Liverpool, New York 13088, USA

PAULA MARIE ALDERMAN or BOUCKLEY, born on 14 October 1959
and residing at 7300 Cedarpost Road, Apartment Cl, Liverpool, New York
13088, USA

NICOLE ELISE BOULANGER, born on 28 October 1967, and residing at
46 Worthington Avenue, Shrewsbury, Massachusetts 01545, USA

FRANCIS BOYER, born on 22 June 1945, and residing at 4 Place De L'Eperon,
Lotissement, Auzeville, Toulosane 31320, France

NICHOLAS BRIGHT, born on 29 August 1956, and residing at 7 Beals Street,
Brookline, Massachusetts 02146, USA

DANIEL SOLOMON BROWNER, (BEER), born on 20 August 1965 and residing at Kibbutz, Parod, Northern Israel

COLLEEN RENEE BRUNNER, born on 4 January 1968 and residing at 7164 Parkside Drive, Hamburg, New York 14075, USA

TIMOTHY GUY BURMAN, born on 9 October 1964, and residing at 49A Hotham Road, London

MICHAEL WARREN BUSER, born on 10 August 1954, and residing at 99 Teaneck Road, Ridgefield Park, New Jersey 07660, USA

WARREN MAX BUSER, born on 22 September 1926, and residing at 169 Hillman Avenue, Glenrock, New Jersey 07452, USA

STEVEN LEE BUTLER, born on 30 August 1953, and residing at 1141 South Clarkson Street, Denver, Colorado 80210, USA

WILLIAM MARTIN CADMAN, born on 10 September 1956, and residing at 13 Surrendale Place, London

FABIANA BENVENUTO or CAFFARONE, born on 30 September 1960, and residing at 21 Donne Place, London

HERMAN LUIS CAFFARONE, born on 14 December 1960, and residing at 21 Donne Place, London

VALERIE CANADY, born on 29 June 1963, and residing at 127 Jackson Avenue, South Park, Morgantown, West Virginia 3 26505-6567, USA

GREGORY JOSEPH CAPASSO, born on 12 December 1967, and residing at 1841 East 33rd Street, Brooklyn, New York 11234, USA

TIMOTHY MICHAEL CARDWELL, born on 5 July 1967, and residing at RD1, Box 203, Cresco, Pennsylvania 18326, USA

BERNT WILMAR CARLSSON, born on 21 November 1938 and residing at Apartment 30, 207 West 106th Street, New York, New York 10025, USA

RICHARD ANTHONY CAWLEY, born on 9 July 1945, and residing at 241 Central Park West, New York, New York 10024, USA

FRANK CIULLA, born on 6 August 1943, and residing at 29 Clifford Drive, Parkridge, New Jersey 97656, USA

THEODORA EUGENIA COHEN, born on 10 September 1968, and residing at 67 Wisconsin, Long Island, New York 11561, USA

ERIC MICHAEL COKER, born on 23 April 1968, and residing at 137 Hilltop Road, Mendham, New Jersey 07945, USA

JASON MICHAEL COKER, born on 23 April 1968, and residing at 137 Hilltop Road, Mendham, New Jersey 07945, USA

GARY LEONARD COLASANTI, born on 1 August 1968, and residing at 60 Garfield Road, Melrose, Massachusetts 02176, USA

BRIDGET MULROY or CONCANNON, born on 13 July 1935, and residing at 20 Nuffield Drive, Banbury, Oxfordshire

SEAN CONCANNON, born on 18 February 1972, and residing at 20 Nuffield Drive, Banbury, Oxfordshire

THOMAS CONCANNON, born on 21 November 1937, and residing at 20 Nuffield Drive, Banbury, Oxfordshire

TRACEY JANE CORNER, born on 4 May 1971, and residing at 12 Springfield Avenue, Millhouses, Sheffield

SCOTT MARSH CORY, born on 27 September 1968, and residing at 25 Chadwick Drive, Old Lyme Court, Connecticut 06371, USA

WILLIS LARRY COURSEY, born on 25 August 1948, and residing at 307 Cresham Drive, San Antonio, Texas 78218, USA

PATRICIA MARY COYLE, born on 4 June 1968, and residing at 62 Seiter Hill Road, Wallingford, Connecticut 06492, USA

JOHN BINNING CUMMOCK, born on 31 May 1950, and residing at 271 Vistalmar Street, Coral Gables, Florida 33143, USA

JOSEPH PATRICK CURRY, born on 21 March 1957, and residing at 885B Beach Street, Fort Devens, Massachusetts 01433, USA

WILLIAM ALAN DANIELS, born on 28 March 1948, and residing at 20 Sweet Briar Court, Belle Mead, New Jersey 08502, USA

GRETCHEN JOYCE DATER, born on 17 May 1968, and residing at 27 Mohawk Drive, Ramsey, New Jersey 07446, USA

SHANNON DAVIS, born on 19 February 1969, and residing at 32 Isinglass Road, Shelton, Connecticut 06484, USA

GABRIELE DELLA-RIPA, born on 3 April 1942, and residing at 406 Plainfield Avenue, Floral Park, New York 11001, USA

OM DIKSHIT, born on 29 December 1933, and residing at 2955 Wylie Drive, Fairborn, Ohio 45324, USA

JOYCE CHRISTINE DIMAURO, born on 9 May 1956, and residing at 352 East 18th Street, New York, New York 10003, USA

GIANFRANCA DINARDO, born on 14 October 1962, and residing at Flat 4, 24 Cranley Gardens, South Kensington, London

PETER THOMAS STANLEY DIX, born on 6 May 1953, and residing at 52 Coborn Road, Bow, London

SHANTI DEVI or DIXIT, born on 14 December 1934, and residing at 2955 Wylie Drive, Fairborn, Ohio 45324, USA

DAVID SCOTT DORNSTEIN, born on 3 April 1963, and residing at 7703 Seminole Avenue, Philadelphia, Pennsylvania 19126, USA

MICHAEL JOSEPH DOYLE, born on 21 May 1958, and residing at 17 Arcadia Drive, Voorhees, New Jersey 08043, USA

EDGAR HOWARD EGGLESTON III, born on 13 October 1964, and residing at RD4, Box 296A, Glen Falls, New York 12801, USA

TURHAN ERGIN, born on 14 May 1966, and residing at 97 Cliffmore Road, West Hartford, Connecticut 06105, USA

CHARLES THOMAS FISHER IV, born on 24 December 1953, and residing at 19 Beaufort Gardens, Flat 4, Chelsea, London

CLAYTON LEE FLICK, born on 23 February 1963, and residing at 68 Rugby Road, Binley Woods, Coventry

JOHN PATRICK FLYNN, born on 24 November 1967, and residing at 10 West Lake Drive, Montville, New Jersey 07045, USA

ARTHUR JAY FONDILER, born on 12 December 1955, and residing at 9 Seymour Place, West Armonk, New York 10504, USA

ROBERT GERARD FORTUNE, born on 24 July 1948, and residing at 34-05 80th Street, Jackson Heights, New York 11372, USA

PAUL MATTHEW STEPHEN FREEMAN, born on 2 April 1963, and residing at 19 Manor Mansions, Belsize Grove, London

JAMES RALPH FULLER, born on 17 September 1938, and residing at 351 Lonepine Court, Bloomfield Hills, Michigan 48013, USA

IBOLYA ROBERTNE DRUCKER or GABOR, born on 14 June 1909 and residing at Wesselenyi 6, Budapest, Hungary

AMY BETH GALLAGHER, born on 30 August 1966, and residing at 246 Vista, Pointe Claire, Quebec, Canada

MATTHEW KEVIN GANNON, born on 11 August 1954, and residing at 611 North Ardmore, Los Angeles, California 90004, USA

KENNETH RAYMOND GARCZYNSKI, born on 17 October 1951, and residing at 1673 Hudson Avenue, North Brunswick, New Jersey 08902, USA

KENNETH JAMES GIBSON, born on 16 February 1968, and residing at 6/502 Infantry Army Post Office, New York, New York 09742, USA

WILLIAM DAVID GIEBLER, born on 8 July 1959, and residing at 52 Radcliffe Square, London

ANDREW CHRISTOPHER GILLIES-WRIGHT, born on 2 May 1964, and residing at 5 Esher Mews, Mitcham, Surrey

OLIVE LEONORA GORDON, born on 9 March 1963, and residing at 182 William Bonney Estate, London

LINDA SUSAN GORDON-GORGACZ, born on 15 September 1949, and residing at 5 Devere Gardens, Kensington, London

ANNE MADELENE CHABACK or GORGACZ, born on 27 September 1912 and residing at 5 East Wallace Avenue, Apartment 201, Newcastle, Pennsylvania 16101, USA

LORETTA ANNE GORGACZ, born on 15 March 1941, and residing at 5 East Wallace Avenue, Apartment 201, Newcastle, Pennsylvania 16101, USA

DAVID JAY GOULD, born on 3 January 1943, and residing at 5883 Bartlett Street, Pittsburg, Pennsylvania 15217, USA

ANDRE NIKOLAI GUEVORGIAN, born on 11 November 1956, and residing at 8 Carrpenter Place, Sea Cliff, Long Island, New York 11579, USA

NICOLA JANE HALL, born on 3 February 1965, and residing at 34 Second Avenue, Illovo, Sandton 2196, South Africa

LORRAINE FRANCES BUSER or HALSCH, born on 6 November 1957, and residing at 24 Camborne Circle, Fairport, New York 14450, USA

LYNNE CAROL HARTUNIAN, born on 13 March 1967, and residing at 5 Tamarack Lane, Schenectady, New York 12309, USA

ANTHONY LACEY HAWKINS, born on 13 November 1931, and residing at 805 East 21st Street, Brooklyn, New York 11210, USA

PAMELA ELAINE HERBERT, born on 27 March 1969, and residing at 378 Parkway Drive, Battle Creek, Michigan 49017, USA

RODNEY PETER HILBERT, born on 19 July 1948, and residing at 117 South Congress Street, Newtown, Pennsylvania 18940, USA

ALFRED HILL, born on 29 June 1959, and residing at Heimenhofenstrasse 3, 8972 Sonthofen, West Germany

KATHERINE AUGUSTA HOLLISTER, born on 26 August 1968, and residing at 64-11 99th Street, Apartment 604, Rego Park, New York 11374, USA

JOSEPHINE LISA HUDSON, born on 14 May 1966, and residing at Flat 4, Arton Wilson House, North Wing, Roehampton Lane, London

MELINA KRISTINA HUDSON, born on 25 January 1972, and residing at 124 Lancaster Street, Albany, New York 12210, USA

SOPHIE AILETTE MIRIAM HUDSON, born on 22 September 1962, and residing at 14 Rue Therese, Paris 75001, France

KAREN LEE HUNT, born on 7 January 1968, and residing at 477 Maplewoods Lane, Webster, New York 14580, USA

ROGER ELWOOD HURST, born on 12 July 1950 and residing at 43 Lake Riconda Drive, Ringwood, New Jersey 07456, USA

ELIZABETH SOPHIE IVELL, born on 21 April 1969, and residing at 24 High Street, Roberts Bridge, East Sussex

KHALED NAZIR JAAFAR, born on 1 May 1968, and residing at 6519 Manor Street, Dearborn, Michigan 48126, USA

ROBERT VAN HOUTEN JECK, born on 8 October 1931, and residing at 145 Lake Drive, Montain Lakes, New Jersey 07046, USA

PAUL AVRON JEFFREYS, born on 13 February 1952, and residing at 8 Orchard Cottages, Clifton Road, Kingston-Upon-Thames, Surrey

RACHEL MARY ELIZABETH JONES or JEFFREYS born on 29 April 1965, and residing at 8 Orchard Cottages, Clifton Road, Kingston-Upon-Thames, Surrey

KATHLEEN MARY JERMYN, born on 27 December 1967, and residing at 35 Sheridan Place, Staten Island, New York 10312, USA

BETH ANN JOHNSON, born on 24 March 1967, and residing at 226 Wren Drive, Greensburg, Pennsylvania 15601, USA

MARY LINCOLN JOHNSON, born on 14 June 1963, and residing at 18 Adams Lane, Wayland, Massachusetts 01778, USA

TIMOTHY BARON JOHNSON, born on 30 November 1967, and residing at 2024 West Lake Avenue, Neptune Township, New Jersey 07753, USA

CHRISTOPHER ANDREW JONES, born on 4 March 1968, and residing at Courts Lane, Claverack, New York 12513, USA

JULIANNE FRANCES KELLY, born on 27 June 1968, and residing at 31 Massachusetts Avenue, Dedham, Massachusetts 02026, USA

JAY JOSEPH KINGHAM, born on 3 March 1944, and residing at 10821 Stanmore Drive, Potomac, Maryland 20854, USA

PATRICIA ANN KLEIN, born on 16 June 1953, and residing at 1108 Hamilton Avenue, Trenton, New Jersey 08629, USA

GREGORY KOSMOWSKI, born on 8 October 1948, and residing at 3253 Tipisco Lake Road, Milford, Michigan 48042, USA

MINAS CHRISTOPHER KULUKUNDIS, born on 17 December 1950, and residing at 6 Shalcomb Street, London

RONALD ALBERT LARIVIERE, born on 19 November 1955, and residing at 200 North Pickett Street, Apartment 903, Alexandria, Virginia 22304, USA

ROBERT MILTON LECKBURG, born on 12 October 1958, and residing at 601 Plainfield Avenue, Piscatawa, New Jersey 08854, USA

WILLIAM CHASE LEYRER, born on 24 August 1942, and residing at 52 Maple Avenue, Bayshore, New York 11706, USA

WENDY ANNE LINCOLN, born on 21 January 1965, and residing at 294 Notch Road, North Adams, Massachusetts 01247, USA

ALEXANDER LOWENSTEIN, born on 25 February 1967, and residing at 24 Old Orchard Road, Mendham Township, Morristown, New Jersey 07960, USA

LLOYD DAVID LUDLOW, born on 6 February 1947, and residing at Headquarters HQ Company, 4th Brigade, Army Post Office, New York, New York 09185, USA

MARIA THERESIA LURBKE, born on 26 November 1963, and residing at Arnsberger Strasse 47, 5983 Balve-Beckum, West Germany

WILLIAM JOHN McALLISTER, born on 18 October 1962, and residing at 124 Peregrine Road, Sunbury on Thames, Middlesex

DANIEL EMMET McCARTHY, born on 2 November 1957, and residing at 127 92nd Street, Brooklyn, New York 11209, USA

ROBERT EUGENE McCOLLUM, born on 12 May 1927, and residing at 1248 Thomas Road, Wayne, Pennsylvania 19087, USA

CHARLES DENNIS McKEE, born on 3 December 1948, and residing at HOS USA Intelligence Section Command, Arlington Hall Station, Virginia 22212, USA

BERNARD JOSEPH McLAUGHLIN, born on 2 December 1958, and residing at 108 Norwood Avenue, Cranston, Rhode Island 02905, USA

WILLIAM EDWARD MACK, born on 24 April 1958, and residing at 202 East 92nd Street, New York, New York 10128, USA

DOUGLAS EUGENE MALICOTE, born on 31 August 1966, and residing at 97th Signal Battalion, Army Post Office, New York, New York 02028, USA

WENDY GAY FORSYTH or MALICOTE, born on 31 July 1967, and residing at 97th Signal Platoon, US Army Base, Mannheim, West Germany

ELIZABETH LILLIAN MAREK, born on 17 February 1958, and residing at 202 West 92nd Street, New York, New York 10025, USA

LOUIS ANTHONY MARENGO, born on 9 February 1955, and residing at 1579 Stoney Creek Drive, Rochester, Michigan 48063, USA

NOEL GEORGE MARTIN, also known as Joseph Emmanuel Barzey, born on 31 May 1961, and residing at 1 Ashdon House, North Old Road, Clapton, Gloucestershire

DIANE MARIE MASLOWSKI, born on 10 August 1958, and residing at 130 Prospect Road, Haddonfield, New Jersey 08033, USA

JANE SUSAN MELBER, born on 1 January 1961, and residing at 17 Melrose Gardens, Burnt Oak, Middlesex

JOHN MERRILL, born on 11 July 1953, and residing at 1 Heath Hall, High Street, Baldock, Hertfordshire

SUZANNE MARIE MIAZGA, born on 31 July 1966, and residing at RD1, Box 221, Benton Road, Marcy, New York 13403, USA

JOSEPH KENNETH MILLER, born on 27 May 1932, and residing at 381 Westwood Road, Woodmere, New York 11598, USA

JEWEL COURTNEY MITCHELL, born on 14 June 1956, and residing at 1154 Union Street, Brooklyn, New York 11225, USA

RICHARD PAUL MONETTI, born on 11 September 1968, and residing at 1615 Longfellow Drive, Cherry Hill, New Jersey 08003, USA

JANE ANN MORGAN, born on 19 March 1951, and residing at Flat 1, 10 Brompton Square, London

EVA INGEBORG FUCHS or MORSON, born on 29 April 1940, and residing at 185 East 85th Street, New York, New York 10028, USA

HELGA RACHAEL MOSEY, born on 21 September 1969, and residing at 42 Titford Road, Oldbury, Warley, West Midlands

INGRID ELISABETH SVENSSON or MULROY, born on 22 April 1963, and residing at Kamnarsvagen 9L126, 22246 Lund, Sweden

JOHN MULROY, born on 1 April 1929, and residing at 35 Cherrywood Drive, East North Port, New York 11731, USA

SEAN KEVIN MULROY, born on 3 May 1963, and residing at Kamnarsvagen, 9L126, 22246 Lund, Sweden

KAREN ELIZABETH NOONAN, born on 26 December 1967, and residing at 11901 Glenmill Road, Potomac, Maryland 20854, USA

DANIEL EMMETT O'CONNOR, born on 22 September 1957, and residing at 17 Lawley Street, Dorchester, Massachusetts 02122, USA

MARY DENICE O'NEILL, born on 2 April 1967, and residing at 1675 Metropolitan Avenue, Bronx, New York 10462, USA

ANNE LINDSEY OTENASEK, born on 13 January 1967, and residing at 110 Tunbridge Road, Baltimore, Maryland 21212, USA

BRYONY ELISE OWEN, born on 29 April 1987, and residing at 59 Chelsea Park, Easton, Bristol

GWYNETH YVONNE MARGARET OWEN, born on 3 May 1959, and residing at 59 Chelsea Park, Easton, Bristol

LAURA ABIGAIL OWENS, born on 8 January 1980, and residing at 101 Rockingham Road, Cherry Hill, New Jersey 08034, USA

MARTHA IVES or OWENS, born on 2 June 1944, and residing at 101 Rockingham Road, Cherry Hill, New Jersey 08034, USA

ROBERT PLACK OWENS, born on 5 March 1943, and residing at 101 Rockingham Road, Cherry Hill, New Jersey 08034, USA

SARAH REBECCA OWENS, born on 9 December 1974, and residing at 101 Rockingham Road, Cherry Hill, New Jersey 08034, USA

ROBERT ITALO PAGNUCCO, born on 20 October 1937, and residing at Oscaleta Road, South Salem, New York 10590, USA

CHRISTOS MICHAEL PAPADOPOULOS, born on 11 November 1943, and residing at 217 Harborview, North Lawrence, New York 12938, USA

PETER RAYMOND PEIRCE, born on 28 September 1948, and residing at 860 East Boundry Street, Perrysburg, Ohio 43551, USA

MICHAEL COSIMO PESCATORE, born on 6 September 1955, and residing at 5482 Banbery Drive, Medina, Solon, Ohio 44139, USA

SARAH SUSANNAN BUCHANAN PHILIPPS, born on 15 August 1968, and residing at 78 Hull Street, Newtonville, Massachusetts 02160, USA

FREDERICK SANDFORD PHILLIPS, born on 8 May 1961, and residing at 12 Van Lee Drive, Little Rock, Arkansas 72205, USA

JAMES ANDREW CAMPBELL PITT, born on 6 November 1964, and residing at 96 College Street, South Hadley, Massachusetts 01075, USA

DAVID PLATT, born on 13 December 1955, and residing at 76 Belfast Avenue, Staten Island, New York 10306, USA

WALTER LEONARD PORTER, born on 10 March 1953, and residing at 85, Remsen Avenue, Brooklyn, New York 11212, USA

PAMELA LYNN POSEN, born on 30 January 1968, and residing at 88 Haviland Road, Harrison, New York 10528, USA

WILLIAM PUGH, born on 29 February 1932, and residing at 103 South Claremont Avenue, Margate City, New Jersey 08402, USA

CRISOSTOMO ESTRELLA QUIGUYAN, born on 16 March 1945, and residing at 37 Park View, Monks Park, Wembley, London

RAJESH TARSIS PRISKEL RAMSES, born on 26 May 1953, and residing at 10 Eastfield Court, Eastile Road, Leicester

ANMOL RATTAN, born on 24 September 1986, and residing at 24301 Panama, Warren, Michigan 48091, USA

GARIMA DIXIT or RATTAN, born on 15 July 1959, and residing at 24301 Panama, Warren, Michigan 48091, USA

SURUCHI RATTAN, born on 20 June 1985, and residing at 24301 Panama, Warren, Michigan 48091, USA

ANITA LYNN REEVES, born on 3 September 1964, and residing at 801 Fairlawn Avenue, Apartment 4, Laurel, Maryland 20707, USA

MARK ALAN REIN, born on 12 February 1944, and residing at 220 East 63rd Street, New York, New York 10021, USA

DIANE MARIE RENCEVICZ, born on 13 July 1967, and residing at 325 West Union Street, Burlington, New Jersey 08016, USA

LOUISE ANN ROGERS, born on 13 February 1967, and residing at 3508 Sundown Farms Way, Olney, Maryland 20832, USA

EDINA ROLLER, born on 24 November 1983, and residing at Vac, Koto Utca 7, H-2600, Hungary

JANOS GABOR ROLLER, born on 26 March 1959, and residing at Vac, Koto Utca 7, H-2600, Hungary

ZSUZSANNA PISAK or ROLLER, born on 21 December 1961, and residing at Vac, Koto Utca 7, H-2600, Hungary

HANNE MARIA MAIJALA or ROOT, born on 15 December 1962, and residing at 20 West 72nd Street, Apartment 609, New York, New York 10023, USA

SAUL MARK ROSEN, born on 24 November 1953, and residing at 116 Burnham Road, Morris Plains, New Jersey 07950, USA

ANDREA VICTORIA ROSENTHAL, born on 5 February 1966, and residing at 784 Park Avenue, New York, New York 10021, USA

DANIEL PETER ROSENTHAL, born on 2 June 1968, and residing at 36 Hamilton Avenue, Staten Island, New York 10301, USA

ARNAUD DAVID RUBIN, born on 18 May 1960, and residing at 68 Avenue Des Croix Du Feu, Waterloo 1410, Belgium

ELYSE JEANNE SARACENI, born on 1 June 1968, and residing at Mews Room 17, 1 Park Crescent Mews East, London

SCOTT CHRISTOPHER SAUNDERS, born on 20 May 1967, and residing at 2996 Macungie Road, Macungie, Pennsylvania 18062, USA;

TERESA ELIZABETH JANE WILSON or SAUNDERS, born on 24 October 1960, and residing at 124 Peregrine Road, Sunbury on Thames, Middlesex

JOHANNES OTTO SCHAEUBLE, born on 8 August 1947, and residing at Kappellenweg 6, 7407 Rottenburg, Wurmlingen, West Germany

ROBERT THOMAS SCHLAGETER, born on August 1968, and residing at 814 West Shore Road, Warwick, Rhode Island 02889, USA

THOMAS BRITTON SCHULTZ, born on 5 January 1968, and residing at 142 Wilton Road, Ridgefield, Connecticut 06877, USA

SALLY ELIZABETH SCOTT, born on 17 January 1966, and residing at 4 Woodvale Lane, Hungtingston, New York 11743, USA

AMY ELIZABETH SHAPIRO, born on 28 October 1967, and residing at 77 Brook Run Lane, Stamford, Connecticut 06905, USA

MRIDULA SHASTRI, born on 12 February 1964, and residing at Room 1, St Johns College, 11 St Johns Street, Oxford

JOAN LICHTENSTEIN or SHEANSHANG, born on 16 December 1942, and residing at 4 East 89th Street, New York, New York 10128, USA

IRVING STANLEY SIGAL, born on 23 May 1953, and residing at 120 East Delaware Avenue, Pennington, New Jersey 08574, USA

MARTIN BERNARD CARRUTHERS SIMPSON, born on 25 October 1936, and residing at 249 Garfield Place, Brooklyn, New York 11215, USA

CYNTHIA JOAN SMITH, born on 6 October 1967, and residing at 340 Brook Road, Milton, Massachusetts 02186, USA

INGRID ANITA LEADGARD or SMITH, born on 12 November 1957, and residing at Malthouse Cottage, Church Lane, Bray, Berkshire

JAMES ALVIN SMITH, born on 11 March 1933, and residing at 139 East 35th Street, New York, New York 10016, USA

MARY EDNA HALL or SMITH, born on 14 July 1954, and residing at 97th Signal Battalion, Army Post Office, New York, New York 09028, USA

GERALDINE ANNE O'GARA or STEVENSON, born on 31 March 1951, and residing at 44 Manor Road, South Hinchley Wood, Esher, Surrey

HANNAH LOUISE STEVENSON, born on 23 September 1978, and residing at 44 Manor Road, South Hinchley Wood, Esher, Surrey

JOHN CHARLES STEVENSON, born on13 September 1950, and residing at 44 Manor Road, South Hinchley Wood, Esher, Surrey

RACHAEL STEVENSON, born on 1 September 1980, and residing at 44 Manor Road, South Hinchley Wood, Esher, Surrey

CHARLOTTE ANN McGUIRE or STINNETT, born on 7 February 1952, and residing at 1526 Lime Leaf Lane, Duncanville, Texas 75137, USA

MICHAEL GARY STINNETT, born on 27 May 1962, and residing at 1526 Lime Leaf Lane, Duncanville, Texas 75137, USA

STACEY LEANNE STINNETT, born on 30 July 1979, and residing at 1526 Lime Leaf Lane, Duncanville, Texas 75137, USA

JAMES RALPH STOW, born on 18 July 1939, and residing at 205 East 95th Street, Apartment 31D, New York, New York 10128, USA

ELIA G STRATIS, born on 17 June 1945, and residing at 57 Longridge Road, Montvale, New Jersey 07645, USA

ANTHONY SELWYN SWAN, born on 15 May 1959, and residing at 41 Halsey Street, Brooklyn, New York 11216, USA

FLORA MacDONALD MARGARET SWIRE, born on 22 December 1964, and residing at William Goodenough House, Mecklenburgh Square, Bloomsbury, London

MARC ALEX TAGER, born on 3 August 1966, and residing at 3 Cedars Close, Hendon, London

HIDEKAZU TANAKA, born on 13 May 1962, and residing at Flat 6, 110 Gloucester Terrace, London

ANDREW ALEXANDER TERAN, born on 31 August 1968, and residing at Pearson College, Yale University, New Haven, Connecticut 06520, USA

ARVA ANTHONY THOMAS, born on 26 April 1971, and residing at 14075 Marlowe, Detroit, Michigan 48227, USA

JONATHAN RYAN THOMAS, born on 29 September 1988, and residing at 15838 Harden Circle, Southfield, Michigan 48075, USA

LAWANDA COLEMAN or THOMAS, born on 17 February 1967, and residing at 15838 Harden Circle, Southfield, Michigan 48075, USA

MARK LAWRENCE TOBIN, born on 4 April 1967, and residing at 36 St Paul's Road, North Hempstead, New York 11550, USA

DAVID WILLIAM TRIMMER-SMITH, born on 26 April 1937, and residing at 222 East 56th Street, Apartment SA, New York, New York 10022, USA

ALEXIA KATHRYN TSAIRIS, born on 6 July 1968, and residing at 379 Vance Avenue, Franklyn Lakes, New Jersey 07417, USA

BARRY JOSEPH VALENTINO, born on 25 February 1960, and residing at 119 Haight Street, Apartment 16, San Francisco, California 94102, USA

TOMAS FLORO VAN TIENHOVEN, born on 30 May 1943, and residing at Jose C Paz, 738 Accassuso, Buenos Aires, Argentina and also at 11 Argylle Road, London

ASAAD EIDI VEJDANY, born on 24 February 1942, and residing at 32 Somerset Drive South, Great Neck, New York 11020, USA

NICHOLAS ANDREAS VRENIOS, born on 20 August 1968, and residing at 6628 32nd Street, NW Washington DC 20015, USA

PETER VULCU, born on 1 August 1967, and residing at 1541 Overlook, Alliance, Ohio 44601, USA

JANINA JOZEFA RUSNIAK or MITKA or WAlDO, born on 19 March 1927, and residing at 2257 North Lavergne Avenue, Chicago, Illinois 60639, USA

THOMAS EDWIN WALKER, born on 11 December 1941, and residing at 192 Taylor Street, Wallaston, Quincy, Massachusetts 02170, USA

KESHA WEEDON, born on 2 October 1968, and residing at 2525 Aqueduct Avenue, Bronx, New York 10468, USA

JEROME LEE WESTON, born on 11 November 1943, and residing at 3134 Eastern Parkway, Baldwin, Long Island, New York 11510, USA

JONATHAN WHITE, born on 14 July 1955, and residing at 11229 Blix Street, North Hollywood, California 91620, USA

BONNIE LEIGH RAFFERTY or WILLIAMS, born on 12 January 1967 and residing at 516th Engineer Company, Army Post Office, New York, New York 09165, USA

BRITTANY LEIGH WILLIAMS, born on 13 October 1988, and residing at 516th Engineer Company, Army Post Office, New York, New York 09165, USA

ERIC JON WILLIAMS, born on 15 August 1964, and residing at 516th Engineer Company, Army Post Office, New York, New York 09165, USA

GEORGE WATERSON WILLIAMS, born on 17 May 1964, and residing at 305 Garnett Road, Joppa, Maryland 21085, USA

STEPHANIE LEIGH WILLIAMS, born on 23 May 1987, and residing at 516th Engineer Company, Army Post Office, New York, New York 09165, USA

MIRIAM LUBY WOLFE, born on 26 September 1968, and residing at 120 Kennedy Drive, Severna Park, Maryland 21146, USA

CHELSEA MARIE WOODS, born on 6 February 1988, and residing at Apartment 1151, 6750 Vogelweh Housing, West Germany

DEDERA LYNN COPELAND or WOODS, born on 4 February 1961, and residing at Apartment 1151, 6750 Vogelweh Housing, West Germany

JOE NATHAN WOODS, born on 5 March 1960, and residing at Apartment 1151, 6750 Vogelweh Housing, West Germany

JOE NATHAN WOODS, JNR, born on 24 September 1986, and residing at Apartment 1151, 6750 Vogelweh Housing, West Germany

MARK JAMES ZWYNENBURG, born on 14 October 1959, and residing at 151 Foxwood Road, West Nyack, New York 10994, USA,

who were passengers on said aircraft, died from multiple injuries at about 1905 hours on Wednesday 21 December 1988 at or near Lockerbie, Dumfriesshire,

(3) That

JOANNE FLANNIGAN, born on 13 June 1978,

KATHLEEN MARY DOOLAN or FLANNIGAN, born on 26 January 1947, and

THOMAS BROWN FLANNIGAN, born on 20 December 1944, all residing at 16 Sherwood Crescent, Lockerbie, Dumfriesshire;

DORA HENRIETTA MOFFAT or HENRY, born on 27 March 1932 and

MAURICE PETER HENRY, born on 18 July 1925, both residing at Arranmore, 13 Sherwood Crescent, Lockerbie, Dumfriesshire;

MARY BROWELL or LANCASTER, born on 12 January 1907, and residing at 11 Sherwood Crescent, Lockerbie, Dumfriesshire;

JEAN AITKEN MURRAY, born on 29 November 1906, and residing at Westerly, 14 Sherwood Crescent, Lockerbie, Dumfriesshire; and

JOHN SOMERVILLE, born on 25 March 1948,

LYNSEY ANNE SOMERVILLE, born on 13 July 1978,

PAUL SOMERVILLE, born on 21 January 1975, and

ROSALEEN LEITER HANNAY or SOMERVILLE born on 31 May 1948, all residing at 15 Sherwood Crescent, Lockerbie, Dumfriesshire,

all died from multiple injuries and/or severe burning at about 1905 hours on Wednesday 21 December 1988 at Sherwood Crescent, Lockerbie, Dumfriesshire.

Extract of Point 4 of the Fatal Accident Report:

(4) That the cause of all the said deaths was the detonation of an improvised explosive device located in luggage container AVE 4041 situated on the left side of the forward hold of said aircraft Registration N739PA. The detonation caused the nose and flight deck of the aircraft to become detached and the rest of the aircraft to descend out of control and to break up, eventually crashing into the ground at or near Lockerbie. The wing and centre fuselage section crashed in the Sherwood Crescent area of the town and caused the deaths referred to in Finding (3) hereof.

The deaths referred to in Findings (1) and (2) hereof resulted from injuries sustained either as a direct result of the explosion and the disintegration of the aircraft or from impact with the ground.

ACKNOWLEDGEMENTS

Many people contributed memories of the Lockerbie tragedy. The author particularly wishes to thank Werner Fischdick, who kindly gave permission to use photographs of civil aircraft from his archive, Jenny Wilson for taking the photos of Lockerbie now and Miguel Mata for help in tracking down photographs not easily found. Especial thanks are due to the well-informed and courageous Swedish journalist Anders Carlgren for updating the activities of various Palestinians and others in Sweden.

In addition this book has benefited from the professional advice of biochemist George Rowlandson, who commented on some effects on the human body of explosive decompression; from Graham Johnson in Toulouse, who commented on aircraft construction and damage; from Chris Turner who gave general aviation advice; and from retired lawyer Richard Evans, who made many helpful observations on the reporting of the trial and appeal. The author freely admits that he has not always taken their advice, but the book would not have been the same without it. As always, any errors or omissions are the author's responsibility.

At The History Press, Commissioning Editor Mark Beynon drove me with a loose rein, as usual, and Project Editor Alex Waite impeccably contributed in its production.

FURTHER READING

Ashton, J., *Megrahi: You Are My Jury: The Lockerbie Evidence* (Edinburgh: Birlinn, 2012)

Chasey, W.C., *Pan Am 103: The Lockerbie Cover-up* (Gresham, Oregon: Bridger House Publishers, 1995)

Crist, D., *The Twilight War: The Secret History of America's Thirty-Year Conflict with Iran* (New York: Penguin, 2013)

Johnston, D., *Lockerbie: The Tragedy of Flight 103* (New York: St Martin's Press, 1989)

Katz, S.M., *Israel Versus Jibril: The Thirty-Year War Against a Master Terrorist* (New York: Paragon, 1993)

Kerr, M.G., *Adequately Explained by Stupidity? Lockerbie, Luggage and Lies* (Kibworth Beauchamp: Matador, 2013)

Leeming, G., *From Borneo to Lockerbie: Memoirs of an RAF Helicopter Pilot* (Barnsley: Pen & Sword, 2013)

MacAskill, K., *The Lockerbie Bombing: The Search for Justice* (London: Biteback Publishing, 2016)

Marquise, R.A. *Scotbom: Evidence and the Lockerbie Investigation* (New York: Algora Publishing, 2006)

NOTES AND SOURCES

Chapter 1: In the Beginning

1   D. Crist, *The Twilight War*, New York, Penguin, 2013, p. 161.
2   Ibid., p. 205.
3   Exhibit 5 attached to the Memorial gave the text of the Iranian law of the 29 August 1934 Executive Regulation on Conditions of the Passage and Stop Overs of Foreign Warships in Iranian Waters and Ports; the 12 April 1959 Act Amending the Act of 15 July 1934 on the Territorial Waters and the Contiguous Zone of Iran; and the 21 July 1973 Decree Law, together with translations of the same reproduced from the UN Legislative Series.
4   Letter from another officer present at those wargames to Captain Carlson after the Airbus shoot-down.
5   Crist, p. 364.
6   Ibid., p. 366.
7   The first sector of its four-sector flight plan, from Tehran to Bandar Abbas, was designated Flight IR451.
8   It was first designated TN 4474 on *Vincennes*, which adopted the number 4131 allocated on *Sides*.

Chapter 2: Medals for Murder

1   Cdr Carlson, writing in *Proceedings* published by US Naval Institute, Vol. 115/9/1039 of September 1989.
2   Ibid., p. 87.
3   Ibid., p. 88.
4   John Barry and Roger Charles, article in *Newsweek*, 12 July 1992.

5 Dan Morales, Dan Craig and Mike Oliver, analysis in Massachussets Institute of Technology publication *Aeronautics and Astronautics*, Spring 2004 edition.

6 Crist, p. 367.

7 G.C.Wilson, article in *Washington Post*, 4 July 1988, p. A01.

8 This and other extracts in this chapter are taken from the Memorial submitted to the International Court of Justice on 24 July 1990, downloadable from http:www.icj-cij.org/docket/files/79/6629.pdf.

9 Preamble to the Memorial to the ICJ [abridged].

10 *Proceedings*, p. 88.

11 Fogarty Report, p. 41, quoted in Crist, p. 369.

12 htttp://www.articles.daily press.com/1990-04-15/news/9004110407_1_uss-vincennes-iranian-airbus-rogers [abridged].

13 Ibid.

14 http://goo.gl/ldjY11.

Chapter 3: The *Qisas*

1 Exodus 21:24.

2 A 'Quote of the Week' in *Newsweek* of 15 August 1988, taken from Bush's speech to the Coalition of American Nationalities at the National Press Club in Washington, DC on 5 August 1988. Also reported by Judy Wiessler in *Houston Chronicle*, 2 August 1988, from a presidential campaign speech by Bush.

3 Mesbahi's story was widely reported in German media.

4 Like everything else about Jibril, there are doubts about his early life. Some sources give other places of birth in 1929.

5 Although Egypt continued to use the name.

6 S. Katz, *Israel versus Jibril*, New York, Paragon House, 1993, p. 22.

7 Sometimes transliterated as 'Kreeshat'.

8 Katz, p. 24.

9 C.R.Whitney, article in *New York Times*, 1 January 1989.

10 Gordon Rayner, chief reporter, article in *The Telegraph*, 10 March 2014

11 Although often said to have studied at Sandhurst, Gaddafi's military training in Britain was on a signals course in Beaconsfield.

12 W.C. Chasey, *Pan Am 103 the Lockerbie Cover-up*, Gresham, Oregon, Bridger House Publishers, 1995, pp. 139–42.

13 Chasey, pp. 146–47.

14 Some sources say fifteen minutes after take-off.

15 Katz, p. 80.

16 Ibid.

17 C.R.Whitney, article in *New York Times*, 23 March 1991.

18 Katz, p. 35.

19 Israeli domestic security organisation.

20 Always trying, the author asked an Israeli friend who works for El Al how many armed air marshals now travel on its flights. It has to be at least two, one covering the door to the flight deck and the other at the rear of the aircraft. The friend's reply was, 'You think I'm mad?'

21 Some reports say he was from Nicaragua.

22 Which became known in the West when used as the name of the terrorists who killed the Israeli athletes at the Munich Olympic Games.

23 R.A. Marquise, *Scotbom: Evidence and the Lockerbie Investigation*, New York, Algora Publishing, 2006, pp. 8–9.

Chapter 4: Of Mules and Malta

1 For a comprehensive history of the Cold War KGB clones, see D. Boyd, *Daughters of the KGB*, Stroud, The History Press, 2015.

2 Katz, pp. 40–46.

3 In camps near Moscow and in Southern Russia.

4 J.S. Bermudez, *North Korea, the Terrorist Connection*, London, Janes, 1988, p. 111.

5 Katz, p. 76.

6 Chasey, p. 151.

7 Chasey, pp. 154–61.

8 Quoted in Chasey, p. 169.

9 Katz, p. 188.

10 Whether sincere or opportunistic, no one can say.

Chapter 5: Autumn Leaves

1 The two German republics were not reunited until 1990.

2 For which he was sentenced on 21 December 1989 to life imprisonment, which means twenty years in Sweden.

3 Katz, p. 200, quoting S. Emerson and B. Duffy, 'Pan Am 103, the German Connection' in *New York Times Sunday Magazine*, 18 March 1990, p. 34.

4 J. Ashton, *Megrahi: You are my Jury*, Edinburgh, Berlinn, 2012, pp. 31–32.

5 Katz, p. 201.

6 Marquise, p. 12.

7 Johnston, p. 102.

8 Marquise, p. 13.

9 Ashton, *Megrahi*, p. 89.

10 Marquise, p. 118.

11 Some sources say the fee was $11 million.

12 Katz, p. 208.

13 Johnston, p. 176.

Chapter 6: The Fatal Last Flight of *Maid of the Seas*

1   A conflation of Prestwick and Shannon.
2   Aircraft Accident Report No. 2/90 [EW/C1094], dated July 1990.
3   AAIB report.
4   C.A. Davies, *Plane Truth*, New York, 2001, pp. 123–24.
5   AAIB report.
6   AAIB report.
7   *MailOnline*, 21 July 2017.

Chapter 7: A Night in Hell

1   AAIB report.
2   G. Leeming, *From Borneo to Lockerbie*, Barnsley, Pen & Sword, 2013, p. 199.
3   First published under the title *Lockerbie: The Real Story* (London: Bloomsbury, 1989), and under the title *Lockerbie: The tragedy of Flight 103* (New York: St Martin's Press, 1989).
4   Ashton, *Megrahi*, p. 54.
5   Johnston, p. 52.

Chapter 8: The Morning After

1   Marquise, p. 29.
2   Leeming, p. 203.
3   Johnston, p. 97.
4   At this latitude the shortest days were 20 and 22 December. A more comprehensive account of the RAF rescue teams' work at Lockerbie may be found in Leeming, pp. 107–206.
5   Marquise, p. 28.
6   Johnston, p. 58 (abridged).
7   Quoted in K. MacAskill, *The Lockerbie Bombing: The Search for Justice*, London, Biteback Publishing, 2016, p. 19.
8   http://news.bbc.co.uk/onthisday/hi/dates/stories/december/26/newsid_2544000/2544147.stm (accessed 27 July 2018).
9   Johnston, p. 119.

Chapter 9: Drugs and Dollars in the Debris

1   Johnston, p. 79.
2   Marquise, pp. 165, 200.
3   Johnston, Postscript.
4   Readers wishing to examine further anomalies in the baggage registration and examination should consult M.G. Kerr, *Adequately Explained by Stupidity? Lockerbie, Luggage and Lies*, Kibworth Beauchamp, Matador, 2013, pp. 19–37.

5   Thought to be a play on the word 'courier'.

6   Patrick Barkham, article in *The Guardian*, 7 April 1999; also Kerr, p. 47.

7   Johnston, p. 70–77.

8   Ashton, *Megrahi*, p. 57–58.

9   Katz, pp. 217–19.

10 Barkham article.

11 The whole of Roy Rowan's article may be downloaded from http://content/time.com/time/magazine/article/0,9171,159513,00.html.

12 Article in *The Guardian*, 28 November 1986.

13 Johnston, p. 122.

14 Johnston, p. 159.

15 AAIB report.

16 Ashton, *Megrahi*, pp. 143–44; *Independent*, 1 October 1996.

17 Kerr, p. 162.

18 For full details, see Kerr, pp. 166–70.

19 Ashton, *Megrahi*, pp. 147–48.

20 R. Holt, article in *Daily Telegraph*, 28 April 2010.

Chapter 10: The Fatal Accident Inquiry

1   *El País*, 5 May 2000.

2   For a complete list of the victims, see Annexe on p. 227.

3   Some reports say 9 January.

4   Kerr, p.?

5   Kerr, pp. 55–56.

6   Kerr, p. 56.

7   Another source records this second baggage handler's name as Tarlochan Sahota, but further Indian names mentioned in this context were 'I. Sidhu' and 'Darshan Sandhu'.

8   Kerr, p. 129.

9   Marquise, p. 36.

10 FAI determination.

11 Ibid.

12 Ibid.

13 Ibid.

14 Ibid.

15 Ibid.

16 Ibid.

17 Ibid.

18 Ibid.

19 Ibid.

20 Ibid.

21 Ibid.

22 Ibid.

23 Ibid. Sherrif Mowat's determination is downloadable from http://www.vet-path.co.uk/lockerbie/fai.pdf.

Chapter 11: Investigating Mass Murder

1   In some accounts reference was to adhesive tape stuck on bags to confirm they had been X-rayed.

2   *Daily Mirror*, 11 September 2001; Gordon Rayner, chief reporter, article in *The Telegraph*, 10 March 2014.

3   Kerr, p. 43.

4   Kerr, p. 30.

5   Marquise, p. 37.

6   Ashton, *Megrahi*, pp. 49–50.

7   Katz, p. 205.

8   Katz, pp. 229–30.

9   R. Wright and R.J. Ostrow, article in *Los Angeles Times*, 25 June 1991.

10 Ibid.

11 Affidavit of Elrich Lumpert made before Walter Wieland, certifying officer at Notariat Alstetten, Zürich, dated 18 July 2007.

12 When giving evidence at the trial as witness 550.

13 David Williams, article on *Mail Online*, 14 August 2009.

14 Affidavit, para. 5, p. 2.

15 Affidavit, para. 6, p. 4.

16 Marquise, p. 115.

Chapter 12: The Plot Thickens

1   The $4 million reward was made up by contributions from the US Air Line Pilots Association, International Air Transport Association and US Department of State.

2   *Times of Malta*, 27 March 2012.

3   Ibid.

4   Chasey, p. 243 (abridged).

5   Ibid, p. 244 (abridged).

Chapter 13: A Unique Solution

1   Ibid.

2   Peter Stanford, article in *The Telegraph*, 21 August 2009.

3   Al-Megrahi writing in Ashton, *Megrahi*, p. 203.

4   Ibid.

5   MacAskill, p. 100.
6   Ashton, *Megrahi*, p. 214.
7   Affidavit.
8   *The Scotsman*, 4 November 1999.

Chapter 14: The Trial

1   *The Scotsman*, 18 November 1999.
2   Ibid.
3   Ibid.
4   Marquise, p. 234.
5   Ashton, *Megrahi*, p. 234–38.
6   Mr Wolchover's professional address at the time of posting was given as 7 Bell Yard, in the heart of London's legal district.
7   Ashton, *Megrahi*, p. 121.
8   Ibid, pp. 248–49.
9   Some accounts give a slightly different interpretation of the telephone message.
10   Chasey, pp. 207, 334, 338–39.
11   Ibid, p. 339 (quoted).

Chapter 15: The Impossible Verdict

1   He was also President of the International Progress Organization, a Vienna-based NGO in consultative status with the United Nations.
2   Downloadable in full from http://i-p-o.org/lockerbie-report.htm.
3   Declaration of Dr. Köchler, 3 February 2001.
4   See Boyd, *The Solitary Spy: A Political Prisoner in Cold War Berlin*, Stroud, The History Press, 2017, pp. 151–81.
5   Report on the Camp Zeist trial by Dr Köchler, addressed to the office of the Secretary General of the UN, Kofi Annan (abridged with author's italics).
6   Under UN Security Council Resolution 435.
7   Alleged to be controlled by the governments of South Africa … and Iran!

Chapter 16: The Most Hated Man in Europe

1   Also called flight despatcher in some countries.
2   Ashton, *Megrahi*, p. 109.
3   Also called the Jamahiriya Security Organisation or JSO.
4   See Further Reading.
5   J. Ashton, article in *The Guardian*, 18 August 2011.
6   *The Scotsman*, 8 September 2003.

7   Ibid.
8   R. Baer, *See No Evil: The True Story of a Ground Soldier in the CIA's War on Terrorism*, London, Arrow Books, 2002.
9   Kerr, p. 18.
10   Quoted in article by Auslan Cramb, *The Telegraph*, 8 February 2002.
11   All extracts quoted are from Report of the Appeal Hearing at Camp Zeist, taken from Dr Köchler's Report to the Office of the Secretary General of the UN.

Chapter 17: The Second Appeal

1   In Britain, this was reported as being £4 million per family.
2   *The Scotsman*, 8 September 2003.
3   Published by Springer Verlag in New York and Vienna, 2003.
4   Dr Köchler, speech at Glasgow Hilton on 18 September 2008 (abridged).
5   This was due to the incorporation into Scots law of the European Convention on Human Rights in 2001, which required him to be told the extent of the 'punishment element' of his sentence.
6   *The Times*, 21 December 2008.
7   S. and D. Cohen, *Pan Am 103: The Bombing, the Betrayals and a Bereaved Family's Search for Justice*, New York, New American Library, 2000, pp. 225–26.
8   Ashton, *Megrahi*, pp. 53–54.
9   MacAskill, p. 150.
10   Ibid., p. 151 (abridged).
11   Mark Townsend and David Smith, article in *The Guardian*, 17 June 2007.
12   Ibid.
13   All details of the ID parade are taken from Kerr, pp. 151–54.
14   Severin Carrell, Scottish correspondent, article in *The Guardian*, 2 October 2009.
15   Ibid.
16   Ibid.
17   Brian Wilson, article in *The Guardian*, 24 June 2014.
18   Severin Carroll, article in *The Guardian*, 3 October 2007.
19   *Times of Malta*, 17 December 2013; *The Telegraph*, 23 December 2017.

Chapter 18: 'Mr Megrahi, You May Go Home!'

1   Dr Köchler's reaction to the review in June 2007.
2   *The Firm*, June 2008.
3   Derived from rhyming slang: 'grasshopper' rhyming with 'copper', the grass informing a policeman of a crime.
4   MacAskill, p. 199.
5   Ibid.

6   Dr Köchler's statement at the Skye meeting of the Lockerbie Justice Group, September 2008 (edited).
7   Ashton, *Megrahi*, p. 350.
8   lockerbiecase.blogspot.com.
9   Quoted in Ashton, *Megrahi*, p. 351.
10 Hugh Miles, article in *The Independent*, 21 December 2008 (abridged).
11 MacAskill, pp. 192–93.
12 Note of meeting of Justice Secretary with Lockerbie victims' relatives, 9 July 2009, published on Scottish Government website (abridged).
13 IPO Press Release ref P/RE/21800c, embargoed until 6 August 2009 .
14 MacAskill, pp. 205–6.

Chapter 19: Late News

1   *The Herald*, 28 August 2009.
2   Author's italics and brackets.
3   J. Ashton, article in *The Guardian*, 18 August 2011.
4   Chasey, p. 340.
5   Ibid.

INDEX